Life thru Lyrics

...the journey to become

PART ONE:

DIAMONDS BENEATH THE DARKNESS

Nicole Danielle

ISBN: 979-8-89109-444-4 - paperback
ISBN: 979-8-89109-445-1 - ebook
ISBN: 979-8-89109-738-4 - hardcover

Library of Congress Control Number: 2023922452

Published in the United States of America.

for Crosby...

Thank You for helping me find my voice.

A NOTE FROM *me* ...

This is life. Right here. Right now. At some point throughout the journey of our lives thus far, we've loved, feared, been excited, cried, lost, won, changed, screamed, laughed, danced, breathed, dreamed—and we've sure as hell been confused and uncertain, but above it all, we have believed.

I'm doing this for my children and for every person out there who needs to know they are not alone. This is for every person who has ever been made to feel like they are not enough. This is for anyone who needs to be reminded what it means to have a dream and who has somehow just gotten really lost along the way. This is for all of you who have let other people's expectations stop you from living your one beautiful life. And yes, it's also for me, but it's first and foremost for my son, Crosby, who needs to know he has a momma who will speak in a way he isn't yet able to. This is his reminder that he has a mom who will not just fight for him or for herself, but for everyone out there who needs to be reminded they too have a voice and their voice, no matter how big or small, matters.

If I'm being honest, which is the only way I intend to write this book series, I've got to let you know up front—I'm never going to claim to know it all about this magnificent yet complex life we get to live. I'm not going to say what I think you want to hear or what you've convinced yourself you need to hear. Instead, I will tell you the truth—the truths I've come to discover about life through my own personal experiences because I was finally able to quiet the noise long enough to realize what's been there all along—*me*.

Life thru Lyrics is a series of self-discovery memoirs, sharing my own journey in this lifetime—and in this first book, ***Diamonds Beneath the Darkness***, I tell some of my stories that contributed to what ultimately became the lowest, darkest point in my life to the awakening of needing to break free from it all in order to save the me that I knew was still in there; the me that's always been there but who somehow allowed the words and actions of others to dim my light. There are many stories to come that were not easy to share, reliving them over and over has been painful at times and there's moments when I don't have the answer, things I'm still working through but I now finally have the strength to speak out loud about them and know, in doing so, can help others in a way I never could have if I continued to stay quiet. I can't always give the perfect discovery moments of how I solved the struggles and challenges within my life, but what I hope I can do is remind you what it feels like to embrace our human experiences and empower you to help your own self get to the other side—however that looks for you.

Through these pages, we can help one another learn to navigate this beautifully maddening world and release the pressure others put on us—because life is amazing, but life can also be really, really hard. Sometimes, all people need to hear is, "Hey, I'm just trying to figure shit out. And maybe my shit doesn't quite look like the shit you're going through, but I get it. So, let's be friends and figure this shit out together."

While this first book in the ***Life thru Lyrics*** series details my personal journey of going from who I felt the world wanted me to be to the awakening of the person I know I'm meant to become, this isn't just about me. I designed this for us. Who can we all be if we just free ourselves from the narratives the world convinced us to believe? Life isn't a direct path to freedom. In order to discover what's been holding you down, you need to first identify all the things in your life that got you to that point where you were face to face with the choice to pivot. This book chronicles many of those things for me.

As I have moments of discovery in my own life, my wish is that you do too for your own—because I meant what I said, let's be friends and figure this shit out together. And more than anything, I want you to know that while none of our experiences are the same, I hope I have written my stories in a way that connects with you so that you know there's someone out there who understands even an ounce of what you have gone through. Someone who is there for you, cheering you on in this lifetime.

There's a reason I named this the *Life thru Lyrics* series and it's because I'm about to take you on an even wilder trip than the words I've written—if you're willing to simply play along. Something to know before you dive in—instead of a quote someone else said to lead you into the pieces of my stories, I'm going to give a song suggestion that is relatable to what I was feeling during these moments of my life, to inspire, perhaps, to give you a deeper level of connection as I bring you along for the ride. Every subchapter in this book is appropriately named after a song that reflects the moment I'm sharing with you. This book wouldn't be possible without Crosby, and since music is a piece of his expressive soul, I hope you will play along. To find out more about this part of my journey, simply scan the code on the next page...

SCAN ME

or visit
www.lifethrulyrics.com

Music is a force, and we all have a soundtrack of our lives.
This is mine, my life—thru lyrics.

XO,

Nicole

CONTENTS

SEVEN The Wrap Up

INTRO.

PANDORA'S BOX

"Little Voice"

For most of my life, I allowed others to make me feel as though I had nothing to bring to the table. So, I just sat and listened. When you are continually *talked at,* you become silenced.

That is, until I became a mom to a beautiful little soul whose name is Crosby, who we also happen to call Croz, who just happens to be labeled as *nonverbal* and who also has autism. Having a child who is struggling to verbally speak with words is pretty much *life* writing me a hall pass to say to all the people who silenced me for so long, "It's now time for you to shut up and listen!" *And damn you for making me get permission in the first place.* My son has given me back my voice, and because of him, life has given me the green light to finally speak.

My seven-year-old son is a constant reminder that I do have a voice and, with that, comes a responsibility to speak for those who cannot. That's life showing me that I can use my voice in a way that connects with others beyond just words. As one of my exes once told me, "Words are just words; it's people who give them meaning." I have never heard my baby boy verbally say, "I love you, Mom," though I constantly fantasize about what his voice would sound like. Yet even without words, I know how much he loves me because I can feel it beyond what three simple words could ever say.

I couldn't have planned for that, but this is life. You choose to embrace it and adapt, or you end up spending a long time in a really dark place. I've seen that dark, even in what should have been the happiest of times—but it's no place to live.

For decades, I have unwillingly found myself surrounded by people who had something to say when I didn't want to hear it, but no one had anything valuable to say when I needed to hear it the most. The noise had gotten too loud, so I got to a point in my life where I was just tired of talking to people. Talking was more exhausting than life itself.

It's not because I didn't care about the people who wanted to *talk* to me. It's just that I started to really see what "talk" was about. When I quieted the noise, I started to see the difference between people who really, truly listened to what I was saying and others who only heard what they wanted to hear. I got tired of trying to talk to people and only getting a blank stare or change of subject in return. So, I stopped talking to those people. I also got really tired of just being talked *at*. Some people walk this earth acting as if they know it all, like they know everything about everything even if they have no fucking clue. So, I stopped giving others the invisible microphone to do so. And I got really tired of providing water cooler conversations for others, especially to people who could never understand what I was going through, so I just stopped talking.

If you are someone in my life who I can sit with in complete silence, and still have an amazing conversation, you're one of *my people*. If you can hear my cries without me telling you, you're one of the true people in my world. My son has taught me this. He has taught me the art of existing within silence. He has shown me the beauty in looking beyond just hearing. And he has allowed me to appreciate strength in the quiet. It's not about being the loudest in the room— the voice that isn't commanding attention is usually the wisest voice; the one that doesn't just hear but actually *listens* is the one that truly speaks. But that also doesn't mean you should allow others to silence you, just because they can't quiet themselves to hear what you have to say.

My entire life I thought it was a parent's job to teach their child. But all Crosby has done since the moment he was placed in my arms has been to show me that he doesn't exist to learn from this world—he's here to teach the world how to live a more beautiful life. And what a powerful thing it is when you learn to quiet the noise of the outside world in order to truly listen to what *the voice within* is trying to say. It goes way beyond the spoken word. The ability to speak, and be heard, is taken for granted so easily.

But even with this newfound strength and fire within me, knowing I needed to take back my power and speak in a way I hadn't been strong enough to do for most of my life, I was still having overwhelming doubts. Because even though I eventually made it through the storm, everything that I finally broke free from was suddenly once again weighing me down.

"Bird Set Free"

"If I do this, I'm opening Pandora's box," I said to my sister, Demi, over the phone.

What was a conversation in my mind suddenly became a real discussion out loud—all my fears just poured out of me. Thankfully, it was my sister on the receiving end. I couldn't control the truth that had been built up inside of me. Everything flooded out.

"If I openly speak of these things, I'm willingly, knowingly putting a lot of my thoughts out there, putting my life stories out there. And in doing so, I'm going to hurt people. I'm going to disappoint people by speaking my truth. I'm really going to piss some people off, and I'm going to get a lot of judgmental comments thrown my way because of it. None of those potential reactions are what writing this book series is for—but regardless, I'm doing this because I *have* to. Because I know my stories can, somehow, help others out there. I wish, at some point, I had heard stories that helped me get through the hardest times of my life. But I didn't, so all I ever felt was alone. I reread these pages I've written, and I say to myself, "Fuck! I needed to hear that." And I'm the one who wrote it. So I know I *need* to do this. But if I do this, I'm going to get a lot of shit for it. Yet, I know this is my purpose right now. This is what everything in life has led me to. Here and now. And, yet, I'm terrified. *Is the wrath of others worth it?*"

Demi said, "Okay. I get that. But think of the alternative. What would it mean if you didn't go through with this and do it?"

Suddenly, I felt like I was burning up inside, like my survival depended on listening to my intuition. I felt like I could throw up from the anxiety I was getting about questioning whether or not to put all this out there. Yet, I was faced with one simple question that I had to answer: *Do I or don't I?*

So I told her, "I don't want anyone to be mad at me, and really, I don't want to be so vulnerable to people who don't know me, and I really don't want to hurt anyone by speaking my truth. These stories are not easy to talk about, reliving some of the darkest moments of my life. But, if I consume my mind with all those fears, then I'm doing the opposite of what I wrote, to live your truth regardless of if it pisses people off because *it's your life*. I was suffocating before, when I wasn't strong enough to live for *me* instead of for everyone else. I climbed out of that, but I can't be okay knowing there are others out there who feel the same way and feel so alone."

My sister paused, the only sound in the room that of my pounding heart.

"So," she asked, "are you willing to open up Pandora's box?"

I smiled, laughing once. "You better fucking believe I am."

For so long, I didn't speak. But because of my son, I finally will.

Crosby Royce,
I love you to the depths of my soul.
Thank you for choosing me in this lifetime.
All of this to come is because of you.

ONE.

The Unmasking

THE CROWN

"You Are My Sunshine"

In order to understand what got me to the darkest, lowest point in my life—we have to start at the beginning.

The earliest memory I have isn't of any I see in photographs. I know myself in those photos and the people who are in them, but there are no emotions I can connect to them. The smiles. The innocence. Family togetherness. Was there ever such happiness that existed? Perhaps. Or perhaps I have just chosen to lock it all away and forget whether the happiness ever did outweigh the pain. For the earliest memory I can recall was on one of the darkest nights.

My brother and I were both really young, and this was when we were still living in our townhouse in Melrose Park, Illinois. It was in the middle of the night when my mother came into my room to wake me up, and as she carried me down the stairs, she said in a voice of panic and fear, "It's okay. It's going to be okay. But we have to go. The bad people are going to get us if we don't."

I was much too young to remember the details of that night and too innocent to understand what it meant to be living in Melrose Park as the daughter of the second-born son in a prominent Italian family. Whatever it was that spooked her enough to wake us up to run into the night was surely something serious. I can't remember the drive, but my next memory of that night was being awake and hiding out in the basement of my papa's house. I remember sitting on an old trunk in the basement, in the darkness. Beyond that, I don't know what happened or how things temporarily worked themselves out, but it wasn't long after before we fled Melrose Park for good and started a new life away from there.

After moving to our new townhome thirty minutes away from my paternal family, a lot of things started to change. My mom had to work extra hard just to keep the lights on, and my father's $37.50-per-week child support checks didn't even cover the grocery bill. My father's family had money, so our weekend visitations quickly became trips to the toy store to pick out things we wanted, anything to make us *happy*, but the deal was it all had to stay there in Melrose Park and none of it could be taken home to our townhome with Mom. A shift started to happen quickly. My brother wanted to be at our father's house more because he was super into everything he had there—he had every video game console and game on the market, so as a young boy, he was in heaven. Also, as the first-born child of the family and our paternal grandfather's namesake, there was a different set of expectations on him, I guess you could say. Before long, nearing the end of our weekend visits, he stayed with our father while I went home to be with Mom. While my brother played his games next to the basement dance floor with a disco ball and flashing strobe lights, I was sitting in the kitchen of our townhome with Mom, illuminated by candlelight. Our only entertainment often became our own voices as we sang "You Are My Sunshine" while I filled out my sticker chore chart.

No matter how dark the nights got, there was always the candlelight. And that flicker was my hope that the hard times would pass.

"Hold On"

One of the last somewhat "happy" memories I have of seeing anyone from my biological father's side was when my paternal grandparents were dropping me off from a weekend visit. Over the last two days, we had gone to a toy store where I got brand-new rollerblades—I spent the weekend playing with my rollerblades and making jewelry, because I was absolutely fascinated with Aunt Nikki's bead collection and loved creating beautiful things. When my paternal grandparents dropped me off at our townhouse, something unexpected happened. I got out of the car, went up to my mom, and said, "I don't want to live with you. I want to live with them. I don't love you anymore."

She looked at me with stone-cold-killer eyes that could make a grown man pee himself, and through the most plastered smile stuck on her face, she said, "Nicole Danielle, get your ass in that house right now!" *It was so terrifying.* I didn't even say goodbye. I didn't even look back. I just ran as fast as I could and hid away in my room. And the next weekend, Mom told me I wasn't going back to my father's house, and that my brother was staying there with them.

While it wasn't the last time I saw them, that is the last *happy memory* I have that involves my father's side of my family. It was the end of what I knew to be the "happy times" with that part of myself. After that, everything associated with them just became part of the darkness.

My brother and I have the same parents but spent more time apart than we ever did together. We were torn apart for reasons we may never fully understand and each raised on a different path in life. It involved a lot of time in the courtroom, a lot of money at play, and ultimately, decisions were made for my brother to go live permanently in Melrose Park with my biological father and for me to stay with our new family, consisting of my mother, my new stepdad and my new baby sister on the way, in the home we built in Gilberts, Illinois.

For two kids who were supposed to always be there for one another, we started venturing down very different paths. And as I continued down the road I was put on, and he continued down the road he was put on, we both just got so far down our own forced-upon roads that one day, when I looked back—he just disappeared.

There was never a "goodbye" moment—not with my biological father, not with my paternal grandparents, and certainly not with my brother. It was all just gone.

And with that, a part of my identity just vanished.

My mom always told me that they brainwashed my brother and me, bribed us with things to buy our love, and they were all terrible human beings. She started to tell me more of *her* truths about my father over the next few years, truths that would support the brainwashing she was actually also doing in her own way. She let me read a part of her journal where one minute my father told her he loved her and the next he threatened that if she continued to shake her ass when she walked, he'd make it so she never could again. She told me about him pushing her down the stairs when she was pregnant with me, and that's why I was born six weeks early. She told me about him intentionally burning down the video store they owned in order to collect the insurance money. She told me I wasn't worth anything more to him than the $37.50 child support checks. Everything that came out of her mouth in regard to that family was just bad, bad, bad. Even so much as to make me believe her when she said, "They chose your brother and I chose you," to justify why I never saw my brother again and why my father apparently didn't want me. She meant for me to hate him, and that was that—but my mind took it as I just wasn't enough.

I developed so much hate around my last name because of what I was told about my father, though never by what I truly felt in my heart. When my paternal grandmother passed away, a part of my heart broke, yet my mother's comment to me was, "Ding dong, the witch is dead." She hated them, and therefore, I learned to hate them too. All I ever knew from my father and his family was love, in their way of what *love* meant. So, why so much hate? My mother could say she was protecting me, but really, she was protecting herself.

My brother was raised by money; I was raised by "love." Or that's what I was made to believe.

My mother convinced me to be ashamed of where I came from—so ashamed that she even encouraged me to drop my father's last name, and at the age of ten years old, I legally became known as *Nicole Danielle*.

"Lucky Star"

When you were ten years old, do you remember what you wanted to be when you grew up?

I wanted to play Susan Lucci's daughter on *All My Children*. Well, at least that's what I told a panel of judges in the USA National Miss pageant.

If you've ever worn a tiara, you know that there are instant expectations that go along with it. You're expected to wear that crown with pride. You're expected to set a good example. You're expected to be a "good girl" because a good girl is a role model for others. You're expected to give back to the community in a way the community expects of you. You're expected to make your presence known, to be in parades, to show up for charity events, to stand tall, to smile—*always smile*—and you're especially expected to know what you want out of life.

The decision to legally drop my last name was a very defining time in my life. At ten years old, I went from being crowned USA National Miss Pre-Teen Illinois and being recognized in all the newspapers, local media, and town parades as Nicole Danielle LaSpisa to moving on to the national competition and, at eleven years old, being crowned USA National Miss Pre-Teen Photogenic as Nicole Danielle. The back of my state sash was embroidered with *Nicole Danielle LaSpisa*, and the back of my national title sash was embroidered with *Nicole Danielle*.

Since I was young, my mother has always said that I was her *Lucky Star*—and no, not just because I have the same birthday as

Madonna. Being a pageant girl is not something I dreamed of for years. My mother presented the idea to me, and it therefore became my reality.

Everywhere I went, I had to wear my crown. Every event became a "photo op," a place to prove I was well rounded and a member of the community, on top of being beautiful. I attended parades, company events, festivals, store grand openings, the Illinois Special Olympics Celebrity Sports Carnival, and the AIDS Walk Chicago—just to name a few. I even had photo ops at my local dance troupe shows and, you bet, at my elementary school. The highlight of my crown-wearing days was when Chicago Bears No. 95 himself, Richard Dent, looked at me in O'Hare airport as I was on my way to President Bill Clinton's inauguration—having to once again wear that damn sash and crown—and said, "Well, who's that cutie?" That made my young Chicago-sports-loving heart beam. That event was followed up by attending Clinton's inauguration with my other invited queens, getting to meet Speaker of the House Tom Foley, seeing Hillary and Chelsea speak from my front-row seat, and parading around the MTV Ball—even getting a wink from President Clinton himself. I was living the experiences most eleven-year-olds would never dream of in their young life.

I didn't go anywhere without that crown.

It's not until after you experience something that you're able to look back and realize how the actions and expectations of others affected your life. That's something you can never plan for. Once my mother signed me up for the pageant, the new plan became to win. You don't just enter something like that and half-ass it. Nobody enters a pageant thinking, *I'm just here to make friends.* No, you're in it to win it. You go all in, because now you're expected to win. I went all in! And I won because I did just that. I got that crown.

But nothing shiny comes without a price.

After the pageant, when people asked me what I wanted to be when I grew up, my answer shifted from playing Susan Lucci's daughter on *All My Children* to "I want to be a model." At the state pageant, I was awarded with trophies for "Prettiest Eyes" and "Best Smile." At nationals, I was crowned USA National Miss Pre-Teen Photogenic for one reason—because I took the most beautiful photos. So, naturally, I was now encouraged to believe that what I was meant to do was go down this modeling path. That was what my mother convinced me to believe and what I fooled others into thinking I wanted for *my* life. Yet, if I had gotten the chance to actually speak up and give the answer I wanted to give, I would have said, "I want to be a lawyer for children's rights."

You see, I was the one who had to be in that courtroom, and I was the one who had to beg to be heard. I was the one who was told my voice didn't matter.

"Read All About It, Pt. III"

The whole feeling-I-didn't-have-a-voice thing isn't something that just randomly came about when I was an adult; it actually started during this time in my childhood. Here I was, a pageant queen with a crown on my head and a platform in which I was able to speak; however, in my real life, I was silenced and told I didn't have a voice.

After the name change, my parents found themselves in court, being sued by my paternal grandparents for "grandparents' rights." My mother made the decision that I was with her, my brother was with them, and that was that. But they weren't going to accept her demands without a fight.

At this point, I had heard about all of the bad things and convinced myself that what my mother spoke about them was the truth. I didn't want to be near them, I didn't want to see them, I just wanted to live this new glorious life Mom and I had with our new family in our big home, just living out the "American Dream." But everything was image; everything presented was surface level. We had the big house, all the toys, all the things, yet my stepdad had to sell his most prized possession, his corvette, in order to pay for the legal fees to protect me. I was only his "daughter" as of a few years by then, but he loved my mom and he loved me, and he was willing to do whatever it took to keep me safe, and make her happy. When you put a man like that up against the ugliness I was told of my father, there was no comparison as to what sort of *love* I was wanting. *Or needing.* While I might have my father's eyes, I learned to see the world through my stepdad's—he's the one who taught me to fight for loyalty and the kind of love a person deserves in life.

During the court battle, I was made to believe I had no rights, no voice. I was reminded of my place in this world—I was a child. *What could a child possibly know?* Only I could have known what I truly wanted beyond the part I was told to play, but no one wanted to let me speak if I wasn't saying what they wanted to hear. So, I always gave the answer my mother told me to give, the answer adults in my life expected me to give in order to keep living by the image being portrayed. I was told to say I wanted nothing to do with my father's family, I hated them, I wanted to be with my mom and my new family in our new big home doing my dance classes and all the what-sounds-on-paper-like-such-a-privileged-life things kids my age growing up in nice suburbs got to do. Whether or not it was the truth, it's what I was convinced to make the world believe. *Everyone is watching—be a good girl, smile, say what we tell you to say.*

The funny thing is, when I described earlier about my final memories I could recall, those weren't actually the final *goodbyes.*

Life carried on, visitations kept happening beyond that, but, as with all childhood traumas, I had grown up to block that pain from my memory, from my life—until I stumbled across letters and poems written in my handwriting from when I was eleven years old, pleading my case to our lawyer, begging just to be heard:

Dear Mr. Hammer,

I am tired of not being listened to. I believe that I have a right to speak in court. Does it say anywhere in the Constitution of America that children have a right to speak in court? If it does, and Judge Hall is not letting me speak in court, I think he will be in big trouble.

People just look at me as a child and don't see who I really am. I have a voice too, and nobody respects that. What else can I do so they will listen to me?

Sincerely,
Nicole Danielle

I then went on to include forty-eight reasons to support my young feelings and reasons why I should be listened to for wanting to stay with my mom and have nothing to do with my biological father and his family. Here are just a few I wrote:

#9 - He has sent two federal express boxes to be delivered overnight: one to give me a little giraffe saying, "Just to let you know I love you," and another one where he mailed a pumpkin with a whole bunch of candy that was junk. It's a bunch of bull.

#20 – A woman with the last name LaSpisa called a lady up and saying that my mom was beating me up and I had bruises all over, and a woman had to check me.

#21 - Another thing was when I was only two or three my dad was beating my mom up and gave her bruises, and the police came over and wouldn't do a thing because my dad had the last name of LaSpisa.

#22 - Also one time I went to visit my dad's house and my mom called to tell my dad he's supposed to bring me home, and he said that he wasn't going to give me back, and also said, "If you ever set foot in Melrose Park again, I'll have you killed."

#32 - When I go there, I have a pull-out bed, and I had one drawer to put my clothes in.

#41 - My father is also a liar & a sneak.

While my letter to our family lawyer didn't allow me to speak in the courtroom what my young heart was begging to say, that letter is what granted me the ability to at least try and plead my own case, separate from that of any adults involved, privately in the judge's chambers. Something so small yet, as a child, a right that I had to fight for.

I was told my grandparents didn't win the right to see me. My parents won—hence why I actually never saw them again.

Looking at those words I had written as a child now through my eyes as an adult, I can see my father tried, in perhaps the only way he knew how. He was fighting for me in his own fucked-up way. I was just convinced to believe it to be something entirely different.

I don't know what side or whose lies were the actual truth, but what I know is that my stepdad always did right by my mom. You didn't want to cross her.

My entire childhood—with a crown on my head, seated in a judge's chambers, being pulled in two different directions, and every adult screaming what was best for me—I sat quiet, listening to the noise. Because the noise was more convincing than the voice I was told I didn't have. So, I gave the answers I was expected to give, shutting down the truth wanting to be set free.

"Easy On Me"

During the time of my name changing, I also transitioned from elementary school to middle school. When I had to go back to school, I went with a crown—which, indeed, comes with some kind of power. I was Nicole Danielle, a *star* in the making. Yet, when I went to my school locker, I was still surrounded by peers in the "L" section of the alphabet, not the "D." It's a natural thing to expect your friends and peers to be happy for your success, but it was quite the opposite for me. A lot of rumors started circling about me because of my name change, including a lot of confrontational remarks from my peers claiming that I was suddenly in the witness protection program. A lot of giggles, whispers, finger pointing—not the kind of stuff a typical eleven-year-old should have to deal with.

The hardest day of middle school came when I was sitting in biology class. I overheard my *friend* asking another student, "Did you hear about the SAND Club?" The other student replied, "No, what's that?" And that's when I heard her say, "the *Students Against Nicole Danielle* Club."

As tears broke from my eyes, behind me all I heard were chuckles.

I've always had pretty thick skin, but I was eleven years old. And that one hurt.

The thing is—nobody saw that pain. By eleven years old, I had mastered the art of wearing a painted smile for the world to see. On the outside, I was fine. I didn't show the hurt. I smiled and waved my way through the obligations and what was expected of me. But inside, I was cracked.

That's the day I realized my "friends" weren't really my friends. I don't know what I did to make people hate me so much and cause them to be so cruel. All I was doing was living by these expectations people put upon me, winning that crown, changing my name for "my safety," and talking of dreams that were never my own. I was just following "the plan," wasn't I? And yet, people didn't like me anymore to the point they created the Students. Against. Nicole. Danielle. Club.

S-A-N-D.

I honestly can say that I don't know what level the *SAND Club* went beyond that comment I heard, but that one comment altered my life. It was the defining moment in my childhood when I learned to shut down from the pain, after realizing how people I thought I trusted could hurt me. I had to carry on as this strong external image I was presenting for the world—yet, I suddenly found myself crawling back internally. I started noticing my friendships changing, so I pulled further away. Even though I so badly just wanted to feel I belonged, all I could do was hold on to this snapshot in my life and mask myself from whatever else was happening behind my back. "What, are you in the witness protection program?" "Haha… the Students Against Nicole Danielle Club"—oh, and the infamous day during gym class when those same "friends" were walking around waving their hands in front of me like pageant queens.

The only way any of that wouldn't have hurt was if I wasn't human.

I know people were doing and saying shitty things just to hurt me, because it made them feel better, and it worked. I'm pretty sure this was the moment in life when my bright light started to dim.

Looking back, whether they did it because they were jealous or just wanting to be shitty 'cause kids can be real assholes, it doesn't matter. But it changed a lot for me in my younger years, and it made me not only question what friendships and relationships meant to me but also made me very cautious of who I truly let know the *real* me.

I never told my parents what I went through. We all have different reasons for what we choose to hide. Sometimes we are ashamed, sometimes we think we can handle it on our own, and sometimes, we are afraid of giving another person more fuel to hurt us. Back then, when I was eleven years old, I couldn't bring that up to my parents. I didn't need it to become an "issue" they went to the school about. Had they gone to the school, kids would have gotten a talking to, it would have become a bigger issue, and resulted in even more heat and even more torment thrown my way. I couldn't deal with anymore of that—there was already too much damn pressure on me with the weight of that crown on my head.

On top of that, I was embarrassed for whatever part I may have played in causing the people I thought were my friends, my peers, to feel that way about me. I was ashamed—here I am, in the eyes of everyone who saw me, a *queen,* letting others emotionally knock me down. But the true core of why I never said anything to my parents is because I thought I would disappoint them. Whether or not I was going to disappoint my parents had become my driving force for everything.

So, I just dealt with it. Before long, I learned the art of becoming numb to it.

"The Sign"

I was twelve years old when my baby sister, Demi, was born. Shortly after her birth, we went on a family cruise. She was way too little to go on a cruise ship, so it was just my mom, my stepdad, my sister, B., and myself that went, while Demi was taken care of at home by other family members. My parents had a lot of trust in me, so while B. was off having playtime in the Fuzzy Wuzzy Room and my parents were off doing whatever parents do when they're without kids on a cruise ship, I went off on my own and found a group of people my age who became instant friends.

The most beautiful thing about meeting such awesome new friends while on vacation was they didn't know anything about my life. I went from feeling like there's no one place I really fit in back home to now being part of a tight little circle of friends. In our one short week together, we snuck off to watch *Braveheart* in the ship's theater and scheduled hangouts so we had something to look forward to after we got back from our off-island adventures with our parents. I maybe even got a little crush, which led to a little hand-holding. He gave me his beaded necklace to take home with me, with promises that we would keep in touch and write to one another. I began to regain my confidence and remember who I was when I wasn't being bullied back home.

But something even bigger happened to me on that cruise ship. I saw a flier that there would be auditions for the cruise play, which was going to be a live performance of *The Wizard of Oz*. I don't know what it was that drew me in, but this was the sign I was needing in my life. I went to the audition, and I got cast as the Scarecrow. Even though I had no real acting chops up to that point—except our fifth-grade movie where I was, ironically, cast as a soap opera star and in my kindergarten class playing Mrs. Santa Clause—I did have an extensive dance background, so I had the ability to express emotions without words. But the Scarecrow? Me, a "pageant queen"? Yet, they wanted me in such a simple role. The most memorable thing I said was, "E=MC squared. Cool, I got a brain!" But the spotlight was on me, and I made the crowd roar with laughter. I did that. I made a packed auditorium of people laugh. It was on that stage that I fell in love with theater. I fell in love with performing. I fell in love with who I was when I was up there in front of a room of people, playing a character that wasn't me, without a shiny crown on my head and, instead, a burlap sack over my face. It was a different kind of spotlight. *I belonged there.*

The art of theater is a funny thing because I felt more alive playing someone else than I did in my daily life. In real life, I felt like I had been playing someone else. On stage, playing the Scarecrow, I finally felt like me.

With a freshly golden tan and a head full of braids and beads, I got home and couldn't shake the feeling that overcame me when I was on that stage. I wasn't a pageant girl, I didn't want to do this modeling thing, and I was tired of my school peers resenting me for it. It was then when I discovered the Children's Theater of Elgin, also known as CTE, and it became my life. I made the best of friends just by being me. Who I was, *Nicole Danielle*.

I had to get lost in a world outside of that "crown" in order to mask the pain of my real life—hence why theater became so important to me.

"Lost Boy"

I spent the next years of my life auditioning for, and being a part of, every season and show of CTE that I could. To say I was addicted to the theater at that point is an understatement. I loved every single part of the entire process. Something within me that I didn't even know existed was suddenly on fire. I was alive! And I couldn't get enough.

I never got cast in the best roles, but I was able to make myself seen in ways I never could have before. I was never a singer; I lacked confidence in that. Where I made my mark was in my abilities to move my body. One of the first musicals I was in with CTE was *Snow White,* and I was cast as one of the "Robinettes"—basically one of Snow White's friendly little red-feathered birds who had a boo-ty-shaking musical performance to the Jackson 5's "Rockin' Robin." While I wasn't cast in a top-bill-worthy role, I made enough of an impact in my performance to be awarded with that season's "Shake 'n Bake" Award—literally given a box of Shake 'n Bake—because I was the best dancer, with a standout performance. And everyone cheered for me, even though I wasn't Snow White.

While *Snow White* was my earliest memory of my time with CTE, one play, one season I could never forget was the one that left the biggest imprint on my heart: *Peter Pan.*

Ironically, I "dated" Peter Pan. It was the fall of 1994, I was just thirteen years old, and we were in CTE's chosen theatrical musical during that time. My first "boyfriend" played the role of Peter Pan in that stage production, and I played one of Tiger Lily's fellow Indians. Once again, I wasn't in a standout role, yet somehow, I stood out to the one who was. We were smitten little things. What was beautiful in the theater world was we got to live out our special moments to-gether, every day during rehearsals and during performances.

There's a weird calmness when you're standing backstage that comes with the darkness and the chaos. It's a comforting "lost" to be in. With the lights from the stage peeking into the back, we would be standing in the dark, our hands just touching enough to say, *Hey, I like you, you like me, and the rest of the world can't see us.* But then, oh, then, he would run away as fast as he could in the direction of that light and fly into the sky toward Neverland. And there I stood, just a young girl in awe that Peter Pan saw *me.*

Although I was cast as one of Tiger Lily's Indians in the play, in real life, I was just a "lost boy," and Peter Pan made me believe I was so much more than what others could see.

During the duration of that show, we spent Halloween night at one of our best friend's houses. Our friends couldn't deny the attrac-tion between us, so they did what theater kids do best and perfectly cued up the music to play "Kiss the Girl" from *The Little Mermaid.*

The room got quiet. All eyes were suddenly upon us, and there he stood next to me. Peter Pan held out his hand and said, "Dance with me?"

Pretty sure I swallowed my heart in that moment—but I grabbed his hand and awkwardly fell into his arms as teenagers do the first time they have a meaningful dance with their crush who had also been crushing on them.

All eyes upon us, as the chorus of "Kiss the Girl" continued to play, suddenly, he leaned in. *Peter Pan kissed me.* With all of our friends cheering us on, my first real kiss ever was something Walt Disney himself would have smiled down upon, that's for sure.

Maybe Peter Pan had it right. *Why do we ever grow up?* Life was so simple back then. Life was a fairytale—and I loved living in the *magic* of it all. But sadly, the magic fades. We start to choose worry over wonder. At some point, we're told it's time to grow up. So we move on, and Neverland becomes a faint star we find ourselves now and then just wishing upon.

Children's theater couldn't last forever; but, through continually playing someone else, I found a big part of my young self that I didn't know was just locked up, screaming to be freed—I found the storyteller in me. Theater was the first time in my life I discovered a part of my expressive soul that went to depths I had never experienced before. The world didn't have to understand because up there on that stage, no one could touch me. No one could convince me of a different narrative, the words I memorized on those pages in those scripts were just words—the performance that came because of that was the reflection of what was hidden within me. In my real life, I could never quite understand how to unleash that part of me. But on the stage, I was set free. I never could have planned for that, but *life*, surely, had it planned for me.

After *Peter Pan* ran its course, so did our sweet little romance. He traded up for a "better role" that involved bigger auditions, better castings, and perkier blondes.

The adventure was fun while it lasted. But now, it was my turn to fly.

THE DREAMER

"Crash Into Me"

I n high school, I wasn't one of the most popular kids, and I didn't excel in any one thing. I kind of found my place being friends with as many different groups of people as I could and put my hands into way more extracurricular activities than one could handle.

Even though by now we were living a much more comfortable life than we had when I was younger, because I went through those tough times growing up when it was just my mom and me, I learned to never take anything for granted. I had a front row seat on my parents' teaching that you had to work really hard for anything you would be given in life.

When I turned sixteen, my parents threw me a pretty epic pool party at our home. It was the merging of two sides of me at the time, a perfect blend of my theater friends I was still really close with and my high school friends who were just good people in my life. During the party, I walked outside and found a car parked in the driveway with a bow on it—a black 1983 Nissan 300ZX with T-tops. My parents bought this car from my uncle for $500 so that they could gift me my own car for my Sweet Sixteenth. Because I was born on August 16th, it was also my *golden birthday*—ya know, the birthday that only happens once in your life when you celebrate in years the same as the date you were born on—so they definitely went above and beyond to do what they could to make it a memorable one.

I loved the car I got on my birthday. I was truly shocked. It was super fun, being able to convert into a semi-convertible when I took the two side top pieces off. But, it was old and definitely wasn't the safest car. Oftentimes, I would be driving and the speedometer would show *zero* miles per hour, no matter how fast or slow I was going. And, because we lived in the midwest, definitely wasn't the best choice for snowy weather.

By junior year, I was focused on two main things: being the executive board vice president of student council, and being a starter on the Jacobs High School Poms Squad, which meant primarily performing during our home football and basketball games. We weren't cheerleaders; we were the halftime entertainment. Performing for a large group of people was a rush, and we never knew who was on the receiving end, watching each one of us.

I spent all four years going to Harry D. Jacobs High School in Algonquin. When you turned into the main entrance to the school, it was a little bit of a stretch down Golden Eagle Drive as you were trying to approach the main entrance and ultimately the parking lot. My junior year, there was one day it was snowing and they hadn't put any salt down yet on the road. I made a left turn in my 300ZX to head toward school, but I ended up fishtailing. I couldn't control the car and ended up sliding right into a school bus that was coming the opposite way. It was terrifying, and thankfully, it was just a little bang-up job, my car wasn't destroyed, and no one was hurt.

By the time I was able to get a hold of myself and park, I was shaking so bad. As a semi-new driver, I was really scared by what had happened, yet I didn't know what I could have done differently. My little snow accident that happened that morning ended up spiraling into quite the gossip fest by the time I made it indoors, and as I was walking through the halls, endless comments were being thrown my way. Out of all of them, there was one that would alter the rest of my high school days—the day I crashed into a school bus, but he chose to crash into me.

Late for school after my lovely, snowy bus accident, I was rushing to get to class. I closed my locker and started to walk down the hall when suddenly a boy I knew but had never really talked to much came up to me, practically pinning me to the inside of a closed door-way by putting his left arm up over the side of the wall and getting right into my face. He asked me, "So, did a mannequin really slide across your car and under the bus and that's what caused the acci-dent? Because that's what I heard."

Really? A fucking mannequin? I thought to myself.

I was so annoyed. Like, so annoyed. But I couldn't resist that smile. He was a senior, a football player, someone I knew of, but I never thought he knew who I was. But that day, he sure let me know he indeed did know I existed.

That was the first interaction I ever had with my high school sweetheart.

After that day, I would suddenly start seeing him throughout the halls and in familiar scenarios I had never noticed him in before. I'd be performing during halftime at the basketball games and would find his face in the crowd, smiling while watching me. One night after a game, he asked me to hang out—and as I sat in my Poms uni-form on his lap, he kissed me for the first time. There was no looking back after that night. I thought high school feelings like this only existed in the movies, but he showed me I was worthy of the real-life version of that.

For the girl who was convinced her father didn't want her, I think a part of my heart grew up feeling that I wasn't worthy of true, mean-ingful love. But my high school sweetheart proved that wrong by showing me just how profoundly I deserved to be loved.

I lost my virginity to him—in a truly beautiful, meaningful way. As I laid in his arms, he became emotional and said to me, "I lost my virginity to someone else. And I wish it didn't happen because it didn't mean anything. And I wish you would have been my first."

That was the first time in my life I saw a guy be so vulnerable in front of me, and the first time I knew what it meant to be loved by someone else in a romantic way. We were in love, and so, giving that part of my story to him—there's no more perfect way it could have been.

"Time After Time"

In the spring of 1998, our prom theme was "Eternity." I wore a red tulle ball gown that had hints of blue and purple under it. With a rhinestone headband at the crown of my head, I stood next to him and saw stars in his eyes. The way he looked at me was—well, it made me feel more like a queen than I ever had when I wore that real crown. As we celebrated a magical night surrounded by our friends, when we danced it was a true happiness I had waited all my young life to feel.

While graduation was upon him, there was no talk of giving up on what we had. We spent that summer together, and come fall, as I entered my senior year of high school and he went off to college away from there, there was no goodbye—we were in it together. We were determined to make the long-distance thing work. I went to his college to visit him and watch him play football. He came home and went with me to my senior-year homecoming. We talked when we both were able to dial into AOL and chat online. We saw each other on the holidays he came home for. But, as winter was coming to an end, our young love ran its course.

We were both on two very different paths, no longer heading in the same direction. I couldn't hold him back, and he would never have dreamed of doing that to me. Even when he was away at college and I was living out my senior year, he never once told me I couldn't do what I wanted to do or be who I wanted to be, and he never tried to ground me. If anything, he was the one convincing me I needed to fly. I had big dreams, and he never would have dreamed of holding me down. And on the flip side, he was paving his own way, and being within reach of his family at that time was important. I could have never asked him to give that up to join me on my journey. He had safe plans for his life, and he knew I was his wild card, unable to be tamed.

Before he graduated from Jacobs, even though we were still to-gether and living out our young puppy love, he gave me a copy of his senior-year photo. On the back of it, he wrote:

> *Don't stop short on any of your goals.*
> *You can do whatever you want to.*
> *- M., Class '98*

I'll always be thankful for this piece of my story, and I'll always carry that message with me.

I can do whatever I want to.

I didn't understand the weight of our relationship ending at that time, nor what that message he wrote me meant. What does young love really know without real heartbreak and life experiences? And I think in the forefront of my mind, I told myself I would always hold on to the hope that "eternity" was a thing. That even though we needed to venture down our own paths at that point in time, once we figured out who we were on our own journeys we were destined to travel along, that our paths would cross again and we would find our way back to one another.

That's what your first love does to you: makes you believe you're worthy of a great love story and that fairytales can exist in real life.

Yet, over time, you may find yourself living a different story.

He was the first person I ever loved, the first person I ever made love to, and the first person whose love broke my heart in a way I couldn't see at the time.

"Dream On"

At the end of high school, I remember my papa saying to me one day, "Theater? Why don't you major in something you'll actually make money in, like business?" While me at the time was too stubborn to listen to the wise advice he was trying to give me, I could hear *his* words in my ear, "You can do whatever you want to." And what I wanted to do was follow my heart, my passion, and the vision was so clear. My dream was to study theater at DePaul University in Chicago and, after graduation, head off to California to make my bigger dreams become a living reality.

But as a life lesson would quickly convince me, it was okay for other people to do what they wanted to do but not me.

After being in Illinois my entire life, my parents made the decision halfway through my senior year of high school to pack up and move to Massachusetts because of a better job offer my stepdad got. He had spent most of his career thus far working for the beloved Marshall Field & Company—that's where he and my mom met, as she did the visual displays for some of the stores. Growing up, I don't know if there was anything better than Christmas time at Marshall Field's. It was instant magic. Once Macy's bought out Marshall Field's, my stepdad got offered a job with this new retail company on the scene called Target. It was my senior year of high school when a better opportunity came about for my stepdad, and so my family packed everything up, left Gilberts behind, and set off to a new life in Northbridge, Massachusetts. Knowing it would be completely unfair to rip me out of the final stretch of my senior year, especially after how hard I had worked all those years, they agreed to let me stay in Illinois and live with my uncle until I graduated.

Before I knew it, high school graduation was upon me, and I had a decision to make. I hadn't heard back about my DePaul application—my dream school—but I had been accepted to Roger Williams University in Rhode Island, which did have an amazing theater program in their "Barn." And, there was partial scholarship money attached. When I sent out my college applications, I didn't want to go to school in Rhode Island. I didn't want to be on the east coast. I didn't care if they gave me some scholarship money; that wasn't my dream. I applied because it was closer to my parents; that's it. My mother pushed the idea of the school, and secretly, their expectation was for me to be closer to my family for college.

Unfortunately, I was coaxed into considering it as an option. DePaul was what was pulling my heart, so to sweeten my moving east in their favor, my parents made me a deal: if I worked hard and got good grades, I would never have to worry about paying back the student loans that I had to have them co-sign to cover what scholarship money did not.

Time was running out, and all my bags at my uncle's house were packed. I couldn't wait, or I would risk not being able to go to college at all. DePaul just didn't get back to me in time, so I didn't have any better choice. I had to fully uproot my life, head to the east coast, accept the journey I committed to and the scholarship I was given, and move forward, paving a new road to ultimately get to my dream of moving to California for my acting career.

So, it was off to Rhode Island. Even though, inside, I secretly just wanted to run away to the west coast.

"Blackbird"

Before moving into my dorm at RWU the fall of 1999, I spent the summer living at my parents' home in Massachusetts. Shortly after making the move, I got a letter in the mail from DePaul University, accepting me into the theater program and offering me scholarship money equivalent to what I was offered from RWU. My dream school wanted me. I was good enough. But as I held that letter in my hand, I looked at my parents' faces—that pretty much told me I wasn't going back.

I guess it could be argued that I was an adult and I had the right to choose what I wanted for my life. But I was a seventeen-year-old living life by way of my parents in the summer of '99. I had spent most of my life doing right by my mother, being a good girl, pleasing my parents, basing my life choices on the societal pressures I felt hammering down on me. As a child, I had seen that "don't fuck with me" look in my mother's eyes, and it terrified me to the point I navigated the decisions for my life based on never wanting to see that again. While I should have had the choice to pack my bags back up and go back to Chicago, to my dream school, I didn't want to disappoint my parents. They offered me a pretty sweet deal. I couldn't see that bone-chilling look my mother could so easily dish out every again. So instead of disappointing them, I chose to please them— and in doing so, made the choice to disappoint me.

I wasn't sure how to respond. I didn't want to throw a fit, but I was upset. I got coaxed into making the decision I did when I should have just stayed patient. If I had, I would have had the ability to choose what I wanted for myself. I did the work. I got the grades. I made the sacrifices. It was my dream. And instead of trusting in myself, I followed someone else's wants for my life and took the deal to do so.

Why did I keep signing on the dotted line, giving other people permission to control my life?

Even though things didn't go in the direction I originally dreamed of, I accepted my decision with grace and created a new plan moving forward. I went to Roger Williams University and I met some of the best people I've ever known, people who became a part of my life for a greater reason than I knew at the time and who have greatly contributed to the woman I am today. So, while I still have this part of me that wonders what my life would have been like had I chosen the path I wanted—to live on my own in the city of Chicago as the bright-eyed, eighteen-year-old me I would have been walking into fall semester of freshman year at DePaul University—I instead had to begin to trust that the universe always has a greater plan for us.

When my parents told me that if I excelled in college and got A's, that I would never have to worry about paying off the balance of my student loans, I knew what my parents would be taking on in order to do that for me. I knew what a financial burden that was going to be. While I had my fun and enjoyed my freedom in college, I took their deal very seriously.

"What A Feeling"

While I was at RWU, I took an acting workshop in Boston with a casting director for *All My Children*—yes, that same soap opera I told the judges during the pageant it was my dream in life to be cast on. I'll never forget that day. It gave me a confidence I had never had as an actor up until that moment in time.

During the workshop, we were paired up with a partner, and everyone was given a different scene to work on and eventually act out in front of the rest of the group. A little secret about me, as much as I love performing on a stage, I was always a freaking wreck before I walked into an audition. I would get so nervous, almost psyching myself out. Yet, when I walked in the audition room or stepped foot on a stage, I would always come to life. Almost like a switch flipped internally, and suddenly, I was "on."

The day of that workshop, I was sitting next to the guy I was paired with; our scene took place in a car. With a room full of other actors of all ages taking the workshop and the guy who was literally a casting director for the show I dreamed of being on in my younger days, I poured everything into that performance. When we finished our scene, our workshop teacher immediately defaulted to first commenting on my male counterpart's performance, praising him for his work and giving him notes on where to improve. Then he looked at me and said one simple thing, "Nicole Danielle... If that was the performance you would have given me in the actual audition for that role, I would have cast you in that role right there on the spot."

Goosebumps.

That was the most praise I had ever gotten in my life, as an actor. All I could do was pick my jaw up off the floor, try not to throw up right there, and simultaneously plot my plan on how to get my ass out of Rhode Island and out to Los Angeles as soon as possible.

While there was nothing I could immediately do to get myself to the City of Angels, that experience, his comment, ignited a fire in me I hadn't even seen in myself before. I decided I wanted to be done with school as fast as possible. I started going to RWU year-round, taking on more classes, working early mornings in the campus library just to make extra money to survive off of while also working at the clothing store Express in Newport when I could. I put every ounce of passion burning inside of me into every single school audition and play, every theater project, every creative writing assignment, every dance performance I was a part of, and also choreographed on my own. He told me he would have cast me. I was that good. And it was time to put everything I had into showing everyone else I was too.

And I did.

At the end of my college years, I ended up graduating from Roger Williams University with a BA in theater, with Magna Cum Laude honors, within three years' time, at twenty years old. I did it. And I held up my end of the bargain. I set crazy goals for myself and crushed them. I took care of my part of the deal, assuming my parents would do the same.

Assumptions are a very dangerous thing.

The funny thing about me moving all the way to the east coast to go to college closer to my family is—just as they did my senior year of high school—my final year of college, my family packed up and moved all the way to Texas for another job opportunity, leaving me alone on the east coast in a place I never wanted to be.

But, whatever. The day I worked so hard for finally came, my name was called, my hand was shaken, and a temporary diploma was placed in my hands. As I hugged my family who was there to support me, and as I said goodbye to the friends who helped shape me into the woman I was walking out into the real world as, while I had a huge smile on my face and a bright twinkle in my eyes, I was really just crying inside.

I wasn't getting on a plane to Los Angeles.

Instead, with my "Dream Box" on my lap, I found myself on a plane to Katy, Texas.

I wasn't going where I wanted to go. I was going to where my parents expected me to go, their new home.

Decades later, I have had to take a step back and question how I let so much of my life be determined by what other people wanted for it. When did I just become a part of someone else's narrative instead of the one I was writing on my own? Simply because I was too afraid of the alternative to speak up and say, "No."

"Daydream"

As children, we were taught to believe in the power of a dream, to use our imagination and make the "impossible" happen. We looked up at the clouds and saw castles there in the sky, while thoughts of actually being able to "catch a falling star" seemed to be our entertainment for the night. But as we grew up and attempted to hold on to that light, it seemed as though the darkened world around us tried to take that light away.

Why was it still okay for my sisters to be able to believe in the magic of Disney and not me? Because they were still kids, and I was now an "adult"? Because everyone else said I had to "grow up"?

Yet, after college, I didn't want to just grow up. I was more alive with my head in the clouds. I've always had a creative soul. Why was the world trying to fit me in a standard-size box?

Ironically, one of my favorite pastimes from my days at RWU and my early twenties was making "Dream Boxes." A Dream Box was my interpretation of a "vision board," except instead of plastering your dreams on the wall for others to visually see, it was a secret place for you to keep them closer to your heart. The Dream Box held my dreams safe for me and protected them from the outside world until I decided I was ready to put it all out there. When I first made mine, I filled it with inspiring images of Hollywood, drawings from my sisters of me winning an Oscar, simple handwritten quotes that in one sentence could keep pushing me forward on my journey. It's where I kept all my original poems, doodles of words and images of what "my soulmate" out there somewhere in the world encompassed.

I filled it with all the things most personal to me—the things that reminded me of how far I'd come and the things that inspired me to keep pushing on in the pursuit of where I knew I was destined to go.

I wanted to give that same feeling as a gift to others. So, I would make a Dream Box by hand for some of the most special people in my life. I would go and get a cardboard-colored box from the craft store, paint the entire exterior black, then I would paint designs on the outside or use some favorite quotes, or song lyrics, or symbols that made it personal to who I was making that specific Dream Box for. I wrote up a little note to include with it, explaining further the concept of what my gift meant.

This was the note:

DREAM BOX

This is a box created just for you, to fill with it all your heart desires ~ what it yearns for, what makes it breathe.

Within this box, place your dreams,
bits of inspiration, feelings held within.
And if ever a time comes when you've lost sight of your dreams,
when you're caught in the line of fire between
the war of your head and heart,
open this box, and you will find the answers
you were searching for all along.

Never forget… dreams are what we live for,
why we awaken day after day
and what meets us in reality during sleep.

NEVER FORGET YOUR DREAMS!
NEVER GIVE UP ON THEM!

*Don't ever let the "outside" world stop you
from being who you truly are, what your purpose is.*

*This box was made specifically for you
because I believe in you!!!*

*Make your dreams the REALITY you've always imagined...
and then you'll truly be living life!*

I did this all throughout college and in my quiet time while living in Texas—and shit, twenty-year-old me was wise. Twenty-year-old me was inspired, passionate, and fearless. Twenty-year-old me wanted to help inspire others and let them know that even when they felt alone, I believed in them. Twenty-year-old me, fearless me, dreamed-bigger-than-the-sky me—she was unstoppable and believed there wasn't a thing she couldn't do. She just had to find her own way to do it.

I wish she never let the world break her spirit.

"Broken"

It didn't take long for the reality of being a college graduate to sink in. Within the first few weeks, I suddenly found myself thrust into this new life in Texas. I had worked my ass off for the past three years of my life in pursuit of my dream, and suddenly I found myself *lost* in this new life I didn't want. As someone who has always had the need to "work toward something," I no longer had anything to work for. I was just existing. When the pressures of adult life started to weigh on me, so did the necessity for the tangible and practical. It was time to get my head out of the clouds, and suddenly, I found myself getting to work at Starbucks by five o'clock in the morning—while my sisters were at home dancing around in their underwear with Disney Princess crowns on their heads.

Shortly after my college graduation, I was on my computer in my room at my parents' house in Texas, when I suddenly found an old familiar face—my high school sweetheart.

We were catching up via the internet. I was filling him in on my life, what I had just accomplished, and where I found myself that day. He told me he was proud of me. *He's always been proud of me.*

But then something happened that unexpectedly kind of rocked my world. He told me, "I'm going to be a dad."

I didn't quite know how to respond to that. My stomach was suddenly in knots, and I definitely didn't write back with an overly excited response to his news. I kind of just listened, I guess. I let him tell me the things he wanted to say. At twenty years old, I wasn't quite sure how to react to my first love telling me he was about to become a dad. I think it was just kind of a moment where I realized that we had grown up into two different people than we had been just a few short years before that. Even though I knew his heart, we were now different people.

During our conversation, he shared with me a vision he had in a dream one day, a vision of the future, a vision so profound there were faces attached to the glimpses he had been shown—a different vision than his new reality. After he told me he was going to be a dad, he mentioned they hadn't known each other long, and being a man of faith and the honorable guy that he is, he told me he was going to do the *right* thing. He was going to marry her and commit to their new family together.

I was proud of him, and in that moment, my heart did smile for him because I knew having a family of his own was always a dream of his one day down the road. It made me cry, but I was truly happy for him that a dream of his was coming true.

I'd be lying if I didn't think for a moment, *What would have happened if that DePaul acceptance letter came just a bit sooner and I stayed in Chicago instead?* But that was just my naive twenty-year-old mind processing the information I had just been given. You can't live your life in the "what if's." *But, what if?*

That still wasn't the most shocking part of what he shared with me. What really did me in was when he said, "And she told me, if I commit to her and our unborn child, I can never speak to you again." But he couldn't just disappear forever from my life without telling me why, so he had to let me know. And in doing so, let me go.

I don't know what was ever said about me or what she knew of our past, but that really fucked me up in the head. That really, really made me sad that my simple existence in this world, in his past, was enough for her to tell him that him committing to her and their unborn child meant he could never speak to me again.

The piece of my heart that always had his name on it shattered that day.

That was our goodbye—and the day I realized "eternity" was never really a thing.

That was the day I first felt that kind of real-life heartbreak I had never experienced just those short years before when we went our separate ways. But on this day, I felt my heart break because now that hope of some great young love story was gone.

That was the day I realized that apparently those words, "You can do whatever you want to," hold limited truth when, quite a few times now, it had been shown how easily other people could somehow control my life.

I don't know why all the things that he told me affected me so much. It's not like we had been in constant touch throughout those past few years, but him just telling me he wasn't supposed to be talking to me, yet he was talking to me to let me know why he no longer would be kind of said enough. I got to a really sad point in my life

I couldn't let anyone see. I spent a lot of time just locked inside my bedroom, with my head back in the clouds—a place I was told I often existed in, yet the one place I preferred to be because life was always brighter and more beautiful up there. Because in my mind, I see in pictures, and when I went to bed that night, I couldn't shake the visions he described to me. I could see a very clear picture of what could have been—but now, would never be.

And sadly, the reality of being an adult kicked in once again, and I needed to put it all away and stop dreaming in pictures that only existed in my mind. I had to stick to what I knew—making coffee and being an actor desperate for a break.

"Feeling Things"

When I was born, I was the fifth generation of women living— me all the way up to my great-great-grandmother, who lived to be 101 years old and died shortly after I was born. The common theme among the women in our family is being proud that we came from a "long line of strong, independent women." So proud, in fact, it was all of us women who carried my great-grandmother's casket out of the church and into the car that took her to be buried. Mimi was the epitome of grace. She was a lady in terms of the standard in which a woman was to uphold. She played the role. Oh goodness, I could only imagine her looking down from wherever she is, shaking her head at me because, clearly, I do not. Regardless, coming from a "long line of strong, independent women" put a lot of pressure on my back from an early age. And yet, you'd think with that mindset being burned into your brain, you'd always have the support of said women around you. Yet, one person in my life constantly found a way to emotionally tear me down instead of build me up, simply because it made herself feel better—that person being, my mother.

Shortly after that day I heard from my high school sweetheart, I managed to book a one-day gig for the BET Network where I was hired to be a background actor/dancer for a live-to-tape show. It was only a one-day gig, and as you often have to do when you're working background jobs, I had to utilize my own clothes for wardrobe. The gig was easy and fun. I danced on stage and got a nonunion pay-check in the mail shortly after for it. When I got home that night of filming, I was still wearing my white hip-hugging pants that I loved with my thick brown belt—it was maybe one of the only pieces of clothing that just fit me so well in my booty area that I was confident in flaunting the goods. I was also still wearing the white BET T-shirt they gave us at the taping over my fitted tank top and still had spar-kles all over my eyes.

During my time at Roger Williams University, the lacrosse guys had nicknamed me "Sparkles" because I always wore glitter around my eyes—but no one ever knew why I often wore them. It was at this point in my life that I started to become really insecure inside and didn't believe I could *shine* on my own. I was never the skinniest nor the prettiest nor the most talented at any one particular thing nor the smartest nor the richest—what I convinced myself of in my mind is who I believed others saw as well. I just needed a way to be seen and *sparkles* became my thing.

Upon coming home from that BET job, I was greeted with a "congratulations" cake from my family. It was a really sweet gesture for my first gig booked in the Texas market. But as things often went with my family, the sweetness only lasted so long before turning sour.

My mother was acting supportive on the surface by way of the cake, but as I stood in the kitchen, in my all-white outfit and *sparkly* eyes just exhausted from a long day of filming, she looked me up and down and said, "You're nothing more than a dime a dozen."

My mother had a way of being my biggest cheerleader and in a flash could be so cruel when she needed to steal a piece of my light in order to make herself feel better. I guess in some fucked up way, putting me down really did lift her up. While she wanted to make me believe she was proud of me at that moment after filming my first project in Texas, she also couldn't allow me to shine so bright. Me shining bright would have forced her to take a hard look at what her life had become—which wasn't much beyond the big house she hid behind. That night, my mother allowed me to feel an ounce of what beauty in the eyes of others could feel like before reminding me of my imperfections and the curves she saw standing before her. She would always tell me I was a "star" or a "bright light" when she wanted to build me up, but when she felt the need to make herself feel better or higher in life, could easily just flip a switch and slam my confidence and self-worth to the ground. Somehow, for some reason, this made her feel better.

I could never imagine putting my children down to make myself feel better. There was really no reason whatsoever for it.

I was really lonely during this time. I didn't have anyone. That's not to discredit the joy I felt in getting to spend time with my sisters nor the few random people I met at work or the gym nor the friendships I was trying hard to hold on to in some form from college—but life was changing, and the more it was changing, the more I was too.

"Live Your Life"

I have a journal from the time of my life just after college graduation. On June 7, 2002, I wrote about dreams and ended the entry with this:

If we don't dream, if we don't challenge ourselves, if we completely lose sight of our imagination and the things that once inspired us when we were children, what is the point of being alive? Why do we exist in the first place, if it is so wrong to dream? My mom often tells me that I am stuck in some fairytale world, that I live with my head in the clouds, but when you think about it, fairytales do exist, for they were first created in the minds of others. Maybe my life isn't a fairytale, but maybe someday, my life will be a tale to tell.

What happened to the girl who *dreamed?* Oh, that's right, I let the expectations of others take hold of me. I allowed other people to convince me that their lies were stronger than my truths.

Why did I ever allow the world to dim that light?

On the outside of that journal is a quote by Maya Angelou that says: "The desire to reach for the stars is ambitious. The desire to reach hearts is wise."

Maybe I was never destined to reach the stars. But, just maybe, I did reach some people's hearts.

So much of my post-college journal is filled with quotes, a handful of which were words said by one of my dearest friends, Erika. Recently, while I was going through that old journal, I DM'd her on Instagram and sent her quotes from a few things she said that really had an impact on my life back then. In return, she sent me a photo of the Dream Box I made for her in college. Two decades later, she still had it and had kept it with her everywhere she went. I cried immediately. She'd kept it, all these years.

You never know the impact you're going to have on someone else's life.

While I never let go of that comment my mother said to me, "You're nothing more than a dime a dozen," I turned it into fuel in my pursuit to prove her wrong. I always believed there was something special about me. In fact, there is something special about every single human who walks this earth. No one person is the same. How boring it would be if we were.

While I tried to respect my parents' wishes for me being in Texas with them, I had to remember the *dreamer* in me who knew there was a life waiting for me somewhere else. I couldn't be in Texas anymore. The longer I stayed there, the quicker I started to lose myself. And if I was never willing to lose myself for the boy I loved, I certainly wasn't willing to watch the woman I was working to become fade away for the expectations of anyone, even if the biggest expectations of all were coming from my mother.

Hearing the news from *him* that he was told to cut me out of his life, hearing my mother so easy tell me I was "nothing more than a dime a dozen," feeling I worked my ass off to do everything that was expected of me and yet there I was just living a life I didn't want—the light inside of me started to dim even more. I knew that there was more to life beyond what I could see at the time—beyond the heartbreak, beyond life's happenings. Maybe it was all a message telling me I wasn't supposed to be stuck somewhere I didn't want to be, and maybe it was time to finally venture off on a new path of my own choosing.

And there his words creeped back in. *I can do whatever I want to.*

It was time to finally fly away from my family's "home." While I wasn't quite ready to venture off to L.A. on my own, there was a more comfortable next step that was pulling at my heart. It was time to head back to Chicago, this time on my own terms.

Maybe I don't have the ability to live dreams so big that I can make an imprint on the whole world, but maybe being who I truly am and genuinely wanting good for others is bigger than any dream I can dream. Inspiring others, in some way, to always believe in their dreams really can change the world.

Personally, the best gift anyone could give me is letting me know they believe in me. That is what keeps me going and lights my fire in the darkest days.

Sometimes all it takes is one person to remind us that our dreams do, indeed, matter. So, let me tell you now—your dreams matter!

P.S.—I believe in you.

TWO.

The X Factor

LOST ANGELS

"Hotel California"

I moved back to Chicago in the fall of 2002. For the girl who was once an overachieving-procrastinating-perfectionist, so focused and tunnel-visioned in life, I quickly lost sight of the bigger picture and got wrapped up in the moment. *Because the moment was so fun.*

I was busting my ass and making a shit ton of money at one of the hottest Irish bars in Lincoln Park, McGee's, but I was out of control—the rebel in me emerged. For the girl who never drank that much, I was drinking every day, pounding Jägerbombs with my customers, sneaking off to the bathroom to share a cigarette with my co-workers, dancing on bar tops with a gold helmet on my head, and carelessly spending all the money I made. I suddenly had this "fuck it" attitude. I never got to just be a kid, ever—so I decided to live with my middle finger up in the air and to hell with anyone who tried to tell me I couldn't do what I wanted.

Don't get me wrong—my two years back in Chicago were fucking fun. Probably some of the best, most carefree years of my life. But the dreams inside of me were slowly vanishing and I started to lose myself.

Shortly after my twenty-third birthday, there was one morning I woke up in an absolute rut, feeling the weight of yet another late night of too many drinks and after-hours nachos clouded my thoughts. While every day had begun feeling like Groundhog Day, this day was different—because I got a call that changed my life. On the other end of that phone was my dear friend, Colin.

Colin and I have a unique history and bond that most people wouldn't be able to understand. When you think of stereotypical relationships in life and what those are supposed to look like, our "relationship" can't be defined by any black-and-white assumption of what a person in someone's life should be. Our story of how we met in college is one of the positive stories of my life, and, to this day, he is one of the relationships I cherish most. While our history runs deep, the one thing he is to me is a constant, a reason not a season. He is the someone who always reminds me of who I am, of the light I have inside me when others try to put that out—and back in 2004, he was the one person who most certainly was not going to allow me to forget what I wanted for my life.

That day he called me, Colin told me that he felt the pull inside of him to move to California. He said that his girlfriend at the time, who eventually became his wife and a confidant of mine, needed to stay back on the east coast for a while longer. He then presented me with this scenario for the two of us to move there together, and be roommates. He found this amazing, gated complex in Santa Monica, with a massive pool, workout facility and a unique one bedroom plus a loft situation we'd have to creatively share.

Oh my goodness, the dream was suddenly once again alive.

I sat on the front stoop of my apartment complex next to Wrightwood Tap and thought about what my life had become. I love Chicago, but was this the life I wanted to be living at twenty-three years old? How sad would the ten-year-old me be to see what I had become?

For the girl who lived her life wanting others to know she believed in them, there I was on the phone with the one person who wasn't going to allow me to give up on my dreams.

Knowing how much Colin believed in me was all I needed at that moment to make the decision to stop dicking around and finally, truly make my dreams come true. And if it weren't for Colin, I don't know if I would have ever had the courage to make it to Los Angeles on my own.

Without hesitation, I said, "I'm in. Let's do this!"

One month later, we both headed west to the land where *dreams come true.*

When we met up in L.A., at our new apartment in the place I dreamed of my whole life living in, we arrived to discover this wasn't Santa Monica at all! This was Ladera Heights?! Wait, the complex was just off the 405 freeway, the Howard Hughes Center was a rock throw away, Magic Johnson's TGI Friday's was just down the road, and the Westfield mall was barely a "mall" at all at this point in time. I thought there was going to be the ocean and sand and the hustle and bustle of all these creative people trying to make it out here in LA LA Land? *This was not the plan!*

But whatever—I was finally, really, truly on the direct path to *living the dream* and trying to get my break in the film industry. But as I quickly came to learn, my dream came with a hefty price tag.

It didn't take long before my head was ripped out of the clouds once again. Without a job, I quickly realized just how far I wasn't going to be able to stretch my savings of $5,000 in 2004. I tried my hardest at first not to resort to finding a job in the service in- dustry because I wanted to focus on my acting career. But, I had responsibilities to take care of on my own so thankfully I was able to get hired at this adorable restaurant right by the ocean in Santa Monica, called Ma'Kai. That alone wasn't always enough, so I also had frequent shifts at the Blu Monkey Lounge in Hollywood as well. Getting a bartending or server gig was never hard for me; getting an actual acting job, now that was.

Los Angeles is a level of expensive that I wasn't prepared for. In the blink of an eye, I was suddenly drowning in debt. I was too stub- born to ask for genuine help, so I had to find a way to figure it out and make it work. That's the thing about working in the restaurant business and living shift by shift—you have to believe in the hope that everything will work out somehow, some way. Usually when you weren't quite sure if you were going to be able to pay the rent, suddenly you got a call that a shift opened up and *it's going to be okay.*

Remember when I said that assumptions are a very dangerous thing? Here's about the time it finally bit me in the ass.

"I'm Fine."

I did have assumptions that my parents would do what they said—having made the deal with me to pay for my student loans if I held up my end of it all and worked hard and got good grades in college. Those assumptions led to me setting goals for myself, higher goals than I ever dreamed I could attain, and I crushed them. What came next is when I truly had to start understanding the art of gratitude in a time when I could have so easily just thrown a tantrum.

It was about four years after living in L.A. when I got a package in the mail that I never expected. I opened the package to find a manilla folder with a Post-it note in my mother's handwriting that just said, "I'm sorry. I can't do it anymore." No further explanation than that. Inside the folder was the information and monthly payments for my student loans from college. The reason I didn't go to my dream school no longer existed. The deal we made, the promise I would never have to worry about my student loans, was broken.

As I held that note in my hand, the note with my mom's handwriting that said, "I'm sorry. I can't do it anymore," I stood there dazed for a moment. Then I glanced over to all of the zeros after the first numbers, and I broke down and cried in panic. "How the hell am I going to afford this?"

Like a madwoman, I grabbed a notebook and began to write out every single account I had, including account number, login information, total balance due I owed, APRs, etc. Once the long list had been tallied, I sat there in complete disbelief. Student loans aside, how the hell did I wrack up over $30,000 in credit card debt in a matter of four years?! What?! Me!? *I'm so much smarter than this,* I thought to myself, but that's where I was wrong. I wasn't smarter than that. Everything I thought I needed in my life to become "someone" in Los Angeles only ended up hurting me instead of helping me.

After my mom wrote that note and mailed my student loans back to me, I wasn't about to blame anyone except myself for the financial position I had gotten myself into. My parents and I made a deal that didn't play out in my favor. Did I throw a fit? Did I complain? Did I call my parents and bitch them out at their broken promises and stomp my foot like I was fucking Veruca Salt? No. Because what good would that do? Seriously. The only reason adults throw tantrums is because for so long all the world did was enable them, so they grew up to be entitled assholes.

So even though I was shocked with this lovely envelope I got in the mail, there definitely was that "OMG, what is this?" moment. I let out maybe some more tears of hurt and frustration simply because I held up my part of the deal, but I never threw a fit about it. Instead, I once again used my mother's actions as more fuel for my fire.

It's in moments like this that your character is defined. This was one of the hardest moments of my life up to this point—I was drowning in debt, already barely getting by in L.A. I couldn't see a way up. But, aside from more debt and broken promises, what this experience did was made me realize I couldn't always count on others, even when I *expected* their word to mean something. Sometimes, all we can do is grab ahold of our own hand and pull ourselves up out of the mess—even if it's just one small step at a time.

"The Climb"

A few years later, one of my best friends, Ryan, and I had this idea that, on the cusp of us Leo ladies turning thirty, we wanted to conquer something big, something that scared us, something we knew would push us into the next decade of our lives with a strong, fierce mindset. So, accompanied by my dear friend Jenne, the three of us headed out to the Grand Canyon. Most people go there just to view it and take some pictures. We decided to be absolute maniacs and hike the thing down and up in the same day!

The Grand Canyon is larger than life. It is stunning in its natural beauty. Hiking down was actually way easier than I expected. If you weren't paying attention, it could be easy to miss, but there were signs that said, "Down is Optional, Up is Mandatory." Basically asking, "Are you really, *really* sure you want to do this?" I snapped a photo of one sign thinking just how *cute* that was. When we finally made it to the bottom, I turned around, looked up, and realized just how oblivious I was. *Holy fuck, I have to climb back up that?!*

Was there a helicopter somewhere that could take me all the way back up to the top? I handled the three-mile hike down like a champ, but three miles back up, no freaking way. Physically I wasn't prepared for this. I wanted to cry, to give up, to throw a tantrum. But then I realized, just like I had done with the student loans, I just had to shift my perspective.

When I look too far into the future, I get overwhelmed. I can scare myself out of doing things I know I can actually do. Thinking too far about how difficult paying off loans would be would have made me panic. I can't think that far in advance because the fears I have can be crippling. So, as I have learned in life, I knew I had to take the Grand Canyon in smaller strides. For me, it's about finding the balance of looking just far enough ahead to prepare, while also enjoying the beauty in every moment of every day, every step. That is all we are guaranteed, after all—this moment, right here.

That day I had no choice. There was no other way out. No one was going to get me out of this but me. I had to reach down and pull myself out of the canyon, and the only way to do that was to look straight ahead and focus on the journey up, one step at a time.

So, I climbed. And I climbed. And I climbed. I chose to take myself down that canyon; it was up to me to climb up out of it.

And I did. It was the most real mind-over-matter experience I had ever lived. It took nine hours to hike down the Grand Canyon and back up, but we fucking did it. When I reached the top, I threw my hands up in the air knowing I just conquered something so much bigger than any of the small shit I thought was defining my life. All that mattered in that moment was that I took what seemed like an impossible situation and I didn't let fear stop me. I didn't become overwhelmed by the big picture, I didn't panic, I didn't throw a tantrum—that would have been the easy thing to do. Instead, I chose to take it one step at a time, breathe through the pain, and push myself in a way I never knew I could. And as I stood at the top, I turned around, looked out upon that vast canyon, and said, "Thank you, Canyon. I fucking did it."

My mother writing that note and sending me my student loan information was, in a way, kind of a gift—it was the handout that didn't pay out. And I was thankful for it.

The day I finally paid them off was one of the best days of my life. Because now, everything I had earned in my life, *everything* I had done in my *adult* life, everything I had was because I worked for it.

I did that, all on my own.

We can't change other people's behaviors, but we can change how we respond and how we react to all situations in life. There's a big division between people who are just entitled and those who work hard yet sometimes get burned along the way. And it's the way in which you handle these moments that build who you become.

Throwing fits might temporarily give us what we want, but at some point, we need to grow up and take ownership of our own life. It's not going to be easy, but getting through the hard things in life, it's always worth the climb.

F.U.

"Hall of Fame"

People always told me I had a way of lighting up a room with a simple smile. But then, the world dimmed me. And for a long time now, I've been that way.

When I was a pre-teen and started getting into acting from a professional standpoint, Chicago didn't have the biggest market, but it certainly had enough opportunities to work and begin to build a resume. I started noticing a pattern when I went to auditions and people would always make comments such as, "Oh, who does she remind you of? Who does she look like?" I was always compared to someone at some level within the industry—as if my identity was somehow connected to someone else's own personal thoughts about that person. Kind of how they say you should never wear a strong-smelling perfume or lotion or cologne to a meeting in case it triggers a hateful memory of someone in the room's ex.

I quickly got tired of the comparison game. I didn't want to be the "next" anyone, I wanted to be the first *me*.

It was 2004 when I made the big move to Los Angeles and, two months after arriving, I was at a casting director workshop. It was actually the same day I met my soon-to-be-best- friend, Madison—a day I will never forget. Not just because she was this tall, blonde, spunky, magnetic New Yorker who was getting all the attention in the room because she had recently been Keira Knightley's double in *Domino*, nor was it because we actually never spoke that day that I first saw her. It was actually what happened to me that would make it unforgettable.

I was all smiles as I walked in the room, excited to show what I prepared for my audition, and the casting director was just staring at me in an unusually awkward long pause sort of way. She then asked me, "Do you know who I am going to say you remind me of?"

Of course I did. This wasn't the first time I heard it, but I played her game. I smiled politely and asked, "No, who?" That's when she said, "You remind me of a young Marisa Tomei. Not just looks, but you embody her energy and her spirit." (Okay. Always a huge compliment—I love Marisa Tomei!)

But then she said, "Nicole Danielle," and looked up from staring at my headshot to the young, bright-brown-eyed girl standing before her, and continued her thought, "Have you ever thought of giving yourself more of an Italian last name? You could really capitalize off that."

I didn't say anything. I just stood there shaking internally, flashing back to me at ten years old, being encouraged to legally change my Italian last name so that I would be completely unidentified from that part of my heritage and the pain associated with it. I snapped out of it when she suggested, "Maybe, Nicole Pacino? Or something like that?"

I couldn't even respond to her comment. I just shook my head, thinking how far I came from that moment when I changed my Italian last name, to this moment here when I was being told it would work in my favor if I gave myself an Italian last name. *Nicole Pacino?* I could hear the comments that would come with that one: "Are you related to Al? Is he your uncle?" No, just *no!*

I arrived home at my modest apartment that night, and I just needed to decompress from it all. Here I was, over a decade after legally changing my last name, and in a single moment of someone knowing nothing about my life, making a comment that sent my entire past rushing back. I poured a glass of Pinot Grigio, lit a candle, put on some music, and sat down at my computer to write some daily thoughts. But, before I started writing, I checked my email and noticed there was an unopened message from my grandma, my mother's mom, which was super weird because Grandma would never send me emails.

The email said, "Nicole. Sorry to be the one to tell you this. Your papa passed away."

"Brown Eyed Girl"

The "papa" she was speaking of was Rocco, my biological father's dad, not my *papa* who I'd grown up with my entire life. Along with her message, she included a link to Rocco's obituary in a Chicago newspaper. But before clicking that simple link that would have confirmed the truth of this unexpected news, I took a moment's pause. At that moment, my mind went to an image of me as a young child sitting on his lap in his office, which was on the lowest level of their triplex in Melrose Park, right across the street from my father's black-and-white house with the pool and all the fun things. My paternal grandfather liked his privacy. That's why his office was on the lowest level, but even though he liked his space, he always let me in there with him when he was doing his "numbers." In the time I spent with my biological father's side, that office was one of my favorite places to be. No matter what I was told to believe, my grandfather always wanted me around. It was our secret place. Even if others made me feel something else, for him, I was *always* enough.

I clicked on the link to the obituary and instantly broke down crying when I saw his picture. I had buried these memories so deep and for so long that it felt more like a previous life. But there he was, and there within him I saw my own bushy eyebrows, dark brown eyes, and warm smile. And there was my name, listed as number two of all the grandchildren surviving in his legacy. There were some other grandchildren I hadn't heard of and honestly did not even know existed. That's how long it had been since I had seen that side of my family.

The news just broke my heart.

I called my mom crying because I didn't know how to handle all these things I was feeling. Things I felt I shouldn't have been feeling, right? I was supposed to hate these people, this part of myself. I wasn't supposed to feel a thing. Yet, all I could do was feel everything.

As I just sat on the phone crying, 2,000 miles away from home, my mom said, "If you want me to, I will go to the funeral for you. I will face those people all over again because you are my precious daughter and he was one of the only decent ones in that entire family."

Knowing the price my mom would have had to pay to be face to face with all of them, including my father and my brother, and knowing the pain that would surface again because of me, I told her I didn't want her to go. Even with the things she has said or done at times that caused me to be hurt, she was my mom, and I would never think to intentionally cause her more pain. With a piece of me slightly shattered, I just kept moving forward and never went back home to say goodbye.

Oh, how I wish I had gone back to say goodbye.

"*Try*"

A few months after I found out my paternal grandfather died, I started to feel the weight of what the pressures of L.A. could do to a young woman. No matter the level of confidence I tried to exude on the outside—with every audition I went on, internally all I could hear was my mother's words being whispered in my ear, "You're noth-ing more than a dime a dozen."

Body issues have been an underlying thing my entire life. I'm an Italian-German-Irish girl who was never built to be rail thin. I have a *body*, and that's just who I am. Throughout my life, there have been a lot of times when what my body looked like was part of the conver-sation. As a dancer, it came built into the expressive part of my soul. As a member of high-school Poms, it was, "Remember in those short skirts, people are looking at your ass!" As an actress, "Don't forget, the camera adds ten pounds." Oh yeah, and then there was that ex of mine who threw a half-full wine glass toward me as he told me I was "a fat fucking pig." Yet, I was only 132 pounds.

So yeah, every time I looked in the mirror, it was impossible to high five myself, as Mel Robbins would say to do, when all I'd heard for so long were the voices of others telling me every version of me was just too "fat" for their idea of what beauty should be.

But I don't think any of these times shaped this story of my life as much as it did when I got cast in a co-starring role in my first feature film.

After a year living in Los Angeles, I had finally gotten what I felt would be my real big first break. My manager got me an audition for a co-starring role in a direct-to-video, independent horror film. It was an opportunity that made me feel as though I wasn't such a small fish in a big pond. I absolutely crushed the audition and *killed* the callback, then finally got the phone call officially offering me the role of "Michelle."

There were just a few caveats. Because I was still non-union at this point in my acting career, and not an official member of the Screen Actors Guild yet, the contract I was offered was for $75 a day. Oh, and I had to be okay with not only the hot-and-heavy, bathing-suit-wearing *love* scene but also the part in the script that in-volved a drunken scene where my character had to flash my friends.

The "gag" was I was wearing pasties over my nips—unlike the other character, who had to be full-on boobs exposed, but ya know, she got paid more than me. All that said, I didn't care. I was ready to work as hard as I had to to make this happen because I was so excited to be cast in my first ever co-starring, full-length feature film. And it was contracted to be released in Blockbuster! While I was not happy about the pay or the questionable scenes, what this offer did was prove to me that I *could* do this, I *deserved* to be here, and I was a good actress. So, yes, I obviously accepted the role.

Our first table read was a breeze. The six actors cast to play this little group of friends just clicked. It was effortless; we really had a blast that first day, and it was instant chemistry. As we were leaving, one of our male executives stopped me outside and gave me some praise about how great I did during the read-through, then just happened to casually tell me, "And, to think we didn't even want you at first." I was really confused—I crushed the audition, and they sent me through to callbacks almost right away, then offered me the role. So, after a great table read, why was I being told that they originally didn't want me?

And he said, "We didn't want you at first because you were too 'curvy' to play Michelle."

That fucking word. How on earth was I considered "curvy"? My bra was a forced B cup and my jeans a size six. But that's what he said.

"We didn't want you at first because you were too curvy to play Michelle, but then you opened your mouth and we had no choice but to cast you. You were the best actress for this role."

So, you're saying I'm a good actress? Even if I'm just a "dime a dozen" and "too curvy" for what you hoped for? But, I'm a good actress, right?! That's what I heard, and that's what mattered the most to me, so I tried my best to push all my insecurities to the side and kept at it.

And I threw those words from him onto the already lit fire that just kept growing.

It all worked out. We made the movie, and I loved every day of filming. I "died" in a bathtub after getting my face clawed off by La Llorona—major shout-out to our SFX guy, Joe, for his brilliant work with making an eyeball dangle halfway down my face and my entire mouth looking removed (haunted for life!). Even though making this film was one of the best experiences I ever had as an actor, there wasn't a day on set I felt confident, even though I had proven myself to be a good actress. Every day I was forced to put on that brown bikini, the only whisper I could hear was "too curvy." It was always right there in my mind. But I pushed through the emotional stuff because this movie was going into Blockbuster, and no way was I going to let the words of others affect the performance I knew I had inside of me to put out there for the world to see.

I wish twenty-year-old *me* would have been a little easier on herself and not listened so much to the chatter of others. Because, damn, she was something!

And she surely was something for *him*…

"California Gurls"

Around the time my horror movie was released in Blockbuster in 2006, I traded in my Nissan Maxima and got a loan for my first car on my own, a Chrysler Sebring convertible—'cause it was Los Angeles, obviously I needed a convertible so my best friend and I could be "top down, screaming out" everywhere we went. Colin's girlfriend moved out west and as they began their new chapter together in a place of their own, Madison and I moved into a super cool loft in downtown L.A., which was located in the old Federal Reserve bank building off Olympic and Grand. We're talking downtown L.A. years before all the hipsterness of hipster things that make downtown L.A.

quasi-cool ever existed. We shared a big space, our beds across the open room from one another, our loft turned into an exposed closet and every night a neon view to remind us that "JESUS SAVES."

I was commuting from downtown L.A. to Manhattan Beach, where I was bartending and serving at a Greek restaurant called Petros, which was just a couple blocks from my favorite beach in SoCal. If you couldn't be all the way up in Malibu, Manhattan Beach was the place you wanted to be. Bustling with beach goers for competitive volleyball and surf competitions to TV set locations for *Weeds*—there was always something to do or see in this beautifully *rich* beach town. At Petros, we would often stay open late for Lakers players, Kings players, and Dodgers players to come in after games. Not only did I get the privilege of serving William Shatner, Magic Johnson, and Khloé and Lamar, but Kevin Nealon and his family were my regulars. Oh, and yes, the most important piece of this part of my story—I was in love. Stupidly in love with one of my co-workers who, just like the restaurant, also happened to be Greek.

The moment I walked into the kitchen for the first time, I knew I was in trouble. I saw him standing behind the "line"—and once I saw him, there was no unseeing him.

Just as my high school sweetheart had done that day I crashed into a school bus and he pinned me inside the doorway, my "dinosaur," as I will refer to him, pinned me inside the employee closet when he was reaching to grab something over my head, wanting me to know he saw me too. His chest was so close to me I could feel his heart beating, and as he looked at me, his eyes said, "I see you. And you're something for me."

It was one of those moments that strike your life and there's no erasing it.

And instantly, I was done. Like, the way I order my bacon *extra crispy* kind of done.

He got me at that moment.

And even though I knew from the beginning we were never going to work out in the end, I was a hopeless romantic who went into every relationship with a sense of hope that maybe, just maybe, this time it would.

Fuck, I convinced myself.

We worked a lot of shifts together and would see each other outside of there when we could. He would drop anything if he heard Toby Keith's "Should've Been a Cowboy," and his Greek ass would wrap me in his arms and dance with me. Most nights after our shifts, we'd meet up at Hennessey's Tavern, where he'd always have a vodka soda, and I would always have a vodka tonic with a lime. He was there by my side when he wanted to be, but he wouldn't give me the level of commitment, as far as a label in a relationship goes, that seemed like a natural expectation after nearly a year of doing this song and dance.

Regardless of that, I held on. Loving him with all I could give, even in the moments I knew I should have walked away.

Less than a year into our relationship, he went to Greece for the summer. Leading up to his trip, a part of me had been waiting and expecting him to ask me to come visit him at some point because, well, that's a natural thing to assume your *boyfriend* would want to see you and show you the country he's from and meet some of the family who still lived there. But no, he never asked me to go. And what he said to me was, "It's up to you to decide if this is worth waiting for."

The passion was undeniable, he made me feel safe in his arms, there was no place off limits to just get at it, and even though he didn't always know how to handle me, he adored me.

So, I chose to wait for him.

The day he got home from his summer away in Greece, I was at his parents' house awaiting his arrival. My heart was aching to see him again, my body consumed with nerves to see him after almost two months without him. When he saw me, tears formed in his eyes, a smile came to his face, and he held on to me as though that moment was the only thing that mattered in life.

He told me, "The thought of you not being in my life makes my stomach turn. I want you to be mine. What do you say?"

A year after being whatever we were and a summer of him in Greece, our relationship was official.

Before Greece, he was not fully committed to me. But after Greece, he was.

"Outnumbered"

There was a day we were at his house—most of his family was there, and they were roasting a whole lamb on a spit in the backyard. At one point my "dinosaur" and a couple others got up and started Greek dancing around the pool, and as they danced, I looked toward where the lamb was being cooked. As the music buzzed in my ears and the dancing before me became a blur, I became fixated on that dead lamb roasting—his face pointed toward me, I couldn't help but feel like I was right there with him. We were the outsiders. And nothing was going to change that. Well, except for him getting eaten by everyone other than me. I'm a visual person, and there's no way I will ever eat something that has the face attached to it, so there was no eating that lamb for me that day.

As I stared at the lamb, I realized the only way I would get out of this without being *eaten up* myself was to finally admit what I knew all along. But just then, before the thoughts could even surface, I saw two of the little girls run over and peel off pieces of the lamb's skin and run off eating it. It was a moment I just couldn't shake. I knew this was a traditional thing, but as I saw them run away eating the lamb skin, I glanced over to my "dinosaur," who was so happy, smiling big while dancing and holding hands with the people around him. And then I thought of all the times he went to Greek events and probably had this same look, this same magnetic energy coming off of him, and I thought about how many other people got to experience that side of him, yet I never would. It was like he was living a double life, and I finally got to see a piece of the other side. He was in his element. *This was his world.* And I couldn't compete for the attention of that—nor ask him to choose. But also, I had to ask myself, *Am I willing to give up what I need for a world where I don't belong?*

Every time he would go off to a friend's party I wasn't asked to go to, every time he would go to a Greek event I wasn't welcomed at, every time his family was gathered together and the conversation changed from English to Greek followed by laughter at the table and eyes looking toward me, every time was a reminder I was never going to be what I know he needed in the end. I never asked to be his priority, but I wanted to know I was important enough for him to show up for. But time and time again, he didn't show up in the small moments when I really needed him to show up because there were other things that were ahead of me on the list.

I truly believed I could have been the one to help inspire him to get to the place in life I knew he was destined to go. And, selfishly, I wanted to be a part of that dream with him. To help him take a chance on the man I knew one day he could become. While I wanted to be the one to stand by his side and see him accomplish all his goals and dreams, it was at this moment I watched him dancing around his pool with a dead lamb roasting in the background that I thought, *maybe there's someone better out there for him. Someone who is also Greek. And just maybe, there's someone better out there for me.*

A year and a half into our relationship, my "dinosaur" and I were at a crossroads. While that was not the day our relationship ended, that was the moment I knew that I loved him enough to let him go.

I was never going to be what he needed me to be—by definition of heritage. I was never going to fit into that world. I was never going to be enough for him. Ever. Because I was never going to be Greek. And to some families and communities, that actually matters. He was never going to leave that world. And I never could have asked him to.

To love someone so much you need to let them go because you know you will never be enough for what they need and, more importantly, you can't become what you will never be—that's a different level of heartbreak.

"What a Time"

About a year after my relationship ended with my "dinosaur," we still communicated now and then and loosely stayed in touch via text.

He knew I had moved to West Hollywood, and one night I got a text from him saying he was going to be in the area with his best friend. He asked if I wanted to meet up for a drink. "Yeah. For sure," I told him. *Of course I wanted to see him.*

Madison and I ended up meeting my "dinosaur" and his best friend at a bar that happened to be just down the street from where I was working on La Cienega Boulevard. I was so nervous to walk into that bar area and see him again, but I put on my big girl pants, slapped on a dose of confidence, and wanted him to secretly regret that we never worked out.

We walked into the bar. Madison and I found our way toward the back where he was hanging out. When I saw him, I nearly stopped in my tracks thinking, *Damn it. Damn him. Ugh, he looks so fucking good.*

I smiled at him. He gave me the look he used to give me, and when he hugged me hello, he really hugged me *hello*.

I missed that hug.

Madison then gave him a hug, while his best friend gave a big one to me. They got us each a drink, and it was suddenly like the good old days.

As I stood next to him, I could see he was different. He had changed. He was growing up, evolving into the person I always knew he could be. He was having more success as a chef at an upscale restaurant while also working toward his dream of opening his own. I closed my eyes and inhaled his smell. I suddenly could remember what it felt like to be lying in his arms. In front of me stood not the boy who I knew had so much potential, but instead the man I knew he could become.

There was never going to be a reunion with us in that way. But there would always be a burning chemistry between us—that was for sure. It was just that kind of passion; anytime we would be near each other it was undeniable. But that was all it was. Two people who could've been but never would be.

It was nothing.

But it was something that I couldn't shake—to the point it royally fucked up my life for the next decade to come.

"Mercy"

A few nights later, Madison and I drove down to Laguna Beach to support my buddy Brett Young's acoustic set at a bar by the ocean. I had met Brett because of a good friend I worked with at Petros. My friend had shared with me Brett's EP, and upon meeting him in person, we became instant friends. Brett was a solid guy, passionate about music and storytelling, and he knew how to pull at a person's heartstrings. *Damn, he knew how to pull at my heartstrings.*

This was pre-country-fame Brett Young—his first EP was so intoxicatingly beautiful that it was well worth the hour drive just to hear him belt out his gutting "Define Me" ballad in person. So, Madison and I drove down to Laguna Beach, sat at a little two-top near the bar, drank wine, and supported his acoustic set.

After having recently seen my "dinosaur," and listening to Brett sing the lyrics to that song, I found myself quickly spiraling. Even after all this time since we had ended, after seeing him again at that bar on La Cienega Boulevard, the wound had been reopened, and I was feeling the burn of the heartbreak I had endured. I just saw him, but I'm not with him, but we talked now and then—so *what was I?* In my mind and in my heart I was convinced I still mattered to him. But I didn't. *Why did I want to matter to him?* I didn't need to matter to him. *But I did. I think.*

Yes, our relationship was long over, but when you have deep feelings about the person you were with to the depths of which our relationship meant to me, the feelings don't just go away. All I did was bury them a little bit and tuck them away in a secret pocket in my heart. Listening to Brett's voice, Brett's lyrics, the wine in my glass, having just seen my "dinosaur's" face in the flesh, his smell, the man I saw he was becoming that I always knew he could become yet I was no longer the one by his side—suddenly my emotions began flooding out, and it didn't take long before I was a full-on hot mess.

After the set was over, Madison and I gave Brett a big hug goodbye, congratulated him on a mesmerizing performance, and got in the car—with me behind the wheel.

I drove us back over an hour from Laguna Beach to West Hollywood, all the while crying out the pain I had been holding in for almost a year, since choosing to leave my Greek love. Seeing him again did a number on me. And even though life had moved on, I had never healed that piece of my heart. The part he still had claim over.

As much as the heartbreak hurt, he wasn't the one who crushed me—he was just the one who led me to my downfall.

"Downfall"

After seeing my "dinosaur" look at me the way he did when we were together, I was having so many doubts. I missed him. I still loved him. I didn't know if I had made the right decision walking away. I was an emotional wreck. Everything I had masked, everything I had bottled up came flooding out of me—with Madison sitting in the passenger seat being forced to listen to my crying babbles of reasons I loved him:

"What the fuck did I do?"

I stopped for more sniffles.

"He once said, 'I don't know how to handle you sometimes,' and you, my best friend, when I told you that, you said, 'If they can't handle us at our worst, they don't deserve us at our best.'"

"But then, I guess he learned how to handle me."

Tears were full-on coming down now.

"Because he loved me. He did. In his fucked-up way of love, he loved me."

"And fuck, who knew sex in the car could be so much fun! Or pools in Palm Springs."

I was just sobbing by now.

"Life wasn't perfect, but he did let me into his world, the only way he knew how. He would look at me and say, "My girl," and I knew how proud of me he was, even when I said he didn't show up. But all the times I thought I wasn't enough for him, that was my own shit—because of the shit with my father—and I need to accept responsibility for that. Because maybe I was enough for him, but I just don't know what that means to be enough for anyone."

And the tears kept coming.

About a mile away from our apartment, I saw the lights flashing behind me.

I was told to pull over my car.

I pulled over to the right of the street, just across from the Beverly Center. With tears streaming down my face, I was shaking uncontrollably. I knew this was bad.

A cop came up to my side and told me to roll down my window. Then the cop said, "Do you know why we pulled you over?" *No, I had no fucking clue other than me being an emotional mess.* "No, I don't," I said in the calmest tone I could speak in.

Then the cop said, "The back half of your right tire crossed over the line."

Okay, the back half of my right tire crossed over the line. That didn't mean anything, really.

I didn't respond because it really didn't seem like a reason to pull me over.

I had been drinking wine, hours ago. But I wasn't drunk. By the look on the cop's face and the mood they were likely in to fill some quota for the night—yeah, this was going to get really bad.

After my lack of response, the cop asked us to get out of the car and take a seat on the sidewalk while my car was inspected.

As I was getting out of the car, something unexpected happened, Madison flung her door open and started begging with the police officer on her side to please turn a blind eye and take her. She said, "She's the good one. Just say I was the one driving. Please, take me instead."

My best friend was literally willing to jeopardize her own record, her own life, to save me. That was a loyalty beyond any blood obligation. That was a friend for life.

I sat there on the curb, with my head in my hands, tears still streaming down my face, waiting to hear my fate. The cops wanted me to do things I wasn't okay with. I wasn't about to say the alphabet backward, and no way was I going to blow into a breathalyzer right there at the scene. So, because I refused to cooperate with what they wanted me to do, they put handcuffs around my wrists, pushed my head down as they put me in the back seat of their cop car, and as we drove off, all I could see in the rearview mirror was my car getting towed, about to be impounded, and my best friend standing alone on the side of the road.

"Jailhouse Rock"

Since I was a kid, others always expected me to be good. Make us proud. Be friends with everyone. Smile. *Always smile.* Other people got to screw up, and I just had to deal with the aftermath. I was never really ever in control. Even that night, the lowest night of my life up to that point, my best friend was pleading with the cops to take her instead because I was "good" and this shouldn't happen to me, and no one would ever have expected this of me.

But secretly inside, I was pleading, *Take me. I need to not feel so good.*

Before long, I was sitting in intake, waiting to be booked. My best friend was standing alone outside the jailhouse after she got a taxi to take her there—she was my one phone call, because I needed someone to talk to who could understand what just happened and her number was actually one of the only ones I knew by heart. As I stood holding on to the jail phone, she said, "What do you do when you realize the only true friend you have in this life is the one sitting in jail?" And then, I started to cry more.

This entire experience was so stupid—and never should have happened. Okay, I learned a valuable lesson, but it was bullshit. When I got to the jail in Beverly Hills—*how L.A. of me*—I was forced to take a blood test since I refused the breathalyzer test at the scene of the "crime" I apparently was being told I committed. As the test was being done, I heard someone wish the intake officer a "Happy Birthday." *How sad. She's working on her birthday,* I thought to myself.

When it was time for me to be called up to take my mugshot, the intake officer got mad at me for trying to smile during it. I couldn't help it—was I not supposed to smile? I mean, that's what you do in photographs, right? Even with mascara stained to my face and swollen eyes from crying so hard, *smile.* That's what I'd been taught my whole life to do. *Just fucking smile.* Although she was annoyed at me for my mugshot photo session, I still wished her a damn "Happy Birthday" as I was being escorted to my cell because that's just the kind of person I am.

Jail was not at all what I thought it was going to be like. I thought I was going to be afraid for my life, having to watch my rear end whenever I needed to bend over to go to the bathroom. I thought there might be a fight because all us fuck-ups were dancing to the tune of Elvis, just living our best *post-living-our-best-life* lives. But nope, I found myself in the community cell all by myself—like a fucking worthless, fucked-up princess in a Beverly Hills jail cell suite.

There I laid on my cot in what felt like a glorified situation since it was a slow night, wearing tight black pants, a crop top, a black pleather jacket, and my hair extensions in a knotted mess, with dried mascara stuck to my face like a football player after sweating profusely on game day, crying over my "dinosaur," crying over being pulled over with Madison in the car, crying over wishing that damn intake officer a "Happy Birthday" and her getting mad at me for smiling—crying, crying, crying. I cried so much that I ran out of tears, and then, all I could do was just laugh, like Joaquin Phoenix *Joker* kind of laughing, because I fucked up. Oh, I fucked up. And all I could do was laugh about it.

This is what it felt like to fuck up.

I was tired of being the good girl. Damn, it felt good to just fuck up for once.

It was at that moment, I finally knew what it felt like to just be human.

"Times Like These"

The next morning as I walked out the door, the sun pierced my eyes. It was so bright I could hardly see, but I felt like it was life whispering—*this is your new beginning*. I had gotten my life to the point I was so low that I had to sleep behind steel bars, in a room made of bricks among a concrete jungle.

This was my wake-up call, and I heard it loud and clear.

The morning after I spent the night in jail, Madison was waiting outside for me, waiting with a friend of ours to take me to get my car out of the impound. Our friend lent me the money to pay the hundreds of dollars it cost to get my car out of impound, knowing I would pay her back. My word meant something, and she knew I would work however hard I had to work to pay back every single dollar.

Because of my arrest, I had to go to court, but I couldn't afford some fancy-ass lawyer, so I had to settle for a public defender. He suggested we do a "blood split" and see what happened. When your blood is taken because of a DUI incident, the blood is actually split into two different containers—one being the sample law enforcement tests to see a person's blood alcohol concentration, the other in case the driver who was arrested wants to independently have their blood tested separately. When the results came back from my independent testing, there was a difference in the results. According to the police testing, my blood was at a .09. According to the second testing we had done, I was at a .08—*point zero eight*—both tests showing I had the lowest blood alcohol level you can have that breaks the law and declared me as legally *driving under the influence*. It confirmed, as I already knew, that I had had wine that night, but I wasn't drunk to the point I should have been pulled over and thrown in jail just because part of my back right tire had crossed over the shoulder line.

Had I been able to afford a proper lawyer and fought to get off the charges, I most likely could have. But I could barely afford to just get by in life at that point, and I also had to pay my friend back the money she lent me, so I had to ride it out with my *free* public defender attorney, who told me the best thing to do would be to just give a plea of "no contest"—assuming responsibility for my actions, without saying I was "guilty."

"I plead no contest, Your Honor," is what I said to the judge.

Because I did that, I got slapped with a guilty misdemeanor charge that resulted in me having to uncomfortably attend AA meetings I didn't need to be at and take classes where I had to watch horrific videos of car accidents related to substance abuse incidents. My license also got suspended, my car insurance got jacked up in price, and I had to spend the next ten years of my life with a big fat *asterisk* next to my name.

Was it reckless of me? Yes. I don't believe anyone should get behind the wheel after a night like that, wine and emotions aside. I'm thankful it was an innocent situation, not even an accident, and the only one whose life it really affected in the long run was my own. I learned a major lesson—nothing is worth being in a situation like that again, because I know for many people situations like that ended much worse.

The only disappointment of that night was that the situation didn't disappoint me; finally I had to just accept that I can't control everything, this was life just happening. I was an adult, who made a decision and had to accept responsibility for doing so. But what I was afraid of, what I was terrified of, was what my parents would think if they found out. And even in my late twenties, I was still terrified of disappointing my parents. *They expected me to be good.*

We all go through things in our lives that we want to hide from others. We all have a F.U., an "I fucked up" moment. We all have a moment that we wish maybe we had chosen differently. We all have regrets. I'd like to believe that even Oprah has fucked up at least once in her life. And that's okay if she did, because that's one of her human experiences. No one is perfect. No one is completely innocent. No one is happy all the time. This is life, and you have got to take the lows with the highs.

During situations like this one, I must believe that the decisions I made were guiding me toward a future I couldn't foresee back then. Although I understood the need to avoid living in the heaviness of my past regrets, on missed opportunities, on what-ifs, I also hoped to discover newfound strength by breaking the cycle from repeating itself.

Life was definitely leading me to an unknown future that I couldn't see at the time.

It was guiding me straight to the one who wrecked me.

SMOKE & MIRRORS

"Use Somebody"

A good guy friend of mine from Chicago once said to me, "You know how I know you're going to be a great actress one day? Because you're beautiful, even when you cry."

As a new someone would soon discover—apparently, that was the truth.

On La Cienega Boulevard existed what we used to refer to as "the trifecta"—three different restaurants that all had one owner's hands in each of them along with his other business partners. So, there was the pizza place my best friend, Madison, was working at, Stone Fire Pizza, the Mexican restaurant I was working at, The Spanish Kitchen, and just down the block was where my other best friend, Ryan, was working, The Belmont.

Never did I plan to spend a decade of my life bartending, but that was how it went. Sadly, I was good at it. Damn good. I was one of the only bartenders on the block who could manage the server well, handle the whole bar, and take a section in the restaurant to serve customers there as well. I was a master at the game, and I survived in a cut-throat town because of it. Yet even in that line of work, there was always going to be someone with something to say, and one night I was told by my colleague, "The only reason you have good shifts is because you have tits."

No, dumbass, I was just that stupidly good at my job!

And everyone on the block knew it, including one very specific patron who I never thought noticed me until one very specific night—let's call this one, *Vick*.

It was a slow weekday night, like so slow I had not one person at the bar, when a friend of mine walked in. After I poured him a whiskey, it was only minutes later before Vick walked in and sat at the bar next to him. They were meeting one another to talk about a project Vick was working on, and of his need to cast an actress in a particular role.

There was no one but them at the bar, and there standing before him, he could clearly see the actress he had been looking for.

We filmed the project at his apartment. My friend was there helping out, along with a small crew and the main actor who I was going to be acting in scenes with. My character's role was intense, which required me to get to a point of crying. Vick was directing it, since it was his project, and as he watched the scene being played out via the viewfinder, with tears streaming down my face, he knew at that moment he had found more than just the actress he'd been looking for—he found the girl he had been waiting for. And I found the boy who I believed saw me through all my imperfections.

Because as Vick later told me, "I'm looking into the viewfinder of the 5D watching you perform and my heart almost exploded. I watched you walk out of the apartment that night and I knew that I had to do whatever I could to see you again."

I guess my friend was right—I was beautiful, even when I cried.

"Slow Hands"

One random night a few weeks after we filmed that project, I was working a shift at The Spanish Kitchen when we ran out of our well tequila. Seeing we were always in cahoots, if one of the trifecta restaurants ran out of something, it was no problem to call up one of the other two and ask to borrow what was needed to just get through the night. Stone Fire had some well tequila they were graciously willing to lend us for our house margaritas, so I asked my co-bartender to cover the server station while I quickly ran across the street to grab a few bottles.

As I happened to be running across La Cienega Boulevard from The Spanish Kitchen to Stone Fire, Vick happened to be running in the opposite direction at the same time from Stone Fire to The Spanish Kitchen. We locked eyes, on one of the busiest streets in WeHo, and at that moment, I knew there was something much more than that one night of filming we had done. When I got back from grabbing the tequila from Stone Fire, Vick was sitting there at my bar and asked me if I wanted to go for a walk after my shift. And I did.

Our conversation led us up the street and back to his apartment on Sweetzer Avenue, just below Sunset Boulevard. There I sat, on his couch, him standing behind me, and then he kissed me, upside down—and well, life just kind of froze.

There was no dancing around anything with this one—he knew what he wanted. And what he wanted was me.

Fast-forward to a few weeks later. I was unsure of what was really going on between us, and the conversation happened:

> Me: "Well, I'm not your girlfriend. Do you want me to be your girlfriend?"

> Vick: "Yeah, I want you to be my girlfriend."

> Me: "Okay, then I'm your girlfriend."

That night, we both said, "I love you."
And that was the beginning of the end.

"You Make My Dreams"

A few months after our relationship began, I was living in a little one-bedroom apartment just a few blocks from where Vick's apartment was. My stepdad had flown out and brought us these two tiny kittens that were born on my parents' property, because Vick had a soft spot for cats. *I'm such a dog person.* We were crazy in love and in such a good place, creating a life together. It was the first time I really felt that. Not that I didn't have serious relationships before, but this was the first time I felt I was building a life with someone I saw a real future with.

About six months into our relationship, he got an incredible opportunity to go work on a show in Canada. With the opportunity came a handsome paycheck and an executive producer title, which is something I knew meant the world to him and something he had been working toward—to be at that level, at that importance, and to feel above the line, not below.

Even though he wanted this opportunity, he wanted me too. "Come with me?" he asked.

Logistically, I didn't know how that was going to look. He had a guaranteed job; I didn't. I knew I couldn't just financially ride his coattails; I needed to make my own money. I figured, at worst, maybe I could find some bar shifts or dust off my old Starbucks hat—just to feel like I was contributing in some way there. Every time we looked up pictures online of the town, of Canada, of a new experience we could experience together, it made my heart flutter. I didn't know the *how*, but I knew the *why*—because it was us having a new adventure, together.

I'm a romantic with a traveler's soul. While I like having roots, feeling there's somewhere I belong, my heart has always had this burning desire to travel, see the world, and experience new things. I like being rooted, but I much prefer to fly. We were madly in love, and here he was, asking me to see a part of the world with him. I was excited about the opportunity to just go away, with each other, and have an adventure doing something new. So, I said, "Fuck yeah. Let's do this."

He accepted the job. And, in the short time we had, got rid of my apartment so we didn't have to pay for two additional rents, packed up my car with the personal items we needed along with our two kittens, and headed to the United States/Canada border where we would cross over an invisible line and really begin our future, experiencing a new world and continuing to make our relationship stronger together on this new adventure.

We were on our way.

We made it through California. We made it through Oregon. We made it through Washington. And there we were, the moment we drove over 1,270 miles for, the moment that we were leaving it all behind for the chance at a new beginning together.

Except—when we got to the border, I wasn't allowed in.

After we pulled my car up, the border patrol asked for both of our passports. We needed clearance in order to enter Canada. He scanned Vick's, handed it back to him, and said, "You're good to go." Then the border patrol agent scanned my passport, looked at me without giving it back, and said, "I need you to pull your car over there and go inside, where your passport will be waiting for you."

My heart was beating out of my chest, and I was on the verge of physically showing all my emotions, from wanting to cry and throw up at the same time. But I stayed calm and tried my best to be positive that whatever was about to be said would still result in us continuing forward with our plan.

I pulled my car over where the officer told me to, I looked at Vick, and with the most apologetic but loving expression on my face, I said, "I'll be right back."

As I walked toward the border patrol office, every ounce of my being shaking uncontrollably, one single thought came to my mind—*Fuck, my past finally caught up with me.*

"Don't Dream It's Over"

There I stood… alone, inside the border patrol office, waiting for them to call my name up to the booth, as the man I loved and was starting a future with sat waiting in the car for me. Waiting to hear our fate. And in that moment, I was haunted by the past years of my life. By the night I let emotions over my "dinosaur," wine, and music collide to the point I ended up in a jail cell, on a cold cot, alone. And there I stood, with the man I now loved in the car with our kittens waiting to begin this next chapter of our lives, and I wasn't just haunted by my past, I was having to come face to face with it.

When they called my name, I tried as hard as I could not to break down crying. The officer behind the desk looked at me as if he knew I wasn't a terrible person, that I was just someone who once made a terrible mistake, a mistake that was about to wreck my life once again, and said, "I'm sorry, but we can't let you cross the border into Canada. You're going to need to turn around and go back where you came from. Here's your passport back."

I knew I couldn't argue with the officer. We knew deep down in the pit of our stomachs there was a chance this could happen, but we held on to hope that if I got flagged, I'd be forgiven and allowed in. We thought our love was bigger than the law, but it wasn't.

While a DUI in the U.S. is considered a misdemeanor, in Canada it's a felony. Canadians who have a DUI can cross the border and enter into the U.S., but U.S. citizens that have a DUI on their record cannot cross that same border into Canada. *How fucked up is that?*

I walked out of the building and just started crying. By the time I got to the car, it was uncontrollable. When I looked at him, I didn't have to explain a thing. He knew.

I found myself once again at a crossroad—all because of my fuck-up, because of my past. It wasn't his fault; it was all mine.

I was told to turn my car around. We didn't have the privilege of extended time to talk things through; they were waving people along to get in and out of there.

He waved down a taxi, grabbed his bags out of the trunk of my car, gave me a quick hug goodbye—not saying anything—and I watched him walk away from me.

Men were really good at making me feel wanted but also, apparently, really easy to walk away from. I knew there wasn't time for a proper goodbye; the Canadian border patrol didn't give a shit about a relationship being ripped apart. I felt like a piece of shit since it was my mistake that put us in this position, but still, he could have hugged me a little bit longer.

As I watched the man I loved walk away, the future we were planning slowly disappeared in front of me. I could feel the pressure down my neck to get back in my car, but I couldn't leave until I knew he did. As I stood there watching his back, carrying his suitcase toward the taxi, a part of me wished he would turn back around, that I would see him running back toward me, choosing to give it all up because I was worth more than what was waiting over that border line. I was wishing he would grab me in his arms and tell me I was enough and everything he really needed in this lifetime, and what we had was worth more than a job with a title and a temporarily nice paycheck. I wanted him to choose me, even though I was the one who fucked up.

But he didn't. He chose what was best for him.

I had to go.

He chose to stay.

I watched him get in the taxi, he waved goodbye, and I was forced to figure out what was next.

I didn't know what this meant for our relationship, I didn't know where I was going back to, I didn't know a damn thing other than I had to get back in my car, turn my car around, and drive forward— with two fucking kittens in my back seat.

"Make It Rain"

While my relationship with my mother was never quite the same after that day she sent me the envelope handing me all my student loans and given she hadn't really been there for me for a long time now in the way a daughter needs her mother, she was still my mom— and to my own fault, was still my default go-to person when things happened in life. So, as I was watching my boyfriend head towards Vancouver, becoming a speck in my unknown future, I sent my mom a simple text just saying, "Plans have changed. I'm not going to Canada." And then, I turned my car around and started the journey back to Los Angeles.

My hands were shaking so bad I could hardly hold on to the steering wheel. Listening to two kittens just cry and meow, I just cried, and I cried, and then I cried some more. My boyfriend was now on his way to Vancouver by himself, and I didn't even have an apartment to go home to. I had already forgiven myself and made peace, thinking this little *oops* in my life would be excused because it was just something that happened. But at that moment, my little mistake became a living nightmare haunting me in real life. My past decision to get behind the wheel of my car that night in Laguna Beach was not something that could just be excused; it was a major fuck-up that just majorly fucked up my life.

And because of my stupid decision before I even met Vick, now my relationship was ripped apart, and we were forced to now be away from each other for about as long as we'd been together.

I cried for so many hours that my eyes were so swollen I could hardly open them, and somewhere between Portland and Seattle, the rain got so bad, yet I couldn't stop the tears. The kittens were going crazy in the back seat, and my mom kept calling, wanting answers to what the hell happened and why wasn't I with him, but I just kept sending my phone to voicemail because my brain couldn't even process words that would even make sense to say to someone at this point.

My phone kept buzzing, and I finally grabbed it to look at it, hoping maybe it was Vick, but it was yet another text from my mom that said, "He is a keeper. You're supposed to be there with him…"

I tossed my phone across the passenger seat, and suddenly, everything was closing in on me. I never told my parents about my DUI, about my night in jail, about not being able to afford to hire a lawyer and have the charges reversed. I was an adult, assuming responsibilities for my adult choice I made that night. And I was terrified of the disappointment I knew would come if I ever told them the truth. I was their *good* girl, who always got *good* grades, who was just the walking epitome of *good*—I wasn't allowed to fuck up because I'd seen how easily they could be disappointed in me in the smallest, stupidest decisions I made in life—like when I got my belly button pierced at twenty years old, my mother flipped out on me and said, "I hope the universe rips that thing right out of your stomach," and then I was grounded because of my decision. And ironically enough, one day in our pool in Texas, my belly button ring actually did rip right out of my stomach, and now I forever have a physical scar to remind me of that. So yeah, knowing how easily I could disappoint my parents definitely was the deciding factor to keep this little secret from them.

But that day, as the rain was coming down, as my phone was buzzing nonstop, as my past and future were colliding right there in that present moment, it all got to be too much. So, I pulled the car off the freeway and finally confessed the truth to my mother about *why* I got turned away at the border. I finally told her the whole truth—as I sat in a Target parking lot just off the freeway, the rain pouring down even harder.

As she took in a breath, about to speak, I cringed, expecting disappointing comments about what an embarrassment of a daughter I was and how I fucked up my whole life. Then she said, "You went to jail? That means you've *lived.*"

And I thought to myself, *Who the hell is this woman, and what have you done with my mother?!*

The woman I had spent most of my life trying to only make proud and never disappoint went on to say that she was actually jealous of me, that my *going to jail fuck-up moment in life* meant that I was just having fun and living my life for once. She started to cry after that, as if realizing the reality of everything her daughter went through alone, and then the mom in her kicked in and said, "I'm just sad that you didn't feel you could tell me this and that I wasn't there for you."

For the first time in so long, I felt like I actually had my *mom* there, supporting me in my life as she had done for so long when I was a young child.

We expect a certain reaction when we tell other people our truths. Yet when we're honest enough with ourselves and when we sit with our truth, no matter how painful or embarrassing or disappointing it may be, we allow for the space to let people surprise us in their response.

I never—not in a million years—would have thought that would have been my mom's reaction. Never. Had I known that, I would have called her that night from jail, when I really needed her to be there for me. But just as I never told her about being bullied in school, at some point in life I just chose to handle the hard things by myself. It was just easier to know I could count on myself, even if that meant facing my own disappointments instead of having to be honest and risk disappointing someone else—especially my parents. Had I told her about my DUI incident and everything I had to face after when it happened, maybe her reaction wouldn't have been the same. Because that day I finally told her, as she could hear the rain hitting my windshield and the tears pouring out of my heart, I felt like she could hear in my voice that I accepted responsibility for my choices. My world was now torn apart because of it, and the depth of my pain was enough punishment.

We're all human. So, I have to believe we all have a moment in our lives that shakes us. Maybe it's not as big as my fuck-up moment that changed the course of my life forever. But, no one is perfect, and we all have moments of regret. We can live with the regret of it, or we can choose to learn from it. I was the hardest on myself, and I had to learn from the choices I made. I got myself into that first mess, which now got me into this mess, and only I could get myself out of it. *Just like I had to do at the Grand Canyon.*

So, I wiped my tears, got back on the freeway, and kept driving.

"American Pie"

After I got back on some sort of path to some unknown destination, I realized something valuable. My DUI and the crumbling of our Canada plan caused just the pause I needed in life to quiet the noise. As I drove 1,270 miles back to L.A., I realized that had I gotten across that border, I would have been choosing to live my life for him, not for me. I was *his* girlfriend following *him* to Vancouver for *his* new opportunity. There was no *me* in any of that.

And now, here I was, turning around. But in turning around, in all the grief of what was being lost and the fear and uncertainty of going back to L.A. alone, ashamed, and embarrassed with nowhere to live and two fucking kittens in my backseat—I knew that my "mistake" was leading me back to my true destiny. I wasn't meant to be the woman who gave up her life to support a man. I was the woman who had to carve her own path in this world, and start making shit happen for herself.

Sometimes our past comes back to haunt us (often in the least opportune times) to remind us of who we are in the most unexpected ways.

While it was a long, lonely drive, I needed the *pause* in life.

I love the pause…

I embrace the pause…

It's what's within the pause that gives us the breath we need to make what comes after the pause mean more.

I needed life to pause.

It did.

And I made it back to L.A.

Since I didn't have an apartment of my own to go back to, Vick told me he talked to one of his best friends, who was also his roommate, and they agreed to let me stay at Vick's apartment in West Hollywood, where his room was still intact, just without the physical presence of him there.

Nothing at all made sense to me by the end of that drive, but that was the one thing that made my arrival back in L.A. a little more of an easier blow to take. I knew the apartment. I knew his room. It was comfortable, and safe. *I just needed to feel safe.*

When I pulled into the driveway at their apartment on Sweet-zer Avenue, Vick's best friend's girlfriend—who had become a dear friend of mine as we bonded quickly because it was two Chicago Bears fans dating two Philadelphia Eagles fans—met me at my car to help get the kittens out. When I finally got upstairs, got the cats settled and thanked our friends for all of their support, I excused myself to head back to my boyfriend's room and just collapsed. I closed the door, fell to the floor, and the tears came rushing back.

I didn't know when I would see Vick again, when I could hug him again, and I didn't know a thing in that moment other than there I was, forcefully back in L.A. I felt so bad for the situation I had put him in, and I felt beyond awful that his best friend inherited three new roommates—me and the two kittens. I knew what a disruptor I was, to Vick's life, to his best friend's life, the inconvenience of just my presence alone, as well as two damn kittens, thrust upon someone else. The guilt was unbearable. None of them asked for any of this. But it was undeniable how much Vick loved me. And while the situation really sucked, we all just sucked it up. I moved into Vick's room and lived there the entire time he was gone.

So yes, while my fuck-up majorly altered the plan, it did not destroy our relationship.

We did that on our own.

With him not physically with me, I started to discover it was a lonely life I was living. I wasn't getting any auditions anymore. Just as I had been doing in Chicago, every day became déjà vu, working back at The Spanish Kitchen and picking up extra shifts when they'd throw them to me at The Belmont. Aside from working nonstop on the block, what was I doing in L.A. if I wasn't actually doing anything in L.A.? Even with friends there, I was lonely. I was depressed after what happened, and even though I knew I wasn't meant to live by his story, I no longer knew what mine was.

"Rewrite This Story"

The last acting role I ever did was for that project Vick had asked me to be a part of—the role where I cried in front of him, leaving an imprint on his heart. A moment in the darkness of the context of the scene, he saw my light. In the ugliness, he saw beauty.

It's not that I stopped loving being an actor. I *love* acting, but the rat race wore me down, and I was tired of walking around saying, "I'm an actor," when, at that point, I should have been walking around saying, "I'm a bartender," with my head held high, proud that I was standing on my own two feet in Los Angeles.

Before Vick ventured off to Vancouver and I got booted back to L.A., he began showing me this other creative side of his life, and I was suddenly fascinated. That's when the career shift happened for me.

Vick was a producer. I saw what he did, and through paying attention to him doing his work, I really began to see a side of the industry I had never really noticed before. I saw how he was able to create from a different side of the camera. One minute, he would be working on scheduling, then he would be on set interviewing cast members, then he'd be at the office late at night in an edit bay just trying to piece something together at the last minute to get to his editor. And then before we knew it, his episodes would be airing on TV. Not only that, but he would be working on his own creative projects with some of our super talented friends, he'd be coming up with his own show ideas and asking me if I could help do some research for him in my spare time, he'd be writing scripts of his own—even writing my own quirks into the main character, like putting on mascara in the car while the male character was driving, which drove him nuts every time I did that.

For most of my life, all I ever knew was how to be a performer, how to wear a crown, how to entertain an audience, and how to make sure a lens was focusing in on me. Yeah, I majored in theater and learned all the behind-the-scenes stuff, but I never really saw the ability to take that kind of passion, that level of creativity, and make magic happen from the other side of the camera, which resulted in the same emotional impact on the lives of viewers.

I quickly put the pieces together. I could still use the creative part of myself but perhaps in a different way than I had originally intended. This "producing" thing could quite possibly be something I could be really good at.

Maybe there was something to this?

Becoming a TV/film producer wasn't my goal when I moved to California—but after six years of not really getting anywhere in my acting career, I was twenty-nine years old and realized I wasn't happy chasing my childhood dream anymore.

Maybe I could start over again. Maybe I could flip the script of the life I always believed I wanted; the life young me dreamed of.

So I decided to at least try. I wouldn't know what I was capable of if I didn't. So I said goodbye to acting, and in doing so, I buried the childhood dream but took with me *the creator* that had always been screaming to be unleashed.

"Try Everything"

I got my first producing job while Vick was in Canada. At that point, I didn't have an ounce of actual "producing" experience and no resume. But I was a good, hard working person, and a mutual friend of ours, who had also worked with Vick on many projects, stuck his neck out and vouched for me. I got hired from his referral for a female mixed martial arts show, and while I didn't know the first thing about using Avid or creating stringouts, or a hundred other "producer" things, I knew how to tell a good story. That got me the job—my undeniable passion for storytelling.

Every day I went into work, I was learning and building my skills, and that was priceless. I made such an impression that my boss ended up keeping me on with his company after that MMA project ended. Before long, I was overseeing all the projects for his company in all stages from development to production to post. One minute, I was helping put together budgets for a scripted feature film about the folklore creature Chupacabra, then I was jumping over to help put together a shoot schedule for a football-food sizzle reel with former Jets' footballer Antonio Cromartie, then I was laying out footage in the edit bay for a documentary about bananas, then I was flying to Louisiana to film with a bunch of crawfish farmers while also sitting in my boss's dad's office learning about branding and product integration. I had my hands in every single aspect of every single project from scripted, non-scripted, and documentary features to scripted and non-scripted television-to-live events and more. I was overseeing it all. At one point, I counted, and it was sixty projects, but I was only making $600 a week and still having to bartend at night and on the weekends to get by.

I was making nothing, and some days, I was feeling like a burden because the producing partners had to get creative with how I was going to get paid. I was handling all their shit for them and working my ass off for pennies, but I did it because I became passionate about producing. I wanted to learn everything I could as fast as I could, hands-on, thrown-in-the-fire style. Every project that went somewhere, I was able to use the producing credit they gave me to build my resume—that alone was invaluable, even though I never saw a single penny from them beyond my $600 paychecks for any project that my hands touched that sold and went somewhere after I was gone.

The biggest thing I could take away from that experience, from that first opportunity, was knowing how good I was at this and the burning feeling inside of me to finally feel what it was like to have success at creating every single day.

I was able to walk through life saying, "I'm a producer."

And finally, I was actually living my truth.

"1 step forward, 3 steps back"

By the time Vick finally made it home from Canada and we were officially living together—finally, moving forward in the same direction—that opportunity I was given while he was away eventually led to me getting hired by a company specifically for one show with a proper title and a corresponding paycheck. But even at that associate producer level with a proper paycheck, I was still bartending when I could just to be able to, for once, have a little comfort in my financial situation.

Vick hated the fact that I was finding my place in our industry as a producer.

There was one day when I was working on an original creative project of my own, and really for no reason, Vick flipped a switch. We got in a fight, and he snapped at me and said, "That's because I thought I was dating an actress, not a reality television producer." Then he told me, "You will never be anything more than what you are right now." He was an executive producer; I was just an associate producer.

In his eyes, I was never going to be anything more than what I was in that moment—beneath him.

The more experience I was getting, and the more I started getting hired to produce more TV shows and projects on my own, the more we started to slowly drift apart. There was an underlying level of competition in our relationship, and not just because he taught me how to be the fantasy football player I am. You should want success for your partner, but when Vick wanted to feel better about himself, he opted to verbally slam me down. *Wow. Just like my mother.* He was quick to always remind me of what my "position" actually was, and how my worth wasn't anything near his, as his bank account would show.

You will never be anything more than what you are right now—those words whispered in my ear every single day from that moment on, crushing my confidence internally in spite of the success I was having.

I should have seen the warning signs from the beginning. Who am I kidding? I saw them; I just ignored them. Since the moment I fell in love with him, I saw his Jekyll and Hyde appear. I've seen his eyes go from kind and warm to dark and cold. One minute, he loved me; the next, he hated me. One minute, he needed me; the next, he just scared me. He could hurt me with the cruelest words I'd ever heard spoken and then say what he knew I needed to hear to make things right again.

He was so good at making things right.

And I was so good at staying.

"Rock Bottom"

About two years into our relationship is when other people could really see just how toxic our relationship was. Well, actually people already knew but most would just turn a blind eye out of respect for their friendship with him. It wasn't really until I was working on a show about spring breakers in Panama City Beach that I realized how blessed I was even in the hard times. I'll forever be thankful for that show and that entire experience because it brought me one of the people I adore the most in my life, Adria.

The first day I met Adria, it was an instant connection with her—one of those paths intentionally crossing that you know the universe made happen for a greater reason beyond that single moment. That show was brutal to work on, but we were in the trenches together, and it bonded us in a way I never knew was possible. We formed a sisterhood, and to this day, she is my ray of light—constantly sending me positive, uplifting, vibrant messages to let me know I'm on her mind and she's out there rooting for me. Somehow her messages always come through when I need them most. And I do the same for her—always cheering her on and having her back no matter what!

When we were down in Panama City Beach filming with crazy-ass drunk spring breakers, for someone "newish" to my life and only knowing pieces of my relationship, it didn't take long for Adria to see how quickly Vick was able to alter my mood, even from thousands of miles away. We would work a thirteen-hour day out in the sun, on our feet all day. At the end of it, Adria and I would just sit there, trying to eat some food and have a glass of wine while we wrapped up our notes for the day and prepared for tomorrow's shoot. And instead of a loving, supportive, proud text, he would say things to me like, "What are you fucking wearing on set that you have tan lines like that?" because I wore a tank top in the sun. That's the kind of support I got from the man who "loved" me.

All I was doing was trying to do my job, in a really rough situation, and I was just trying to get through it—yet there I was looking at Adria with tears streaming down my face.

She would just sit there, shake her head, and say, "Oh, honey. I don't like this for you. You don't deserve that. Not at all."

And it happened all the fucking time. He could build me up so high and then emotionally slam me down to the ground in a single second. He could make me feel so valued, then so damn small. He could shower me with love, then make me feel disposable. And in the times he wanted me to know he wasn't happy with me, he put so much fear in me. I was terrified to let my light shine, so I quickly started to dim even darker. Over and over and over again. Hit after hit after hit. I stayed because we had a life we built together. And I saw the good in the love we had, but the dark was so scarily dark. But I fucking loved him, so I took the emotional hits.

That's what an emotionally abusive relationship does to you.

"Pass You By"

In the beautiful times, Vick and I went on vacations, traveled to our families' homes for the holidays, and created a "family" with amazing friends in L.A. One minute, he would show me support and encourage me to believe in my creative abilities while I would be inspiring him to write and help him do whatever he needed to further his own success. We could just lie in each other's arms with our two kittens in our condo we bought and talk of dreams, ideas, and the kind of life we could have one day, while the outside world just faded away.

But in the dark times, he would tell me I was a *fat fucking pig* to the point he made me so insecure I found myself, at 132 pounds, on a crazy diet, consisting of only drinking protein drinks on weekdays except one green salad on a Wednesday and a diet coke for a treat. I quickly saw myself fading away. When he wanted to flex his power, he would constantly remind me it was *his* condo since it was *his* money for the down payment. He would go out alone with our friends and fuck with my heart, staying out all night after his phone had died while I was left up alone, worrying if he was okay until the next day when he walked back in the door. Oh yea, and that time he flipped out on me in the middle of LAX airport and left me stranded with a suitcase in my hand and tears streaming down my face.

He made me so insecure—and while he did, as I mentioned, inspire me to become a producer, he would shit on me if I wasn't making a lot of money, so I would struggle to balance my new producing career while picking up more bar shifts. I couldn't keep up.

Around the three-year mark, there was one night I could never forget. It was the moment that really shook me up to the point I had to come face to face with all these truths...

A note from me: Just before sending my book to production, I decided to pull the truth of this story out. I just couldn't let it exist in print. I went into writing this series with the freedom to finally speak some truths, but I realized at the final hour that I couldn't share this one. The night I'm speaking of was the darkest night of our relationship and, while those who know us will know who this story is about, I don't want anyone, especially his family, to ever see that side of his darkness I lived with back then. I guess, all these years later, I still want to protect him from that and the emotional pain I still feel from that night—and that comes from a sincere place of respect, and love. All I will say is that it was enough to leave me shaking on the ground, while he walked away from me and went back to our friends who were at our condo that night, acting as though nothing ever happened. That's all I will say about it.

And, I never got an apology for that night.

What did I ever do to him?

"Reason To Stay"

I loved him so much. We had our home, a life we were building together. Hearing those words whispered in my ear that night as I was forced to the ground, thinking of years of cruel things he said to me and how easily he could knock me down to make himself feel better, even as tears streamed down my face—seriously, what was I doing? I didn't know what to do. But I knew only one person could tell me the truth I needed to hear—my other best friend, Ryan. This was around 11:30 at night, and she didn't hesitate to immediately text me back:

> "You always have a job at The Belmont. You will never be homeless as long as I'm around.
>
> The average woman in the US is a size fourteen, you are WAY under that!
>
> And for the past three years he has never known how to love you back."

I didn't have much at that point. We had sold most of my stuff and bought all new things for our *home*, together. So it physically wouldn't have taken a lot to leave, though emotionally it would have.

Shortly after that night, I ended up packing up my stuff, and Ryan let me live on her couch until I figured things out.

For the few weeks I stayed with Ryan, I tried my hardest to focus on the bad, not the good, but it was impossible to do. I knew he had gone away on a ski trip to Colorado, showing that his life could so easily move on without me. He even had one of his best friends move into our guest bedroom. As I would sit out on Ryan's balcony, looking out onto West Hollywood from above, my heart would ache so bad. I wondered where he was out there, and I didn't know who I was anymore without him. Even in the pain, my identity was intertwined with his. So without him, a huge part of who I had become was missing.

I would sit on Ryan's couch, just listening to all the music that meant something to our relationship. I looked at our photos over and over. And I was so fucking sad, every single day. It was like I couldn't breathe without him.

One night, we made plans for me to go over to the condo just to hang out. The condo felt different. The bedroom felt cold. The cats felt distant. *This was no longer my home.* As we caught up on that week's episode of *Game of Thrones,* Vick and I sat on the couch next to one another with great tension and heartbreak sitting between us—lovers who no longer were lovers but were clearly still in love. We knew how damaged we were. But we also had hope for what we could become. And I knew in the center of my heart that if we could just work through the hard things, the hurt, the broken trust, the disrespect, the drinking too much—if we could just work together to be better and make the changes I knew we were both capable of, that there was something there worth fighting for. Even in the times he wanted me to believe our life couldn't be "romantic comedy movie" worthy, he knew we had something you don't just find every day— something anyone would be lucky enough to find in their lifetime. *The good was that good.*

It wasn't easy, and it wasn't instant, but we decided to give our relationship a second chance. And I moved back into *our* condo.

"Lose You to Love Me"

Over the course of our relationship, I tried to own up to my part in the destruction of us because I greatly contributed to our emotional undoing—but fuck, things didn't change. Just a month or so after I moved back into the condo, I was bawling my eyes out to Madison, feeling so defeated, and she asked me, "Does he make you happy more than he makes you sad?" And he did. Make me happy. But the sad was so *sad*.

You can only take being called a *cunt* so many times.

But don't forget, as he once told me, "words are just words; it's people who give them meaning." So I was the one to blame for being sensitive and upset that he could so easily call me a *fucking cunt*.

It was a verbally abusive relationship, and he made me addicted to him. I knew what we could be, together. I held on to that hope that maybe one day it would be better, yet for three and a half years, Vick took a sledgehammer to those dreams and tried to convince me fairytales didn't exist.

There isn't one specific moment that I can pinpoint when I knew there was no saving us. It wasn't the first time I moved out of our condo and was treated so inferior to him before ultimately we agreed to give it another go, nor was it the night I found myself on our closet floor after the dark night I just couldn't put in print, nor was it the day he flipped out on me because I had strappy tan lines from wearing a thin tank top after filming outside on location, nor was it the day he called me a *fat fucking pig*, nor the countless times he got in my face and told me I was a *fucking cunt*. Maybe it was the moment after I moved back in and we were working on a second chance, and after showing him the gift I made for him, a video of memories over the course of our three-plus-year relationship, his response to what I made for him was, "I feel like I'm at a fucking funeral." *Yeah, maybe that was it.*

For three and a half years, I stayed with someone who could hurt me so deeply and then somehow make it all okay in a single moment. Of all the men and relationships that had been in my life up to this point, no one could hurt me like he did. Because we built a life together. He was the first, true *forever* kind of "adult" relationship I ever had—the one I saw a future with, *the one I wanted a future with,* and the one I gave my heart to, who then absolutely crushed it.

He was good, but he had demons in his past that came out and triggered the demons in mine. In the good, he let the best parts of me shine. In the bad, he brought out a side of me that scared me at times, and unleashed this dark side of me that I didn't even know was locked in there. And I couldn't control it. He made me quite hostile at times because I couldn't just sit there and take his verbal punches.

We both contributed to what ultimately became the collapse of us. I had learned to emotionally hit back. I learned to be combative. When the wounds healed from one fight, the bell ding'd, and it was time for round two. The longer our relationship went on, the harder we hit, the longer the rounds lasted but the more love existed, and we fought harder because the good that was there and the love we had was so much stronger than the pain.

I loved him so much. I really, truly did—like genuine, real, earth-shaking kind of love. And I loved his family so much. I loved the life we created for ourselves with a group of friends who became *family* to us there, who we spent holidays and Sunday Fundays with and cheered each other on in an otherwise very lonely town. This part of it all became a huge part of my identity, and I knew, if I walked away for good, I was going to lose all of that. *How could I lose that?*

I gave him every ounce of me, and I fought for us to the end.

Until I just couldn't fight anymore.

I wasn't enough for an industry I loved. I wasn't enough for my father. At times, I wasn't even enough for my own mother. I wasn't enough for my high school sweetheart to say to his unborn baby's momma, "No, she's too important not to be in my life in some way"—nor enough for my "dinosaur" because I was never going to be able to change the fact that I wasn't Greek. And, I certainly wasn't enough for Vick, who I loved with everything I had in me but who didn't want to change for the better to be with me.

All of the "not enough for love" just chipped away at my soul.

So, I made the choice to finally try and become enough for *me*.

"Wrecking Ball"

I knew if I was going to leave, it was for good this time. There wasn't going to be a round three. But I needed to be prepared. I had to be sure. Losing everything, leaving everything—I needed to know I could do this on my own.

Just down the street from where our condo was, Adria lived in a charming little bungalow on Poinsettia Place, near Melrose Avenue. I knew it well, as I had been there a few times to visit her since our spring break show. We were catching up one day, and she told me she was going to be moving out of there and into a new place with her boyfriend, so her cozy cottage apartment would be available. Adria vouched for me with her landlord, and without having to go through a massive application battle with others, he offered me the apartment if I wanted it. With a new adorable apartment I could call my own, I stood, looking at a relationship I knew was never going to change, and had to make a choice.

I had fought with every ounce of what I had inside of me for my relationship with Vick, but I couldn't punch back anymore because if

I kept on going, there was going to be no sliver of me left. One more emotional punch and there would be no getting up the next time. It was one of the hardest decisions I've ever made, but I couldn't justify losing myself completely. I was still in there, *somewhere*, and I had to take back my life. I had to stop trying to save someone else and realize I had to fucking save myself. I had to stop fighting for that relationship, and I had to start fighting for *me*. I had to realize I was worth more and I deserved more, not just from him but from myself.

So I took the keys to the apartment on Poinsettia Place, and in doing so, chose *me*.

My relationship with Vick defined a pivotal time in my life when I had to learn to walk away—for myself, because I knew I deserved more. No matter how much love there was, the only way to stay true to myself was to walk away, even if that meant turning around, facing a road of charcoal, lighting a fire, and standing there with bare feet. And still choosing to walk forward. No matter how bad it burns. No matter how much it fucking hurts. Walk forward. Because there's no way I could go back.

Walking away from him was an unbearable pain. But I couldn't let that outweigh the pain I would have felt had I stayed.

I knew how much he loved me. But sometimes, love really isn't enough.

Even though I was the one who ultimately chose to leave, I don't think anyone had destroyed my heart the way Vick did.

I wasn't enough for him until I walked out the door. And then, he tried to argue I was—but this time, it was just too late.

"Apologize"

None of us are the past versions of ourselves or our past mistakes. This piece of my story was a very difficult one to open up about, and in doing so, there was no intention to open old wounds or cause any pain. And yet, all it has done is release all the pain I'd pushed down for so long now because I just kept it buried inside of me—so this has been hard to relive. It was a very beautiful yet very painful season of my life. A lot of fun, a lot of love, but a lot of pain. And a lot of moments I'm not proud of. We're all human and do things in moments we can't always justify. But what we take from it and how we grow is the most important thing of all.

Neither of us are now who we were back then. I know for certain that people are capable of change. Sometimes you're just not the one for your person to want to change for, or fight for, and that's a hard thought to grasp—that after your relationship they will move on and find someone who they hopefully can be that person for, or someone who will just accept them. But you can't force someone to change. The only person you can change is yourself.

After I was gone, Vick sent me a letter, apologizing for some things. He admitted things I never thought I would ever hear him say. In that letter, he wrote:

> I regret a lot of things that I have done and said over the years. But one thing that I will always be sorry for telling you is that "life is not a fairytale" or "romantic comedy" or whatever I said. I am overwhelmed with regret that I said that to you—someone who believes that life should be a fairytale—and now only as I'm truly faced with losing you, I realize that the thing that made me fall in love with you is your belief that life can be a fairytale. In

so many ways, that is the essence of Nicole, that is what makes you so much better than any other woman I've ever met. You've loved me so much more than I could ever ask you to. And I've made you feel disposable.

Vick, it wasn't just you. It was the world that made me feel that way.

While other people had spent years making me believe I wasn't enough, I had no choice but to convince myself their narrative was anything but the truth—because I was nowhere around, trying to write myself a different story.

The craziest fucking thing is that all the years of my life leading up to this point, I was always enough. I just had to stop allowing myself to let others convince me I wasn't.

But how do I do that?

Despite the pain, I have so much gratitude for this time in my life—for the love I was able to feel in the good, the strength that came from being beat down, and the lessons I was able to take with me when I walked away.

For over three years, I lived with the pain of what I went through while we were together, never once, not even now, talking of the depths of it. I let the actions and words of a very abusive relationship get burned so deep in my brain that for the next ten years after I was gone, I let his whispers control me. And it took this long to have the strength to speak out loud about a small part of it—because I'm tired of limiting myself in this one lifetime just because a boy thought it was okay to be so fucking cruel.

Whether he meant the words he wrote to me or not, I got some form of an apology. It doesn't make anything that happened okay, but what it makes me realize is that not everyone who goes through something like that probably got an email like I did. And so, to you my reader, if you have ever gone through some form of abuse and never had someone help you out of a really hard time, like Ryan and Adria did for me, and if you never got an apology from the person who hurt you in a way you never dreamed possible, I guess I just want to say—I'm sorry. I'm so sorry you ever had to feel that. I'm so sorry someone else hurt you to the point you allowed them to make you feel below them or not enough. I'm so sorry no one was there to help you get out. I'm so sorry you didn't feel you had another choice than to take the punches thrown your way. *I'm so sorry.*

We all have stories that we've lived through that are really hard to relive. While some of it is manageable to deal with, some of it just hits really deep.

Please know, just because others have beat you down at times doesn't mean you don't have the strength within you to stand back up and keep moving forward.

You are so much stronger than you know.

That's really what I want to say to you.

Because—being able to say that to you, was worth the pain of reliving this story.

And in case you need a little bit of hope, a reminder, let me tell you now, *I promise, you are more than enough.*

THREE.

The Unthinkables

AMAZING CRAZY

"Ocean Eyes"

My friend Chris once said to me, "You should go after the person you'd feel lucky to be with." It's an ironic thing because I had never gone after a single man. The only one I ever *went after* was the one who married me.

As my relationship with Vick was coming to an end and I was turning the key to the door of a new life waiting for me, I promised myself I was going to take the time to focus on me—but then, something kind of unexpected happened.

The minute I walked in the room for the show I was hired as a producer on, I walked past an open door and froze. I locked eyes with *him,* and my heart skipped a beat. In all the loves I had experienced in my life, I had never felt that kind of feeling before. It was as if my soul whispered, *You found him.*

I went to my desk and sat there, but I couldn't shake that feeling. I couldn't unsee his eyes. I had to find an excuse to go back to that room because I had to make sense of this feeling. So, I grabbed my computer, and with my heart practically exploding out of my chest, walked into his room.

"Hi. I'm Nicole, the new producer starting today. Can you help me get my computer set up on the Wi-Fi and printer here?" I nervously said to him.

Not even looking up at me, he just barked orders to his coordinator, "Buscemi, take care of this, please."

Ewww. He legit wanted nothing to do with me. So he pawned me off onto his coordinator to "take care of me."

He had such a shitty attitude and was probably one of the grump-iest people I'd ever met in my life. Here I was like Little Miss *fucking* Sunshine on my first day on the show, and he was the cloud that came in and rained all over my day.

But the thing about me is, I actually love the rain. So, I wasn't going to let his misery stop me from listening to what my intuition was telling me—*you found him.*

Over the next weeks, I kept finding ways to position myself around him. In Las Vegas, I asked him for my cast members' per diem they were owed for the week, and as he walked with me to bring it to them in their hotel rooms, instead of making small talk with me on the walk, the only thing he said was, "You smell like the Vegas strip."

In Wine Country, I asked him if he wanted to meet me and an-other producer in the lobby and have some pizza with us while we prepped for the next shoot day. He declined, yet I found him stand-ing with his crew drinking beers, right in front of my hotel door.

In Los Angeles, I would hang around offering my help if there was anything I could do to help production out and help make their lives easier, which is something producers never did, and he would always say, "We're good," even though I knew he wasn't sleeping and was drowning in the stress of the show.

And in Orange County, when I asked him if he wanted to join us at dinner and take a break, he said, "No thanks." But it turned out he went to a restaurant right across from where us producers were eating. *Nicole, take a hint, girl!* He clearly wanted nothing to do with me. Yet, all I found myself wanting was for him to want everything to do with me.

Every time I was near him, the feeling only intensified. None of this made any sense. Like, zero. I was supposed to be focused on the show and myself, yet it was *myself* telling me, *This is the one.*

But he didn't see me. Or so it seemed. Later, he confided that he *definitely* saw me that moment I first walked through the door. That moment my eyes locked with his. Every time I thought he didn't notice me around, he did. He saw me more than I knew.

As I would come to learn, he just couldn't show it.

"*Iris*"

One day, we were all gathered together on the basement level of our hotel in Las Vegas. Everyone was stressed out to the max. Our call sheet still wasn't ready for the morning, and the crew was scrambling to get the logistics together so everyone could be released and go to bed. But I knew even after everyone went to bed, *he* wouldn't be sleeping. He never slept. He was the first one on set every day and the last one to leave. He was on overdrive. I'm not sure how he was functioning, but it was like he was programmed to push through and make sure not just his but everyone else's jobs were done. He was that good at what he did.

I ripped a piece of paper out of my notebook and wrote something down on it. I folded it in half, and as he sat there on his computer, I dropped the piece of paper on his keyboard. I didn't even make eye contact with him. I just turned around and walked back to my bag and started packing up for the night. Trying not to let him know I was watching him—*but I was watching him*—as I packed up my laptop and my things, I saw him open the piece of paper. And then as I saw him fold the paper back up, he looked at me, shook his head—and then he smiled.

On that piece of paper, the only thing I wrote was one simple word: *Smile.*

That was the first time in weeks I had seen him smile. I cracked him.

Seeing him smile in that way made me smile too. It was the first time I had smiled like that in so long—like my light was back, like he was helping me remember who I was after being so broken and beaten down.

After seeing him smile like that, I found myself walking toward him before heading to my room for the night. I went right up to him, still seated in front of his computer, and said, "I'm going to make it my personal mission to make you smile every single day for the rest of your life," because what I had to admit to myself was that *in my new pursuit to make him smile, he was giving me a reason to smile too.*

Afterward, whenever my eyes would scan the room looking for him, I would see him looking for me too. Every time our eyes met, suddenly a smile appeared on both of our faces. Not a single word needed to be spoken. *He found me too.*

The following week, we were again back in L.A. Our base camp was set up in a conference room not far from Universal Studios. I was walking through the parking lot with one of my fellow producers toward the hotel, and as we were waiting for the elevators, I saw *him* walking on the sidewalk down below. I wanted the elevators to hurry up so maybe I could casually bump into him before the day got started. I couldn't say any of this out loud, because the *smile* was our little secret, just us two.

But my co-worker noticed him too and said, "He's here early." Followed by a pause, so awkward as though she was deep in thought. Then she said, "Adam doesn't really seem like the kind of guy who would be married."

I almost threw up.

Everything in my body started shaking, but I couldn't let it show. What the fuck was *life* doing to me? What the fuck was I doing? *He's married?!*

"He's married? Weird. He doesn't wear a ring," is what I said back, trying to react like a normal person.

My co-worker nodded, then mentioned something about seeing his wife drop him off the other day. I can't even remember the exact words because it all became a blur just hearing *him* and *wife* in one sentence.

He's married.

"Untouchable Face"

When I was younger, I believed so deeply that there was one soulmate out there for each of us. I even wrote poems about it. But then I grew up, and the more I experienced in life, the more I started to discover new beliefs. I no longer believe there is one soulmate for every individual, but rather that there are multiple *soul mates* out there for each of us. To me, soulmates are those people you find over and over again across many lifetimes, the ones you come to find in different shapes and sizes and bodies time and time again—a mother, a best friend, a lover, a child, a coworker, a stranger who you meet once but leaves an imprint on your heart. To me, a soulmate is someone you are supposed to have in your life for some reason, someone who, against all odds, keeps coming back. Someone who needs no introduction—it's an immediate connection and you just know. There's this overwhelming sense of something that comes over you and allows you to pick up where you left off a lifetime ago.

To some, this may seem absurd, for not everyone believes in the idea of reincarnation or multiple lifetimes, but to the ones who believe in infinite possibilities, in destiny, in purpose and meaning, in more than this one life—no explanation is needed. I know you understand. Because for me, the way I love, the amount of love I give and the depths to which I love in this lifetime—I have to believe there's more beyond just this.

That's what I meant when my intuition said, *You found him.*

But then real life said, *He's married.*

I did my best to avoid him that day. It wasn't that I was feeling any sort of negativity about what I learned; I was just processing the reality that the human I believed was the one I had been waiting to find again, was indeed married. I couldn't understand the meaning of why this was happening, but I had to believe there was more that I wasn't seeing.

It was getting toward the end of the night at the hotel by Universal Studios, the crew was wrapping up, and our large group started to dwindle down. We were gathered in a small conference room in the hotel, I was seated on the floor across from the same producer I was with earlier that morning, and we were both finishing up our notes for the day. After I gathered up my stuff and as I walked over to the table to turn in my walkie for the day, that's when he stopped me—to make me smile. He knew I wore this brown strappy wrap bracelet around my wrist every day that had inspirational words on it. I found it at a small shop on Melrose Avenue and loved it so much it became a part of my daily wardrobe. When I was leaving that night, he gestured down to his wrist—where he was wearing a set of four rubber bands and on one of them, he had written the word "smile."

I got lost in those baby blue eyes of his and wanted nothing more than for him to tear my clothes off and pin me up against the wall right there in front of everyone. But that couldn't happen. So, I nervously laughed at his attempt to now be the one to try and make me *smile*, I said goodnight, and I walked away.

In the few conversations I did have with Adam up to that point, I learned a few things. He grew up four hours from where I grew up. He moved to L.A. the same month and year I did. His baseball team was the Cincinnati Reds and football team the Indianapolis Colts, which didn't sit well with me being a Chicago Cubs and Chicago Bears fan. The year before, when I was working on that spring break show where I met Adria, Adam was supposed to work on that show too. My desk was right next to our line producer's desk, who Adam was literally on the phone with one day—but he ended up not taking the job. If our paths had crossed back then, there would have been no way we would have seen one another in this way. Life clearly had a different plan for not allowing our paths to cross the year before.

But what was that plan? Why were our paths crossing now? He was fucking married—what was *life* doing to me? What message was the universe trying to send me?

The next week, we all traveled down to Orange County because that was where the next location was to film at. That night, we found quite the interesting little blend of the crew seated around a table after a long day of filming. We were playing games, talking, laughing, drinking, and to my left was Adam, seated next to me. He was engaging with his side of the table, and I was engaging with my side, but I could feel him staring, seemingly a reaction to the way some of the other guys were talking to me. As if he was a little jealous. He had no right to be, but I could feel it. And maybe I flirted back a little bit with the other guys, hoping just maybe he would be a little jealous.

I don't know what gave me the courage to just out of the blue turn to him and say, "You're married? Like, for real, you're married?"

It got awkward at the table. This came out of nowhere and would have made no sense to anyone other than him and me. He leaned over, and whispered to me, "Yes, but it's complicated."

Everyone went back to the conversations they were having before I completely disrupted the mood. Married but complicated... but married. *Fuuuuuuck.*

The next day was set for another full day of filming, so people started to call it a night. I was trying to get Adam to get up and leave at the same time as me so I could actually talk to him, but when I got up, one of the other guys got up with me and walked me to the elevator instead. His intentions were to follow me to my room, yet I turned back and stared at the one I wished had.

Luckily, I was able to talk my way out of that elevator and made it back to my room, alone.

"Wine Glass"

I got to my hotel room. My head was spinning, not from the wine but the confusion of what the hell was going on emotionally. The room was dark, so I flicked on the first light switch by the door and I dropped my bag down by the desk. And as I looked out of the window, that's when I noticed my view for the first time.

When I looked down, I saw my view below just so happened to be of the patio table we were just sitting at. And I could still see Adam sitting there, laughing with his crew. And me, watching, wondering, *What was all of this?*

My heart was aching for someone I couldn't have. I had never felt this before in my life. My heart was actually *aching*.

As I stood there, staring at him, smiling—that smile I longed to see for weeks and then finally did because of the note I wrote him. Below me, I saw him smiling with other people on our crew—not me.

As I watched him, I thought of that day I first walked into the office—when I walked down the hallway wearing my tie-dye maxi dress and jean jacket and nearly tripped over my flip-flops as I looked into an open doorway and saw his eyes, and he was sitting there behind his laptop in a white T-shirt and New Balance gym shoes. I didn't know how it was possible a heart could stop and also flutter with butterflies at the same time, but that's what happened that day.

Even in the shittiness he exuded, somehow I was the one who eventually could make him smile.

But I couldn't be with him. *Why can't I be with him?* I wasn't supposed to be with him. *I need to be with him.* I had to stay away from him. *I don't want to stay away from him.*

I shook my head. *Forget it.* I really didn't have the time or energy for any of this. I was over it. *I was not over it.*

I looked out the window one last time. He was so close, but he was so far away. But I knew I had to let go of whatever these feelings were inside. Whatever this pull was between us, that wasn't supposed to be happening. *It can't happen.* It couldn't happen.

So, I walked away from the window and changed into my pajamas, got my bag ready for the next day, and got myself ready to just pass out from mental exhaustion. I climbed into bed.

And then, there was a knock at my door. And it was *him.*

I opened the door. I said, "What are you doing here?"

He didn't say a thing. He just grabbed hold of me and kissed me with what felt like decades of built-up desire.

Oh…he kissed me. And kissed me. And he kissed me some more.

He broke away and told me he was married. Yes. But they weren't in a good place. They had been together since high school. He proposed because it was the next thing to do. There was a lot of deep shit they were dealing with and had been going through. He had been sleeping on the couch for the past year. It was basically over even though it wasn't really *over.*

I guess that made what was to come next a little more *forgivable?*

I grabbed him and kissed him.

I think we slept two hours that night.

"What Have I Done"

When I opened my eyes in the morning, he was staring at me. His eyes were smiling. He whispered, "Hi."

I whispered, "Hi," back.

His phone rang, and it was his coordinator. This was the first morning Adam didn't go to set early. He was okay with that—he finally had a reason to stay in bed.

That day, we were filming on a pier at the beach. It was excruciating, an elimination day; both of my cast members were the top favorites in the running to win the entire season, so I was locked in and bouncing all over the place. But when I had a moment to take a breath and look around at the beautiful views of the ocean, I turned around and noticed something I had never seen before—there was Adam, standing in the parking lot at the end of the pier, watching what was happening on set. He never went onto set where things were being filmed; he always stayed behind in his safe production space where he didn't have to be bothered when everyone else was out doing their job. When people asked him what he was doing out there that day, he said he was just making sure things were running smoothly. But really, he was standing there watching me.

That night, we didn't hang out with the rest of the crew. We sat outside by the hotel gazebo, drank wine, listened to music, and talked as if we were picking up where we left off a lifetime ago.

That night in my hotel bed, we laid in each other's arms naked under the covers. And as I discovered the natural groove in his chest that seemed to exist just for me, we talked of dreams—big and small. We talked of our passions and hopes for the future—both of us admitting we didn't believe Los Angeles was the place we wanted to spend the rest of our lives. "I don't know if I would want to raise my kids here," he told me, "but it's hard because our work is here. I went to school for this business, and a part of me always wanted to be a cinematographer for feature films. But here I am, production managing reality TV instead."

After really listening to what he said, I suggested, "Why don't you try to transition into features then? Why don't you get a camera and just start filming stuff like you used to in school?"

"Because this is comfortable. It's what I know, and I can see the direct path forward from here. It's a lot harder to transition into features from reality TV," he told me almost with a sense of defeat in his tone.

A small awkward pause happened when both of us processed this moment.

"I don't know if I want to stay here forever either," I then told him. "I have this burning desire in my soul that knows there's a whole world out there, and I want to see it. I sometimes fantasize of what that would look like—to just go and not have to explain a thing to anyone."

"Where would you go?" he asked me.

Without a single hesitation, I said, "Italy! Hands down, my number-one place I need to visit in this lifetime."

He laughed awkwardly, then told me that was one of the only countries he had ever been to—because that's where he went on his honeymoon. *Lovely,* I thought to myself. *Just a lovely reminder I'm lying in the arms of a man who's technically still married.*

I knew in the eyes of the world, this was wrong. *But how could something so wrong feel so right?* There was no undoing what had been done. We had to hide it from the world—from everyone. It was our secret. And I was okay with that—because the moments together, the smiles, the beauty life brought back to my heart and soul was worth it all.

He helped me reclaim my light.

But he was married.

Seriously, what have I done?

Yet, as wrong as we knew it was, we both knew we had found that something special our hearts had been waiting for. It was instant. It was effortless. We weren't looking, just existing, and in a moment, we opened our eyes to what was right in front of us. We couldn't deny the force that was pulling us together. It didn't seem real. It truly was "love at first sight" but not in the way you would expect. Adam was not a shallow person and didn't exist at a surface-level idea of what *love* could mean. It was something so much deeper. It was our souls pulling at one another, an undeniable love that could make no sense to anyone other than us. *We just knew.*

A month after that first night in Orange County, we both knew we needed an escape. While we found each other, we were both *lost* in a sense in life. We knew we needed out of L.A., and so we each packed a bag, got in his truck, and hit the open road, headed toward Napa Valley.

"Best Days"

There's a gazillion different versions of the idea that the "road to nowhere leads to somewhere," or however you prefer that saying to go.

I'm going to tell you a version I know:

> Two *lost angels* who were burned out from Los Angeles escaped to a place where the outside world couldn't find them. They didn't know where they were going to go, but they knew they really liked wine, the open road, music, and each other. So, they escaped to find a little treehouse to hide

out in for a simple moment in time. Instead of a treehouse, they found a barn in the middle of a vineyard—a cozy barn with a wine and cheese basket waiting for them right along a dirt path that was surrounded by lush green vineyards where they could wander freely without expectations, without a plan, without others needing them to be anything other than who they were in that moment in time. For the first time in a long time, they weren't running toward the next to-do on the list, but instead, content in roaming in this unfamiliar place. It's in this place they decided to be free enough from the chains that weighed them down and to just have *fun*. Fun. Such a simple idea, but as the angels had gotten older, they had forgotten what it felt like. From that day forward, they vowed to never forget again.

Their main goal became to, simply, smile. That's it. To smile. And with that, to feel alive. To rediscover a piece of self that had been buried. Others would not have approved of these two being there together—shame on them for steering off course, for taking the road less traveled, for discovering happiness. But they were there, no matter what others said, no matter what was expected of them, and it was there where they were granted the freedom to just exist among a vineyard that became their playground.

This was the story of Adam and me shortly after admitting how strong our passion was for one another. On a dirt path to nowhere in the middle of Napa Valley, we discovered our *somewhere*.

On that trip to wine country, with an old tape camcorder in one hand and a glass of red wine in another, I filmed Adam and said, "Tell me a story."

He played along. He just wanted to make me smile. He looked into the camera and said, "I've never done anything like this. Ever. This is probably the best thing I've ever done with probably the best person I've ever met, and I can safely say that, honestly. Life throws you a lot of shit, right? Sometimes they throw you a good one. A good shit. And *them* shits are the ones you need to hang on to. I almost stopped believing in that."

This was a raw, honest moment full of true emotion. The look in his eyes was making me so flushed—but that didn't stop him. He looked past the lens of the camera and into my eyes, smiled, and said, "I've never been happier than this moment."

The truth I couldn't tell him at the time—I had never been happier than I was at that moment.

There's a photo I have of me from that day, that he took, that I can honestly say I felt more beautiful in than I ever felt wearing that crown. It's a bit blurred, I'm wearing a sun hat, and a tank top dress. I'm looking deep into the camera, with a smirk on my face that can catch an onlooker's attention enough to wonder, *What is she thinking?* And the reason I love this photo so much is because of what the expression on my face signifies: "It's just me, looking at you, looking at me." That's the best way I can describe it. The expression on my face was the reflection of Adam looking at me. And it was beautiful.

It was the moment I knew I was so much more than enough.

"Purple Horizon"

There was another clip from this day that I captured as I was messing around with the zoom button, just trying to get a handle of a camcorder I never used. I zoomed out and zoomed in and saw the long dirt path that sat within two sides of the vineyard. Behind the camera you could hear me say, "The path to nowhere, right?—leads to somewhere."

As Adam started walking backward down the dirt path, looking at the camera, he said, "So it's really just a path to *somewhere,* if you think about it."

And without a breath, I said out loud, "Somewhere Road, that would be the name of my road, if I got to name a road. Somewhere Road."

Sometimes you have to get away, to find your way. Somewhere Road is the point along a journey that seems like nowhere to most, but being nowhere is somewhere. Being *lost* isn't a bad thing—it's taking the pause in life that's needed to just exist as yourself without the noise of the outside world beating you down. It's a place we discovered within a space we needed to be allowed to stand in and realize it's in these moments of that which, whether or not they make sense to the outside world, they make sense to us and this space in itself is *somewhere.*

Here we were, lost amongst the vineyards, lost from the reality of our lives back in L.A., in a secret place where we were able to roam freely without the constraints of the world holding us down or screaming at us to do what they wanted us to do and be who they wanted us to be. Here, we were just free to wander in this safe space and take the pause we needed to in life to discover, see, and feel beyond the noise. So, I will always embrace this space in life to exist and be okay with being *lost*—because lost is a much better place to exist than being "stuck."

And it's along this journey where you're lost, that you are found.

That little dirt path sparked an invaluable belief that was yearning to be discovered: the idea that a road doesn't have to be a start and finish point but can be a space within itself. It may seem like nowhere, but nowhere is *somewhere.*

By that, I mean that a path that might seem like it leads nowhere may actually be the place we needed to stand in to grow into who we are *becoming*. We must realize that it's these precious moments of "nothing" that make the most sense to our inner selves. This space of inner knowing is, in itself, *somewhere*.

So, my version of that road to somewhere or path to nowhere is this:

The road to nowhere is actually somewhere. It's—Somewhere Road.

"Of Crows and Crowns"

Upon returning back to my charming cottage apartment on Poinsettia Place in West Hollywood, the place we called "Old Yeller" because I had bought this cozy little yellow couch that was just the right size for the space and just big enough to spend the best times snuggled up with Adam—that night we got back from Napa, I had a glass of wine sitting on the wine cork tabletop I made, and he had an IPA in his hand. I looked over my left shoulder to see what he was so preoccupied with, and that's when I noticed he drew a "green heart emoji + finger pointing emoji" on my chalkboard wall above my desk. I looked at him, wondering what that was all about, and that's when he said to me, "I *think* I have love for you."

The next morning, I woke to find Adam nowhere to be found. He had to leave early to go back to his apartment in Burbank and gather himself before heading off to work that day. But while he wasn't physically there, he had left something on my dresser. It was a paper airplane he made. It was addressed to "Love at first sight," and inside of it was a handwritten letter telling me how happy his heart was and that he was indeed in love with me.

Just because we were "easy," didn't mean life was. Loving Adam was easy, but it was also hard. It was easy because I didn't have to convince him to love me. I didn't have to give him ultimatums. I didn't have to fight for it. It happened, naturally and with ease. But even in the ease of loving him and him loving me came daily hard things—that's just life. No life is perfect; there's always the hard things, the pain, the past that constantly finds its way into your here and now, no matter how hard you try not to think about it.

We both had a lot of shit to deal with and work through on our own before we could really move forward together, hand in hand, in the same direction. We had an abundance of immediate happiness and love but also extreme sadness, heartbreak, and forgiveness. For many months it felt like we were together, but we weren't truly *together*. We weren't allowed to be together, until after his divorce was final. And once it was, it didn't take long before Adam helped me pack up Old Yeller and moved me from West Hollywood to Burbank, to be with him. While the beginning of our story wasn't right by the standards of others, it was always *right* in our hearts. It was the greatest lesson of learning to just live our lives for us—even if it wasn't what others expected us to be doing.

The thing we really had to discover was that the "hard times" are constantly there, but it's essential to find *happy* in the hard.

Happiness starts with you. In you. In the good times and in the hard times. It's the beauty in the breakdown. Just because you have to deal with some hard shit doesn't mean you can't find happiness within it.

People asked us back then how we knew. How could we define what we had when it was still all so very new? And all we could say with the biggest smiles on our faces was, "It's *amazing*. It's *crazy*." And so, *amazing crazy* became our thing. Those two words have shaped our journey together in this lifetime. Living became an everyday adventure, and a paper airplane became the symbol of our life together.

Adam never knew this, but after I made him smile that very first time, I suddenly found myself writing the word "Smile" on my arm, on the inside of my hand, on a Post-it note on my computer—I left myself little reminders everywhere because I wanted to keep feeling what I felt in that moment when he finally did. And it worked every time. Because even though we couldn't be together at that point in time, I was thankful for his existence in any form in my life.

Gratitude is finding happiness in the hard, and a *smile* got us both there almost every time.

UNSUNG LULLABY

"Three Little Birds"

M any people think they're invincible, that nothing bad will ever happen to them. They hear stories of what others have gone through but never think the same will happen to them.

Until the day it does.

Less than a year or so after that first night in Orange County, when Adam knocked on my hotel room door, life revealed a true gift we were being given.

On May 12, 2014, I got confirmation of the news we were secretly hoping for. I remember looking at that stick, and after only a month of *trying*, I thought, *Oh shit, how do I give him the news he's going to be a dad?* It may have seemed fast, especially without a ring on my finger, but it never, ever felt too fast for us. It was about us together on our own journey, knowing we found *forever* and wanted to begin to build a future together. The night I got confirmation via those two pink lines, Adam was still asleep. I snuck back into the bedroom and, without thinking, shook him 'til he had woken. I then put the stick in his face.

The first words out of my mouth were, "So, this is happening!"

He just looked at me, his eyes smiling, and asked, "Are you serious?"

I nodded. He wrapped me in his arms, pulled me down into the bed, kissed my forehead, and said, "I'm so happy."

I didn't want to jinx things. I kind of had nervous emotions about it being so early. Just like I would never share an unborn child's name or embroider an item ahead of time, I needed to keep this beautiful little secret of ours close to our hearts. Adam was a "close to the chest" kind of guy; he taught me how to be that way. While we wanted to keep my pregnancy a secret, there was one person I absolutely could not keep this from—Madison. She had just given birth to her first son, my honorary nephew, so I knew her post-pregnancy emotions would be bursting with excitement. Our hearts were wanting this moment so much. And now, it was happening. I couldn't hide that from my best friend.

So, I texted her the photo of my positive pregnancy test. To which she wrote back:

"(He's) gonna have a girlfriend!!!!!! Holy Shutballlllllsssssssss!!!!! Omgomg NOT SOMETHING YOU NONCHALANTLY TEXT UR BEST FRIEND!!!!!! Omgomg"

"I'm planning their wedding, I'M GONNA BE AN AUNT!!!!"

"Ahhhhh"

While we were overjoyed, the timing absolutely stunk. We had both just started working on a really demanding new TV show called *Car Matchmaker,* and every day we were based out of a location in Venice Beach, having to commute from our home in Burbank. Also, we had a massive family trip coming up—for Adam's cousin's wedding in Indiana and also a family gathering at my home in Chicago, that had already been contributing to more stress in my life at that point.

"Brave"

When I was a child, my mom was a really good mom. She was there for everything, even when she worked nonstop just to make sure there was a peanut butter and jelly sandwich on the table for me. We didn't have a lot of possessions, but we had a lot of love. We danced endlessly to Madonna, and aside from the shitty comments she could throw out now and then and keeping me from really knowing my Italian roots, she was my best friend. At one point, I actually idolized my mom and wished when I grew up, I would be a mom like her. When she wasn't the one causing it, her love could heal any and all pain, even if temporarily.

But having been a mom since she was seventeen years old, one day for who knows what emotionally breaking reason, she flipped a switch, and decided it was time to live the life she wanted to live. She had married a man who gave her the life she always wanted and who became my "dad," but ultimately, he wasn't enough for her, her children weren't enough for her, and she divorced him. Then she started getting flirtier than she ever was before, even keeping in touch with ex-boyfriends of mine if there was some way their existence in this world could benefit her somehow. I got nasty attitude thrown my way when I got my first tattoo—yet, suddenly, she was becoming covered in them. She couldn't fly out to L.A. to see her daughter, who was struggling just to survive on her own, yet she could suddenly start taking my sister, B., on trips around the world. I would be given crap for not being there for things in Illinois, yet they were never around for me. She evolved into this persona for the work she was doing with fish and started getting people to write her checks to support her mission—she did what she felt she had to do to get what she wanted, and to hell with everyone else. It didn't matter who she hurt to get what she wanted at that point, but she made sure the world only saw her "light." My mother was too wrapped up in her own life to notice she hurt the people she was put on this earth to love.

I'm all for people living their own life, but you can still live your life and be a good mom. She chose not to.

At this point in time as I found myself newly pregnant and we were gearing up to fly back to both our homes, my mom and I were fine, I guess. She was trying to act supportive about meeting Adam for the first time. We had just had another blowout with one another thanks to social media. She asked me if I had seen one of her posts about her business and questioned, if I did, why I hadn't "like'd" it yet? I was confused, as I hadn't been on social media, so I went onto Facebook to see what she was talking about. And that's when I saw something that shocked the complete fuck out of me and really just added a new slice to my skin by my mother's own doing—she reunited with my brother. I was happy for her, that she reconciled with her first born child after twenty years of not talking to him. What hurt was the way she handled it and my finding out via a post on Facebook; telling the world before she told her own daughter.

Some words were exchanged via text and then, the conversation just stopped. And we did what our family does best—lash out and say all the things, then just sweep all the dirt under the rug, never getting to the root or talking about the bigger issues. It's the Band-Aid—put a Band-Aid on it and move on.

Yet, Band-Aids are just that—a temporary fix.

So, the timing really stunk. Me just finding out I was pregnant. A new job, stress with my mother, seeing tons of family, meeting all the important people in Adam's life, lots of events planned. It was going to be a lot, because we weren't ready to share our news with anyone else. So this was going to be tough. I just had to trust it was all going to be all right.

Everything will be alright.

"Take Me to Church"

Three days after finding out I was pregnant, we hopped on a plane and headed to Indiana. That was our first stop, since Adam's cousin's wedding also happened to be the same day as Adam's birthday. This would be the first time I met most of Adam's extended family, which was already overwhelming me with nervousness as to what they would think of Adam's new love, when all they had ever known was his first wife. But more than any of his family members, there was one person specifically I was terrified to meet—his best friend, *Gary*. I was scared shitless what he was going to think of me. Would he like me? Would he approve of me being with Adam? These guys have known each other their entire lives—inseparable, have gone through it all together. I was the *girl*. The girl who Adam fell for the minute he saw her when he wasn't supposed to be looking. The girl who didn't wreck his marriage, but his already failing marriage ended after our paths crossed.

But there I was in May of 2014, secretly pregnant with this precious little bean our hearts were so hoping for, without a ring on my finger, stepping into a situation where none of these people had seen Adam in years—who knows what rumors or truths they were told, and here she is! *Fuck me.*

We showed up to a bar in Indianapolis the night before Adam's birthday/his cousin's wedding to find *Gary* and their other good friend waiting for us. As we walked in, I just took a deep breath, trying to dodge whatever unwelcome, judgmental looks and comments were about to come my way. But then, I was shocked—the opposite happened. *Gary* ran up to me, picked me up, and bear-hugged me as though we had known each other our entire lives. Like a real, brother hug. After he put me down and we were face to face, he said, "Thank you for making him so happy."

His best friend on the entire planet, who I had never met, didn't care about any of the petty shit; he just cared about Adam's happiness. And he could see how happy his best friend finally was—and that made him happy in return. And *Gary* just wanted me to know. He welcomed me, and I belonged.

The four of us sat at a table, laughing, catching up on old times, the guys sharing stories with me about their childhood, *Gary* and I engaging in conversation about our mutual deep love for the Chicago Cubs. Adam shared a deep bond with the people he considered "best friends" in life. That evening, their love affair was undeniable as they reunited in the same room. Adam was a complete goober just being in *Gary's* presence, which made it effortless to avoid any attention being drawn to the fact that I wasn't drinking my glass of wine. *Dodged that bullet.*

That night gave me some hope that I would be able to get through the wedding weekend without anyone knowing a baby was growing inside of me—except when it came to Adam's mom and grandma. We really weren't ready to tell anyone else yet because it was still so early—but damn, those two were good! Apparently being crazy in love was a very different glow than a pregnancy one. They sniffed it out of us and were over-the-moon ecstatic with endless happy tears to discover a new grandbaby was on the way. *And I was just secretly hoping their happy tears weren't going to fall into Grammy's B's and G's she was making.* Thanks to them, and my future father-in-law, I had a few people sneaking me watered-down apple juice during the wedding reception, to pass for a chardonnay, so no one asked questions as to why Adam's new girlfriend wasn't drunk on the dance floor participating in some wedding dollar bills dance with everyone else.

"Coming Home, Pt. II"

It had been two years since I'd seen my mom and some of my other family. Unfortunately, when you're the one who moves away from home, you're also the one expected to always travel back.

After the wedding in Indy, we headed to Chicago, where Adam and I spent the day taking in the city together. I took him to my old workplace, McGee's, in Lincoln Park, and then we ventured over to Soldier Field, where Colts-fan baby daddy bought a Brandon Marshall Bears jersey for our little one at the gift shop. (Big deal here for my Chicago sports-loving heart!) Once our quick rendezvous in the city was over, we had to head out to St. Charles, to my mom's house, for what was intended to be a birthday celebration for Adam. However, it ended up being just another classic Mom surprise, changing the narrative of the story based on how she wanted social media to perceive it.

That "party" for Adam's birthday, sure, there were some balloons, which was also to celebrate the rest of my family meeting him for the first time and me being home after years, but it ended up becoming a "first time me and my four kids are ever together" moment. Which, to be fair, it was. But she turned it into that on her own, and we weren't made aware that my brother was going to be there until we showed up.

This was not the first time I had seen my brother since we were separated as kids. The first time we reunited since we were young was when I was with my ex, Vick. We came to Chicago once around Christmas time and went to dinner with my brother and my aunt Julie one night. My brother was feeding us shots the whole time, so the details are hard to remember beyond the photo I have of my brother, Julie and me together. After that night, my brother and I got to a communicative point we were good at for a while, even trying to do some creative work together. But my mom never knew about that. *Some things you need to hold extra close to the chest.*

But this was certainly a surprise to see him in our mother's house for the first time—with all of us together, and the first time in our entire lives he was ever meeting our sister, Demi. Needless to say, after the not-so-pleasant text exchanges with my mother after seeing her post to Facebook that she had reunited with him, I guess I shouldn't have been so shocked to see him in our house. But I think what hurt me the most was realizing my mom and I really weren't as close as we used to be. She talked to me when there was no one around to listen to her. And when she didn't need me anymore, I was informed about the things in life just as everyone else in the world was—via a social media post.

As we were gathered around the table after dinner, my brother was doing his usual big personality, loud-mouth spiel and decided to call me out for not drinking the glass of wine he poured for me. Drinking was never a big thing in my house growing up. My stepdad maybe had a beer now and then, and if my mom took a single sip of a mixed drink, she'd suddenly become overly dramatic and flirty, making sure everyone in the room noticed her. So nothing would have ever been said had he not opened his mouth when, for once, he should have kept it shut.

I guess I should have been more ready with an excuse to why I wasn't drinking my wine that night, but the day was already overwhelming, and I wasn't thinking on my toes. My brother forced my hand to admit that I was pregnant, which we were not ready to do with my family at this point.

"Love the Way You Lie, Pt. III"

Here I was, super early in my pregnancy and working a stressful new job. We just went through days with Adam's family, and now this with mine, my brother who hadn't been around most of my life pressuring me, my mother who had slowly been suffocating me and testing my patience, growing shittier over the years and proving our mother-daughter relationship was nothing like it used to be when I was younger—everything was closing in on me. And here I was, having been the *oldest child* in this family for most of my life, now being shoved to the side because suddenly my older brother was standing in front of me. I'm not entirely proud of what came next and take ownership in my part of it. Sometimes our backs get so pinned against the wall that all we can do is attack.

I'm a Leo. I felt like my back was pinned to the wall. And I attacked.

"Yes. *Yes.* I'm pregnant. We're having a baby. We just found out days ago. But yes, I'm fucking pregnant."

My brother blurted out, "I fucking knew it." And everyone else was just kind of silent in the room; no one knew quite how to respond.

My mother decided to make it all about her when she said, "How could you keep this secret from me? You're pregnant with my grandchild? I'm going to be a grandmother? How could you not tell me?"

Oh my fucking you know what...

Why, why, *why* was it always about someone else?

Leading up to that moment, there had been way too many "taking something that's about someone else and making it about yourself" moments with my mother—and I just snapped.

I told her what a shitty mother she had become. To which she replied, "How could you speak to me like that?"

And then I said, "Maybe if you knew how to act like a mom, I'd start treating you like one."

The truth is she hadn't really been there for me, truly been there for me as a mom, in a very, very long time. After she divorced my stepdad, she had become consumed with her own life. She cared more about what her "friends" on social media thought, the image she portrayed to the world that wasn't anything close to reality, than she did the real people she brought into this world. Everything was about "look at me" in the eyes of the world, yet she didn't give two shits about the relationships that should have mattered. And I was so sick of it all.

I think this is the point I started to really be triggered by "surface-level" people—the ugliness that people can project, thinking it's something desirable in the eyes of others. Yet all it does is pushes the people who would be there for them further away. And all the while you're wasting your energy convincing the outside world of a life that isn't real, you're actually missing out on what's truly important—your real life.

As I said that to her, "Maybe if you knew how to act like a mom, I'd start treating you like one," she just stared at me, with those same eyes she stared at me with when I was a child and she told me to get my ass in the house and I ran away from my biological father's family.

I couldn't take it anymore. Years of lies, deceit, bullshit, real love but real pain—I just snapped. Which turned into a full-blown screaming match between the two of us, and everyone just watched from the sidelines. No one was going to step in, no one was going to stop this—it was decades of pain waiting to be unleashed. I can't even remember the words, but I can never forget the shaking my body was going through as I just screamed at my mother for becoming such a shitty fucking mom.

My sister, Demi, saved me from destruction that night. She grabbed me and Adam, and pulled me into her bedroom to get me away from my mother. She had her own shit with our family separate from mine, and I don't even know the extent of it, but she knew me well enough and loved me enough to know that I needed to be pulled away from what was hurting me. Demi locked me in her bedroom that night, knowing I couldn't be anywhere near my mother again. I was overwhelmed. I was beyond upset. I laid down. I looked at both Adam and Demi, still shaking from the fight with my mother, and told them both how much I loved them. And thanked them for being by my side.

I put my hand on my stomach and, with tears streaming down my face, just knew life wasn't going to be the same.

"Family"

The morning after that fight, I woke up and wanted nothing more than to sneak down to the basement because I just wanted a few things from my childhood. I knew it was that bad. I didn't know if I could ever step foot in that house again. But when I walked out of Demi's room, I saw my mother standing at the front door with it open, with her overly plastered fake "everything is more than *fine* voice" on as she was talking to her friend at the door. She looked at me and spoke to me as if nothing had happened the night before. That terrified me—how good she was at masking the reality of the truth. I used this as my opportunity to escape in the moment. Adam and Demi grabbed our stuff and got it in the car while I played the role, pretending to be the *good* daughter and saying, "Hi," to her friend. And as I wore that painted smile I knew how to wear so well—we got out of that house. And I let go of everything in my childhood that would remain.

Demi got in the car with us because, before that major blowout, we had a bigger plan my mother didn't know about. We were going back down to Chicago to go to a Cubs game. I wasn't about to leave my *home* without experiencing a game with Adam at Wrigley Field. My aunt Julie was there, my papa and Grandma Sue were there, many of my family was there, Demi, my brother, and even my sister, B., showed up. Without the drama of my mother, and me trying to fake the shots my brother was trying to force onto everyone—this was the true reunion we had been waiting for. In the city, our Chicago roots, together, laughing, having fun, no drama. I wasn't going to let the drama of my mother from the day before allow me to leave Chicago with a negative mindset. Instead, I turned it around, I embraced the moment we were living in, and we had the best day. I danced with Cubs legendary icon Ronnie "Woo Woo," while my family took their shots at the table. I got to take Adam (and our little babe) to Wrigley for the first time. It rained. The Cubs won. Reds-fan Adam started singing along to the "Go Cubs Go" song—and we ended it all on a high note.

As we said goodbye, we left Chicago and headed home—focused on our little family of three.

> A note from *me:* *I want to say now that my intent with writing these stories of my life is not to trigger anyone to deal with deep trauma they didn't expect to be forced to face, upon making the choice to read this book. My deepest reason for doing this is so that others know they're not alone in the experiences they go through in life. What's to come was probably one of the hardest things I've had to write about, and I share some painful details. What should have been a beautiful time in life, ended up being a very lonely time for me because of what I'm about to share*

that I went through—that I didn't know was okay to talk out loud about at the time. While there's great story moments during this next part of the book, taking care of other people's hearts is what is most important to me at this point. So—if anything pertaining to miscarriage or the loss of a child is just too painful to experience through the lens of what someone else went through, I encourage you to skip ahead to the section that says "The Rainbow Connection." I promise there's a happy ending to come out of what comes next, but to get there I had to finally be strong enough to talk about what happened.

"Stand by Me"

Come June, our excitement continued to grow. We had just celebrated Adam's first Father's Day, and we were both settling into the reality of becoming parents. I was starting to hang up the small pile of things I had collected for the baby thus far and smiled as I held the baby's little Chicago Bears Brandon Marshall jersey in my hands. Our small little bundle of awesomeness was growing. And so was our love.

Around this time, my sister, B.'s college graduation was coming up, but Adam and I were both crazily wrapped up in the demanding car show we were working on, and since we had just been back in Chicago the month prior, the timing just didn't work out for another trip back to the Midwest to be there in person.

Also, after that blowout with my mother, I wasn't emotionally ready to deal with round two.

I didn't really hear much from my mom after that night. People don't really talk about things in my family. Someone is in your life one minute, then something happens and they're not—it's never talked through; it's just one and done until one day someone is delusional enough to think everything is *fine*, that enough time passed and pick up where they left off.

But around that time of B.'s college graduation, I tried to focus not on my fight with Mom, but on the positives in life—having gratitude for the job I had and our baby growing inside of me. Even though the job was physically and mentally draining, I was thankful Adam and I had each other. When it comes to producing TV, he deals more with the logistical side of things, and I deal more with the creative. We're a great balance for one another. And during this time in life, I don't know if I could have gotten through it without my partner being right there with me, every moment of the day by my side.

Pregnancy is such a crazy reality—there's a tiny human growing inside of you, and it's a beautifully weird thing that a lot of people will never understand. But now I did. Madison nicknamed the baby Embry, a gender-neutral name, since we didn't know if it would be a boy or a girl. And, as she liked to remind me, my two-month old honorary nephew couldn't wait for the day "Embry" was to come into this world. My favorite picture of myself from this time is of me holding him in my arms—knowing my little one was growing inside of me. That moment made one of the biggest imprints on my heart. One that will last forever.

My pregnancy had started out at a crazy speed, and I had gained twenty pounds in the first two months. When I wasn't at work, I could barely move off the couch—drained entirely as if a little vampire baby was inside me, sucking everything out of me. But I knew all the bad days would be worth it to hold our precious babe in my arms.

Then the day we had been excitedly anticipating for over a month was finally here—our first real doctor's appointment and first ultrasound. We walked into the doctor's office located in the Kaiser

Permanente building on Sunset Boulevard, where I had to do the usual things like pee in a cup and get my blood pressure taken, and then we were escorted to the back room.

Since it was still early, I couldn't have the over-the-stomach ultrasound. So, the doctor slid this microscope up through my vagina, and *holy shit,* here we go, the moment we'd been waiting to experience for almost two months. I didn't know what to expect. Then all of a sudden, I saw a little peanut-shaped form, and it was the most surreal moment knowing this little creation was inside of me, like really inside of me. There were no words to fully justify what this moment of actually seeing our tiny little baby for the first time meant to us.

The doctor told us that our baby was growing at a perfect rate, like in fact even a day or two bigger than should be at nine and a half weeks.

But then, I heard the scariest words I've ever heard in my life. "Something's wrong. There's no heartbeat."

"Let It Be"

The doctor's face became like stone. I looked at Adam, not knowing what she was really talking about, and out of nowhere, the tears started pouring out of my eyes. I couldn't process what on earth she meant.

"What do you mean there's no heartbeat?" I whispered, my voice panicked. "You just said the baby was bigger than expected, and now you're saying you can't find a heartbeat? I see the baby, right there in front of me. What are you talking about? Why are you saying this? Babies have heartbeats!"

This wasn't supposed to happen. This was not the plan.

The doctor began to attempt to make sense of this realization by then telling us, "At any moment leading up to this day, even this morning, something just *happened*. The baby just stopped growing."

There was no answer to my *"Why?"*

That's all she could give me. That was it. No explanation. Just that. Until I saw the shift happen in her from someone who was having compassion to someone who needed to do her job. She said, "I'm so sorry to tell you this. But it happens in one out of every four pregnancies."

I knew that was the typical, default reasoning she had probably delivered to other mothers before, mothers who just had their dreams come crashing down in a matter of thirty seconds.

Yeah, that didn't matter to me; this was my life, and this wasn't supposed to happen. I finally found the man whose love was the greatest gift I had ever been given in this lifetime and we were setting our future in action, and now—now, the life growing inside of me was, most likely, nothing more than a strawberry-sized reminder of the beautiful hope we once had.

I couldn't even respond. I was frozen. This wasn't real, *right?*

What she said next, I will never forget. Because while she was looking at us, she was staring at Adam. She couldn't look me in the eyes. "I want you to wait ten days and come back in again."

I couldn't even look at Adam. I didn't know how to process the words that were coming out of her mouth. But that was when she hooked me. That was when she made me believe this wasn't a nightmare. "Sometimes these tests aren't accurate. It would take a miracle if the next time there was a heartbeat. But it has happened. I've seen it. Miracles do happen."

With my heart pounding uncontrollably, I closed my eyes and said to myself, "Miracles do happen."

I opened my eyes, and finally looked at Adam, as tears started to stream down both sides of my face.

Okay. Miracles do happen, right? Wait *ten* days.

I had no other choice than to pull myself up off that table and put my clothes on. We had to get to work.

On the thirty-minute commute from the hospital in Hollywood to Venice Beach, I was struggling with a major battle going on inside of me—my head telling me the news of what we just found out and the truth my body had accepted and was living with.

I pulled up the text chain that we had going between my mother and my two sisters, and sent them a simple text letting them know that it was a painful day. I told them there was no heartbeat and a good chance I was going to lose the baby, but the doctor said miracles do happen and I had to wait ten more days.

My mother was the first one to respond, and her text simply said, "This day isn't about you. It's about your sister's graduation."

I think that might have been the lowest moment of my entire life, up until that point.

All I could do was look out the window, wiping away the tears that wouldn't stop pouring out of me. I didn't tell Adam she said that. Even in her most hurtful of times, I still tried to hide her ugliness.

"Let It Go"

We made it to Venice Beach and walked in late, with painted smiles on our faces—but painted smiles only last until the makeup wears off.

About four times throughout the course of that day, I ran out back and broke down crying. "Why is this happening to us?" I cried. "We are good people. We have both been through so much in life. We work hard, we love hard, and we are thankful for everything in our lives. Why us?!"

The next ten days led up to what could potentially be the absolute worst day of my life. But I kept reminding myself what the doctor said, *Miracles do happen.*

Every day Adam and I went into work, we continued to smile through the pain. This show was exhausting. I took pride in all I did, so I tended to pick up the slack of others. My partner in life and work was the same way. That week, Adam and I were working seventeen-hour days on top of everything we were dealing with personally.

I was the only female producer there every day on the show. I could handle the boys club, that's for sure, but during the worst two weeks of our lives, there were moments when it was unbearable, moments when I just wanted to walk away. People were rude, mean, and just awful during that week. Some of my male bosses above me weren't doing what needed to be done, so I was having to pick up the slack. I was constantly in the middle of a "whose dick is bigger" contest, and the only way to ensure the next shoot day was going to happen was to go above my pay grade and make sure shit was getting done. Adam and I would stay there until all hours of the night just helping one another make sure shit was set up okay for the next day because if we didn't, it would be a *car* wreck. But that's what we did—we were always great partners who had each other's backs in every avenue of life. *Even if it was killing us.*

But that week challenged me, mentally and physically. I ran outside and cried more than I could ever admit. While the boys club was gossiping about whose cocaine was found in the women's bathroom, I was running to the bathroom just to try and hide my tears from the unknown reality going on inside of me. Adam and I were trying to give every ounce of everything we had, sleeping only three hours a day, for a show that didn't really matter, all the while knowing our baby was, most likely, just sitting dead inside of me. Even though at any given moment I could miscarry, we still put work above that and found ourselves hoping it didn't happen during filming.

Such a fucked-up way to think, but when you work in the business we work in, every day matters. Every paycheck matters. But sometimes you have to ask yourself, *At what cost?*

Adam and I were working around the clock, seven days a week at this point. We finally got a day off, and it happened to be the day after we were set to go back to the doctor. We left work early on that Monday to go to our afternoon appointment. The afternoon L.A. traffic that day made the drive about an hour long, but it felt like the longest hour of my life. I was in a complete daze; all I could do was say to myself over and over, "Miracles do happen. Miracles do happen." *Miracles do happen, right?*

We went in and met with a new doctor I had never seen. He repeated the same procedure as the doctor before.

No miracle here.

No change.

The only confirmation we got was that our baby had been dead within me for the past ten days.

The doctor gave us three options—the most ridiculous being, "Well, just wait it out and it will happen naturally over the course of the next two to three months." *Are you fucking kidding me!?!?* The hospital option just freaked me out more, and also, because of work, *time* wasn't really on our side. So, I decided on the at-home option, where at least we could be in our own space while grieving the loss of our baby.

"Save Tonight"

Please know, this is a sensitive topic, and every woman will have their own opinion on what is morally, physically, emotionally best for them. I'm sure there will be people who will disagree with my decision to go the pill route and not let nature run its course. But the emotional and physical pain was so much, I couldn't do that to my body or my mind. I chose the healthiest decision out of the three options that was best for *me*. My decision may not be the *right* method for others. Then again, I hope none of you ever have to ever make that kind of decision.

Sometime between the doctor confirming our baby was gone and picking up the pills at the pharmacy, I picked up my phone, debating whether to text my mother and my sisters about what was happening. But I couldn't. I was still too hurt by what my mother had said. But even that hurt was nowhere near comparable to the pain my heart was feeling. I did text my sister, Demi, just us two. I texted my best friends, Madison and Ryan. And I texted Adam's parents. That was it. Then I put my phone away and shut down—because nothing else in the world mattered other than what we were about to face.

That night, Adam had to help insert four pills up through my vagina and let science take its course. At about 3:00 a.m., I woke up in excruciating pain. At about 5:00 a.m., it hit me full force. I won't even begin to explain what it is like, but I will say it's probably one of the absolute worst things a woman could ever physically go through. It is beyond brutal.

I would like to say it was a blur, but there's zero truth in that.

I remember it all.

The most profound moment of that entire experience did not come from the ten hours I spent curled up in the bathroom or blood clots the size of golf balls or the heartbreaking loss that was happening in front of my eyes. It wasn't even the time I spent wondering if I was going to see my strawberry-sized baby drifting in a pool of blood in the toilet. The moment I remember most about that day is the reason I fully believe that everything in life happens for a reason, and that somehow you find the strength to get through the hardest times in life, even when you don't think you can.

A little after 5:00 a.m., I was so sick I couldn't even make it to the bathroom. I puked all over the floor in our very short hallway. I continued on running to the bathroom because I was dealing with worse bodily issues than puke. When I was able to gather myself off the floor and came out, I saw Adam on his hands and knees cleaning up my vomit. I was in so much pain, I just curled myself back up in bed and tried crying myself to sleep, as if sleeping was even possible that day. Through the tears and puke and all kinds of gnarly mess going on, I remembered those words my mother texted: *This day isn't about you.* I bawled my eyes out, the deep pain colliding with the pain of releasing our baby from my body.

Then Adam climbed into bed, pulled me into him, looked me in the eyes, and said, "You're the most beautiful thing I've ever seen. I love you. And that's the most important thing."

At that moment, I realized, that's what we wait for. That's what we hope for. That's what we trust in. That's what we believe in. *That's love.*

"Bigger Than The Whole Sky"

I will never forget the words my mom texted. I was living, real time, one of the most traumatic experiences of my life, and she made me out to be selfish. Maybe I put unrealistic expectations on others without realizing it. Maybe, as others expect things of me, I expect too much out of the people I should be able to count on to be there for me in my life. But what I *expect* is simple—I expect a partner to act like a partner, a best friend to be a best friend, and above all, for a mother to be a mother. Not even this, the worst thing I'd ever experienced, was enough for her to get on a plane and be there for me—at that point in time, she hadn't gotten on a plane for me in nine years.

All I wanted to do was curl up in a ball and cry, cry, cry until I had no more tears left to cry. But because of Adam's unconditional love, because of my best friends, because of my sister, Demi, because of my aunt Julie, and Adam's wonderful parents, and some of our incredible friends—knowing we had the love around us and the *family* that we created for ourselves supporting us, made it possible to just push through.

While we did push through, I was in a dark place for a long time. I walked around in a fog, once again just wearing that damn painted smile I had learned to master at ten years old. I couldn't expect people to remember my pain or think about my trauma, but it was killing me inside. I was surrounded by the ignorance of others, so I was forced to put more bandages over the wounds. I have never been one to intentionally play the victim, so I let the world move on while I stayed still. I remember the first time I hugged my honorary nephew afterward—I cried because "Embry" wasn't there, and would never be there like that photo had promised.

The loss of our baby didn't magically get easier. I would be lying if I said it did. All I knew was for about seventy-two days I got to be a mom for the first time to a tiny little soul we called "Embry." Though it was only seventy-two days, it will forever be a tiny scar on my heart. I would never be able to sing to Embry, would never be able to hold Embry, would never be able to kiss Embry's baby-soft forehead, or ever hear Embry's giggles. That year, I had about ten friends who brought beautiful babies into this world, and more came soon after. But for me, that wasn't meant to be. And I will never know *why*. There's no explanation other than perhaps it wasn't, simply, meant to be. To live with a pain like that and never have an answer is a really hard thing. To try and hold onto the belief that *life* always has a bigger plan and life's happenings unfold exactly as they're supposed to, can sometimes seem impossible.

I couldn't freeze time while I worked through this grief so, I had no choice but to try and move forward. I had to pack it all up, all the emotions, all the feelings, all the pain, and shove it away on the top shelf of our closet—because that's what others expected me to do.

But you see, I couldn't do that.

In my heart, I knew our baby was a girl. I met her in my dreams, imagined what she would smell like, and I could hear her laughter. I could feel her cradled into my chest. When I woke up, I had a real name for her:

Emmelia Grace.

Six months after the loss of "Embry," Adam and I were on a good path forward. While the pain of losing our baby remained a buried ache within me, our relationship was stronger than ever. Overcoming such a profound loss together made me believe that we could endure almost anything. Yet, as we moved forward in our life journey, the universe sure found a way to challenge me emotionally—by once again making me confront my past.

"Over You"

I'll never forget the last time I saw Vick. It was well over a year and a half since our relationship ended. It was six months after I lost "Embry." It was on a Sunday, in December, in Redondo Beach. I knew Vick would be at that place, at that time, on that day. It was our friends' wedding—and he was the co-best man.

On the day of the wedding, Adam was in Georgia for a work commitment so he wasn't able to attend as my plus-one. I knew it was going to be somewhat daunting to walk into an emotionally charged setting by myself—but there was no way I wasn't going to be there for my friend, who I truly cherish in this lifetime. We had a friendship that wouldn't be broken just because my relationship with Vick ended. So I went, on my own. I got my own hotel room and I pretended to be confident and brave, knowing I would have to see Vick. And see him, *happy* with someone new.

That I was not prepared for.

Upon opening my hotel room door, I practically ran into Vick's new girlfriend, en route to the ceremony accompanied by another dear friend of mine. My friend texted me ahead of time to let me know she would be with her—a kind gesture that showed consideration for my feelings, given her obligation to Vick as a result of her marriage to his other best friend.

It's not that my friend didn't want to come have a drink with me ahead of time, it's just that—well, I was the *old*, she was the *new* and oh, the skies were so blue that day.

I had no choice but to tread lightly behind them as we were all rushing to make it to the ceremony on time. I let them walk towards the open outdoor space first. I wasn't going to be the one to make that entrance for everyone else to see. Yet, he surely did.

Standing at the altar, dressed in his suit, Vick's gauze shifted from his new girlfriend to me. And for a moment, life froze—just as it did the night we were both running across La Cienega Boulevard at the same time. He was staring in my eyes and my heart literally sank to the pit of my stomach as I stood there on my own with everyone looking at me.

It was a suspended moment in time; one of those moments that didn't last long, but lasted so much longer than real time. It was one of those "this is what it could have been like" moments in life. For just a second—me standing at an open entryway by myself, him standing up at an altar and the rest of the world just disappearing from view. I think we both remembered what we could have been, if I hadn't walked away.

This is what it could have been.

I took a deep breath, which snapped me back to the present moment, both of us haunted by a glimpse into an unrealized future.

With a nod, I respectfully acknowledged Vick's presence for others to see and then I dashed as fast as I could to the first open seat I could find. Surrounded by so many of my old friends, that "family" we created together, for years—it was killing me inside.

Despite the happiness Vick and I had separately found, my heart couldn't help but find itself sad.

How could it not have been? *I'm human.*

Moments later, my dear friend was standing in her white dress at that same entryway. She looked stunning; radiating pure joy on her wedding day. There was so much love circling the air and it was impossible not to inhale the happiness of that moment. I watched her walk toward her forever, toward the friend who was my roommate after the dumb choices of my past booted me back from Canada—and as I saw her grab his hands, it was impossible not to smile. And it was equally impossible to avoid the presence of Vick standing up there next to them.

At one point, my eyes shifted from him to his new girlfriend, who was smiling at him. This was my living hell and I was burning up inside. But when my eyes made their way back to the bride and groom, my body got an overwhelming sensation that someone was staring at me. And when I shifted my eyes just a little, there Vick's eyes found mine. Locked in, unable to break away, I suddenly remembered another piece of his apology letter—and it was as though he was speaking those words to me right at that moment:

> *I am sorry that after 3.5 years you've had to watch other couples get together and get engaged and married. I'm sorry that I tried to poison you on the idea of marriage. I'm sorry for making you feel like you weren't enough for me. I know now that the reality is that I wasn't enough for you. You stayed by my side because you*

loved me so much. I am sorry that I failed you as you waited pa-
tiently for me. And I will be sorry until the day that I die for the
pain that I have caused you—the most beautiful person inside
and out that I have ever been lucky enough to meet. Taking your
love for granted will be the biggest mistake I make in this life. I
believe that with all my heart.

Our eyes only looking at one another, it took every ounce of me to fight back the tears internally wanting to be released. My phone buzzed with a new text notification and I broke away from Vick's gaze. The words on my screen were from Adam:

I'm so sorry I'm not there with you. I hate that you are there alone and you have to face all of that all over again by your-self. Tell her Congratulations from me. I love you—and I will see you soon.

I took a deep breath; holding on tightly to my phone as I started to scan the outdoor venue. As I looked at the faces of the people and the life happening around me, an unexpected revelation dawned upon me—a simple reminder of how far I had come from where I had once been. This was my past; and it was time to finally say *good-bye.*

I took a sip of my wine and smiled, thankful for this moment in time.

Two weeks later, Adam proposed to me.

Good thing I never stopped believing in fairytales.

"Cry Pretty"

Two weeks after my friend's wedding, with a moonstone engagement ring on my left finger, I got a phone call from someone we had known for a while. I thought she was calling to congratulate us on our engagement, so I answered. To my surprise, she was hysterical and just started word-vomiting all this stuff to me—admitting to me that, after six months together, she had been snooping through her boyfriend's computer and found inappropriate messages between him and some girl on an online website.

I didn't even get a chance to respond because then she told me something that struck a nerve when she said, "And I was pregnant, and he *made me* have an abortion."

To this day, I've never been able to let that go.

As I was on the phone with her, I knew she was looking for some sort of sympathy card to be thrown her way, but all I could do was start spiraling emotionally. I started mouthing to Adam in so much anger what was being told to me, her saying *he made her have the abortion.* Adam didn't believe it himself because he knew her boyfriend. A lot of things that would come out of this person's mouth were often a lie, so neither of us wanted to believe this to be true.

Whether or not it was the truth or a lie, this wasn't about the act of whatever decisions people made for their own lives; it was the ignorance I could never get over. Because having learned this information, I was suddenly supposed to care—when she couldn't think to remember my pain.

There I was, having just experienced a monumental moment in my life, a moment I dreamed of my whole life for someone to say to me the words Adam said when he got down on one knee after the painful year we had—and within a single piece of information

I never asked to be thrust into my awareness, suddenly all the emotions I pushed down for the past six months surfaced. Because it forced me to remember the pain of losing our baby; a pain that had never healed. *A pain I didn't choose.*

When I hung up the phone, I just broke. I fucking broke down to my knees crying so hard, almost screaming. And after six months of keeping the pain locked inside, I finally snapped—and Adam just happened to be the one standing in the room…

"I lost my baby. I didn't choose that. Yet, I had to just fucking accept it and move on, hurting every single fucking day because of it. I lost a child, and now she is forcing this 'my boyfriend *made me* have an abortion' shit my way that I didn't fucking care to even know about regardless if it's true. She's the psycho one snooping through his computer, and now I'm the one emotionally suffering because of it. I can't fucking take this shit. I'm supposed to care? When no one cares about my pain. And I'm in so much pain. I was the one who made us lose our baby."

I guess I just needed to finally say it out loud—*I was the one who made us lose our baby.* Adam couldn't say a thing. All he could do in that moment was exactly what he did—sat on the floor next to me, pulled me into his arms, and held me, giving me the permission I needed to finally just cry it all out.

Other people's ignorance + your deep pain = the kind of things that aren't easy to just get over or *let go* of. No matter how much time has passed, the pain doesn't just go away because the baby did.

"One Day at a Time"

I resisted talking to anyone about this time in my life because women didn't talk openly about pain like this; society had already conditioned me to suppress such deep suffering. I was already convinced I didn't have a voice, or that my voice didn't matter, so there was no desire in seeking out any sort of mental help to help me through this hard thing. So instead, what I did was bury the emotional pain from losing a baby, from my mother's cruel words, and from saying *goodbye* to a past love that would forever sting—slapping on a shit ton of Band-Aids so I could keep coasting through life. By no means is that the healthy thing to do—but that's what I chose to do to stop the bleeding for the time being.

But here's the thing about putting a Band-Aid over the wound— it's just a Band-Aid, a temporary solution to mask the pain. One day, when we wake up and that Band-Aid has fallen off and the wound has healed on a surface level, we convince ourselves we're fine, so we continue skating through life because it's the easy thing to do. Yet, what people often forget, or look past because sometimes pain runs so deep, is nothing can ever properly heal without the deeper, excruciating agony that comes with properly cleaning out the emotional wounds. No Band-Aid, no pill, can ever heal you.

Acknowledging the deep pain, suffering and grief is the first step on the path to true, authentic healing in order for the wounds to close in a healthy way—and I was just not brave enough to do that.

Because, at that point in time, the pain was just too real to have to deal with.

The pain was just all too real.

This may be about my pain and my story throughout great loss in my life, but it by no means discredits the pain my husband went through as well. Adam lost that baby too, and the emotions and grief he had to go through with not only experiencing that loss but also seeing the person he loved go through it, knowing there was nothing he could do to help or make it have a different outcome. I can never speak to how it made him feel because, honestly, I still don't know.

It's an experience and a pain he buried, and it's part of his own story separate from the one we share together.

Human kindness is so important. People mask their pain in different ways. And no one, *no one*, not even your partner in life, will truly, fully ever know what you're going through. So be kind, have patience, and above all, love with everything you've got—because life is just too damn precious not to.

To all the women out there reading this who have ever dealt with infertility and loss, and to the partners who've navigated their own emotional mazes, I encourage you to share your stories. It can be a lonely time, and you may feel empty, but the one thing you are *not* is alone. While I often masked my pain, it's a suffering many of us deal with—and we can help each other heal.

Even if your story resonates with and helps one single soul out there, maybe that was the plan *life* had for you instead of the life you had planned.

"The Rainbow Connection"

For over two years since losing "Embry," I carried my personal pain just below the surface. I had to play the "I'm okay, life has moved on" role for everyone else to see. Others expected me to move on. I tried to meet that expectation, but if you looked into my eyes, the pain was always right there.

I couldn't feel an ounce of peace from losing "Embry" until 2:12 p.m. on August 3, 2016—which was the moment our baby boy, Crosby Royce, was placed in my arms. It wasn't until my son was born and safely in my arms that I could start to be okay-ish with the past. The moment I finally held Crosby, the moment my beautiful boy, my rainbow baby, looked me in the eyes, I knew in that moment the only "why" I needed to finally find some peace. If "Embry" had come into this world, I would never have had Crosby, and I believe, more than anything, that his soul chose me in this lifetime to be his momma. He needed me, and oh goodness, I needed him.

I guess that Kaiser doctor was right. *Miracles do happen.*

There's a cliché that "time heals all wounds." Many people jump to say they disagree with that; I did too for such a long time. But when you stop to really think about it, the cliché isn't saying time forgives, time forgets, time makes it disappear, or time lets you move on. Time, actually, does heal wounds. Wounds do heal, and when they do, *they leave scars.* Physical scars. Emotional scars. And we are meant to live with these scars. The moment Crosby was born, I was able to finally make peace with the loss of "Embry," but that baby is a scar that will forever be on my heart. Scars are nothing to be ashamed of. They create character. Every scar has a story, and it's about time we wear them proudly.

But some wounds take much longer to heal, because when it's wound after wound after wound that just gets reopened and cut deeper because of someone in your life who just continually causes you pain—for me, that's my mother. Even though I graciously allowed her to be present at my wedding in Hawaii, because she was my mom, the emotional wounds I wore because of her were always right there. Aside from her making so much of my wedding about her, my mother not being there for me during that dark time of losing a baby, the words she said to me back then, "This day isn't about you," only added to the deep pile of pain she had been putting on my back, and in my heart, for my entire life. And the wounds would keep coming, until the day years from this time when they finally turned into a scar. But not a scar I could ever wear proudly—one I have had to hide from the world.

MY MOTHER'S DAUGHTER

"Numb"

I don't know why but it seems that the people who hurt me the most in my life have always been the ones I gave my *love* to in some way—the deepest of all, falling under the category of "family." It seems fair that, as a child, you naturally expect your parents to be there for you, always. Until *the shift* happens in life when you realize your well-being is in jeopardy just by keeping them in your life.

In honoring my truth of everything that got me to the darkest point in my life, I have to be honest about my mother's existence in it. While I won't ever stoop to her level of being okay hurting someone you're supposed to love—I will tell you the story of when I finally snapped. When everything caved in on me. When I realized I needed her out of my fucking life. It's not the worst thing she has ever done, but it was the moment when I realized that I could no longer let someone else, even my mother, affect my life to such depths that it could cause me to lose another baby.

When I was about seven months pregnant with Crosby, our baby shower was coming up and my mother was overwhelming me. She was trying to contribute in certain ways—I will give her credit for that. Her and my sister, B., made some party favors to hand out. When the box arrived at our apartment in Burbank, I opened it to find all the wood pieces coming unglued, the jelly beans were thrown into bags that were falling apart and warping together with other ones. It looked like a half-assed attempt to contribute in some way, but it was an embarrassment of a gift to hand out to our guests. So, I ended up going out and buying cute little milk bottles with straws and redoing all their "gifts" myself. It was the last thing I wanted to be doing—so pregnant and in temperatures near 100 degrees in Burbank—but I did it because so much thought was being put into every other aspect of showering our *little lion baby* that I couldn't let people take home those favors the way they showed up.

As our baby shower was approaching, my mother's random, last-minute excuse as to why she couldn't be there was, "I can't make it. (some guy I'm seeing) invited me to a blues concert in Chicago, and we're going."

No, not kidding.

Okay, some random dude (*news to your daughter*) invited you to a blues concert (*since when do you listen to blues music?*), and therefore you cannot come to your daughter's baby shower for your *first* grandchild?

It takes a lot for me in moments like this to calm my emotions because if I said the things I wanted to say, it would probably end with me punching a wall. I had sat with her—when we had nothing, when it was me and her living by candlelight and mac and cheese dinners and my bottles that she filled with Pepsi. We got through the hard times together because it was me and her. I was supposedly her *lucky star* and gift to the world. She put me through emotional hell at times, she put unrealistic expectations on me my whole life, she made me lose a lifetime of knowing my father—but I stood by her side, even after I lost a child, because she was my mom. And everything I went through up to that moment, as her first grandchild was close to being born—we weren't enough for her to do for once what a daughter needed her mother to do. Just be there. Just be there without it being about her or needing attention from others, and for fucking once, just actually be there for me.

And here's the thing—I'm an adult. I understand everyone has emotions and feelings about things that others can't understand. If there was a deeper rooted reason for not getting on that plane, I was her daughter, and if she really knew me, she knew she could talk to me about anything. And sure, while I still might have been disappointed she wasn't there to support us, I would have understood and gotten over my own shit because I'm a very understanding and reasonable person when people are being honest. But the truth is, I wasn't enough. My baby wasn't enough. Some dude with tickets to a blues concert was. The plans weren't going to change because of her—but life certainly did.

"No More Drama"

Growing up, I had a front row seat at my mother's ability to just cut people out of our lives. It was truly an art form how easily she could turn off that emotional piece of her heart; almost like tasking out your day and scheduling your week, a line item casually became, "Who *aren't* we talking to this week?" One day, this person isn't talking to that person but two weeks later those people we weren't talking to are coming over to grill and swim in the pool this weekend. But no, we're not going to Papa's house this year for Thanksgiving because Mom is just mad at everyone but the dogs.

There was always an excuse with my mother, and if there wasn't an excuse, then it was always someone else's fault. Why would you take ownership for your own part in anything when it's so easy to just point the finger and blame someone else, right? She was never wrong, and everyone was always out to get her.

Until she needed something from someone. Oh, that's the most dangerous side of all. My mother could be pissed at you but then realize you could help her in some way, usually in the form of money or connections or fancy cars to take selfies in front of, and then she would turn on the charm and work the situation in her favor. She could make you feel like the most important person in her entire world—until she got what she wanted. Then she had no problem throwing you out with the trash. The world was always revolving around her, and we had no choice but to live by her way of life.

Shit—now I realize why certain people in my life can trigger me so easily. Because they remind me of my mother.

In that "blues concert" moment when I was seven months pregnant with Crosby, I was done. It might seem like a really petty reason to finally say that, but it came after decades of built-up shit. I wasn't about to throw a damn tantrum because I wasn't getting my way that neither I nor the baby inside of me were important enough for my mother to get on a damn plane for (more than once now). So, I simply decided that I could no longer live like this. I could no longer allow anyone, especially my mother, to affect me so much. I could no longer tolerate ignorance in my life. At that point, I just stopped caring who anyone was as far as a "title" in my life. If they were a shitty person and they'd shown that time and time again, I didn't need the negativity around me. I chose to no longer think, "She's my mother, so she's supposed to be there!" *Fucking expectations. Shame on me too.* No more. I lost one child, and I wasn't about to allow anyone to put me in a place so physically or mentally stressful that it could jeopardize the child inside of me or my own health.

That was the moment I made my baby a promise—to always put him first and do right by him in this life, no matter how hard the decisions I had to make might be. While I appreciate my mother for giving me life, she became toxic to my own well-being. And while we spent our entire lives seeing my mother so easily cut people out of our lives based on who pissed her off or welcome them back in when she needed something from them—I finally realized it was time to take control and make the move to just cut it off at the source, that source being my mother.

So, I had to do what I had to do to protect myself and my family and ensure a healthy delivery of our baby boy. I had to cut my mother out of my life.

After her blues concert text, I sent her messages telling her to leave me alone. I told her I could no longer allow her to negatively affect me. Knowing she had Adam's number if she desperately wanted to make things right and get ahold of me, I had to go to the extremes in order to give her some wake-up call—so I blocked her from my phone, I blocked her from all my social media accounts, and I cut her off from my life.

And, my husband never got a phone call.

Sometimes we have to be brave enough to make the toughest decisions in order to save ourselves, and put our own mental and physical health first. If something or someone is damaging your soul, you have to remove from your life what is negatively affecting it. No one ever enjoys cutting someone out of their lives, but you get to a point when sometimes your lifeline depends on it.

I love my mom, deeply. So, this was probably the hardest decision I'd ever had to make in my life, but my own family's survival depended on it. My role as a mom depended on it. And my own life depended on it.

I would never want to hurt her. But I could no longer be hurt by her.

"Not Ready to Make Nice"

Seven years after telling my mother I could no longer allow her to negatively affect my life—I still do not have a relationship with her.

When your child wants nothing to do with you, you would think it would force a mother to take a step back and question things. But even that wasn't enough for her to see someone else's version of the truth.

I'm not proud of the way some of the things come out of my mouth when I speak about her. A lot of it is anger, disappointment, frustration—but at the core of that, it's just sadness.

Over the past seven years, there have been so many moments I have cried because I needed my mom. As a grown-ass woman, I have needed her more than I could ever admit to needing her. But what I really needed was for my mom to just be *my mom* and be there, without saying a thing about her own selfish agendas. I just needed Mom, but my mother was not around. So, I learned to handle all the hard things life had thrown at me on my own. I learned the only person I could truly count on was myself, the only person my family could count on was me, so I had to become the superhero of my own story. I needed to protect all of us and become indestructible for my children.

But I really just fucking needed my mom.

To the day of writing this, my mother knowingly has two grand-children on this earth that she has never met, and that's still not enough for her to try and make peace or do better. I've learned to be okay with *me* not being enough for someone, but my kids, I can't even begin to entertain that thought. They will never know that sort of nasty energy in their lives because I will not allow it to touch them. I will never let anyone, especially so-called "family," ever allow them to feel disposable, unimportant, or second best. Ever. So I will continue to love them with everything I have inside of me—because they deserve a more beautiful story than the one I had to live.

I can't fault people, ever, for the decisions they make for themselves. That's their own doing. But I can choose how I adjust my life because of it.

Because here's the greatest truth I've had to learn about this shitty piece of my life—I may be my mother's daughter, but I am not my mother. I am not my husband's mother. I am not my great-grandmother. I am not my best friends, or their mothers. I am not any mother to ever come before. I am not the choices anyone before me made, nor am I any longer obligated to live as though I am. I am *me*. My husband and I chose each other—and I am the one who fights for our family every single day because I am who our children chose to be their momma in this lifetime.

Strength is born out of the hard things in life. And without the hard, we cannot appreciate the good. I have had to make some of the absolute hardest decisions in my life by myself, but I did them for my kids, because they have made me strong. I did them for my sister, Demi, I did them for my aunt Julie, I did them for the women who send a sparkle my way when I need it most and to whom I try to always send that magic back when they need a reminder we're in this thing-called-life together. I don't discredit any "hard things" my mother has done, or any woman, but it is a different kind of *hard* to say to the woman who is 50 percent responsible for giving me life that *I can no longer allow you to share this air with me because you suffocate me.*

I love my mother-in-law and am thankful I got dealt a good one—but her and I will butt heads on this forever. She's a big believer in blood-family relationships, that "blood is thicker than water," but when you've experienced what I've gone through—no one can tell me to "do right" because "my mom is my mom" and that's more important than anything else. At this point in my life, the vows I gave to my husband and the *family* we have created for our own selves is the absolute, most important thing in life.

And yea, sure, I could have fought harder to "make it right"—but it's not my responsibility to parent my parent.

My mother cut my father out of my life for her own survival, and I had to cut my mother out of my life for mine—well, isn't that some full-circle shit right there.

Ironically enough, the original proverb was "The blood of the covenant is thicker than the water of the womb," meaning the deep bond you have with companions in your life, the people you choose, is stronger than the family you're born into. Somewhere along the way, a disgruntled family member who wasn't getting what they wanted twisted the whole thing around as a way for others to be guilted for their own poor behavior.

While blood might be thicker than water to some people, sometimes it's the *family* you make for yourself that is the one you can count on to never hurt you in the way your own "family" can.

Here's the other thing I've had to realize—we can choose to let others hurt us or not. Just because someone is related to you or forced into your life somehow, it does not mean you have to continue to choose to let them hurt you. It's actually up to us to take ownership of this because the only people who can choose how other people affect our lives is us. I'm tired of saying, "Shame on you for hurting me." Shame on me for allowing people into my life who do so.

FOUR.

The Messy Middle

REALITY

"Hollywood's Bleeding"

Whenever I was asked why I wanted to be an actor, my answer was always very clear—because it didn't matter whether I made someone laugh or I made them cry, what mattered was that I made them feel something *real*. I wanted to make people feel something, escape their own *reality* for a little while, and be transported somewhere else. I love that feeling of being able to do that for others. It has always made me feel so alive.

I feel those same feelings when I'm producing the best possible stories, the moments that make people so overwhelmed with heartfelt emotion that they cry, pee their pants a little from laughing, or hold on to the edge of their seat, not knowing what's coming next in a moment of suspense. I don't just love the title, the paycheck, or the recognition that comes from it—I love the entire process of creating it. Being a storyteller is a magical thing.

However, it takes a lot of passion and also a few hefty doses of insanity to be an "unscripted" TV producer. As a reality TV producer, I have the gift of being able to turn a pile of shit into gold. I shouldn't be so proud of that, but it's what I do. But over time, a scary truth came to light—the more successful I got at producing reality TV, the further I started drifting from myself. I was so busy "writing" life for others, I couldn't even write about my own life, memories, and feelings. I was too drained to journal anymore. I had no energy to reflect on moments of gratitude. I stopped working on my screenplays and couldn't find enough silence to even scribe a little poetry. I was thankful for the opportunities, the paychecks, and the ability to discover a new something I was really good at. But I could no longer quiet the noise to be alone with just my thoughts and my words.

However, apparently, some people around me had discovered the ability to do so.

One day on set, I looked around the table and noticed our assistant camera operator wasn't around. I asked my crew if they knew where Austin was and one of the guys said he was off meditating—that he used his lunch break to take a break for himself every day and recharge. In the intense situations our industry can bring, it was his way of doing a stressful job but making sure he prioritized his mental health.

Why did I not know he did this? How is no one else doing this? Why isn't this built into our daily schedules as a specific line item for the day on the call sheet? And why was he having to sacrifice his own lunchtime for his mental health?

I didn't realize the importance of that time Austin took for himself back then, but now, I applaud him. It's not an easy thing to do in a soul-sucking business. *A sometimes soul-sucking world.*

"Waiting On the World to Change"

It could be argued that there's more unreal about reality television than real. Most "reality" television is to some degree actually scripted. People like me script out how we would like to see a season play out. We track every character, find big-event moments to center things around, figure out how we can force drama 'cause "drama sells," and if we don't get everything we planned for, we somehow magically "fix it in post." Don't think a cast member actually had an appointment on her own to go get her asshole bleached—that was all set up by producers for *shock* value and, weirdly, comic relief.

We certainly are masters in our craft, I will tell you that. If you're a good producer, you can make anyone believe anything you want them to. For all you lovely trashy TV watchers out there who keep us employed, you might want to take note of what I'm saying before you start to believe everything the Housewives or the Kardashians or the Jersey Shorers are saying. (I'm guilty of it too. *Family Reunion* is a weekly watch in our house thanks to my husband.) I say this because you need to realize that this is the "reality" you're sitting at home comparing your *real* life to. So, take everything when it comes to this maddening world of reality TV with a grain—or, really, a heavy sprinkle—of salt. *I prefer Pink Himalayan!*

My husband hates watching this kind of mindless TV with me because I call out all the editorial screwups, the major holes in the story, the overproduced moments, and—above all—continuity issues. It can legit make me go crazy how in one shot a girl's hair will be up in a ponytail and the next cutaway it's somehow miraculously down, never seeing her pull the scrunchie out of her now-perfect-looking hair. Or better yet, there sits two people at a table having a conversation, and when you first see them, their glasses are full of wine, and by the end of their first sentence the glasses are practically empty. So stupid—and yet, there's lots of people out there getting paid a shit ton of money to say, "Whatever, no one will notice," and give the okay to ship the episode.

This is how you begin to separate the talented producers from the amateur ones who were given the *title* to just shut them up as a compromise for not wanting to pay them more.

Unfortunately, I have a talent for turning shit into sparkly diamonds.

But it caught up to me.

Summer of 2016, toward the end of my pregnancy with Crosby, I was starting to really question what I was doing in this "reality" TV world. The episode I had been working so hard on was once again blown up because someone else's episode wasn't working the way they had planned. So now, all of my hard work was being ripped away from me and sent off to make someone else's episode better. And it quickly became another long night.

Adam and I were still working at the same company at this point, on the same show, and his office was just down the hall from mine, but he was done with the bulk of his work. Since we rode together to the office, he was just relaxing on the community couch waiting for our pizza he ordered to be delivered.

I was sitting in my office in complete darkness with the exception of one Anthropologie candle burning beside me. I was struggling to make sense of my newly shredded shell of a once *great* episode, and all the while, I was struggling with my morals too. I had once again just experienced a cast member's personal life blow up, and we had all celebrated that we were there in time to capture this "gold." But it wasn't working now the way they wanted it to work.

Well, my job was to *make it work*. And somehow, *somehow*—I managed to pull it off.

I put together a scene that never happened.

"Free"

I'm not the kind of producer who just scrubs through the raw footage putting together the obvious moments—while it's more time consuming, if time is on my side, I actually go through and listen to every piece of audio that's there, even if the cameras are showing an empty black screen. A lot of times that's where you find the little nuggets to put something unexpected together, when others couldn't be bothered to just do a little extra work.

Because I had listened to every piece of one particular shoot day, I knew there was audio other people didn't know existed. I was able to steal audio from the mics of cast members talking in the bathroom when they didn't think to realize their mics were still *hot*, laid the audio over a dinner scene, which allowed for a distracting backdrop, put in cutaways of looks from some of the cast to create bitchy tension, and cheated in other shots to make it look like some people were there for this, who were not. I was being a good producer, knowing how to manipulate reality to create a complete non-reality that you're supposed to think actually happened. A little polishing from my editor, a great music track, some additional dramatic cues, and *voila!* Beyond the interior workings of our team and the cast members, no one would have known this wasn't *real*. Not even the network.

The best part was the network wanted more of this drama, and we had to dance around their request, knowing there wasn't any more content because this never actually happened in *reality*.

All this effort was for perhaps a ten-to-twenty-second act-out moment; the moment just before a commercial break. Damn, with what seemed like nothing to work with, I somehow miraculously gave them a great act-out moment. Look at me, turning nothing into something.

I was in my office late that night, so pregnant, so tired, so disgusted at what I actually pulled off. Adam walked in to bring me a piece of pizza and found me *literally* banging my head against the wall. I looked at him, with tears in my eyes, and said, "I don't know if I can keep doing this. I feel like a terrible person. I'm ruining people's lives." He said the usual, "Well, they signed up for this shit," comment, but I just broke and said, "I don't care. I get that, but they're human, and I'm sitting here making someone look like a monster when this never happened." And in a stern but very loving way, he said, "Maybe you're just too nice for this business."

Maybe I'm too nice for this business?

That's when it finally hit me. It wasn't that I was too nice for this business; it wasn't that I didn't love producing—I was just so fucking tired of producing shit television. I was tired of justifying the paycheck for the crap. I was tired of the kind of work I had been doing, because it made me feel dirty. I was tired of wandering aimlessly through my days because I was uninspired by the content, and I was so annoyed that people actually sat around, wasting their precious lives, watching this garbage.

I was tired of seeing my cast and crew sacrifice their mental health for *reality.*

On the flip side, the cast in those overly produced scenes don't usually give two shits. I just created a great TV moment for them, which only led to more Instagram followers and more money.

Pretty sure they slept just fine the night that episode aired.

"Where Is The Love?"

On top of my husband telling me I'm "too nice" for this business, I'd had people tell me some of my original ideas were "too soft" because they were about positive, uplifting content and giving back to the world.

When did being a woman in this business come to mean you had to be a bitch and only produce shitty TV? Why was being a good person and wanting to tell good stories a negative thing? Why can't we take chances on something meaningful, even if it's *soft,* if it means helping to inspire others to make humanity better? Why can't we take a gamble on a new kind of format instead of just what fits within the same, boring, overproduced box? Just because we work in *entertainment* doesn't mean we have to be monsters and lie, cheat, and steal to make the work we do matter.

Making entertainment for others is supposed to be *fun*. But somewhere along the way, for me, it started to become anything but that. It wasn't that I stopped loving creating and producing television—I was just tired of producing absolute dog shit and being forced to make it something desirable to others.

But sadly, that's the reality of this "world." Being freelance, you take what you can get. You don't always get to be choosy with the opportunities offered to you, and most of the time, it's the only offer at that moment, so you say, "Okay. But this is the last time." But it's never the last time. You become addicted to the work because you become addicted to the paycheck. You don't know if another job will line up just as this one is ending. You finally go on a vacation, but the phone never leaves your hand because you're expected to be at everyone else's disposal 24/7.

The kicker is, unlike crew members and editors, freelance producers have no union to protect us; there is a guild but no union. There's no overtime pay. No health insurance. No 401(k) contribution. No vacation time. Now, depending where you fall on the line of producers, the weekly rates can be phenomenal, but when you break down the number of hours you put in, you start to weigh the cost of a lot of things. You can only try and explain so many times why you can't just hang out on a Sunday because no, for real, we're drowning in work that has to get done. You sacrifice your own health and happiness because if you're not going to do the work the way they want you to, then get out of the way because you better believe there's 200 other people in line behind you who will.

But yeah, maybe I was too nice for this business because I cared about people. Even those wanting to be "Insta-famous" and selling their souls for their fifteen minutes and one million followers have shit going on behind the scenes that no one knows about. I've seen a lot of darkness go on when the lights are shining somewhere else.

Caring about my cast—yeah, maybe that did make me too nice for this business.

I carried the weight of this with me for years, still taking meaningless jobs for the paycheck when I could. Until one day, I was finally working on a project I was truly passionate about. A project I was excited to wake up for and felt honored to be a part of because I was finally able to feel like a real storyteller. The heaviness of all these feelings had been buzzing around in me for years, but one moment became almost too much to deal with—when I really had to question what I was doing.

After shipping a cut of my episode to the network the night before, I knew something was up when my boss called me the next morning. We never talked the morning after a cut was sent to network, as the network needed time to watch the episode and send notes back. When I answered my phone, I could hear in his voice something wasn't right. My boss then told me that one of our cast members was dead. He took his own life. It had nothing to do with the show but was some deep-rooted personal shit.

I never met him in person, but I'd watched and rewound every ounce of him that was captured on film—because I was the closest to his storyline. Yet, I never saw signs of something like this ever possibly happening—just like so many do in life, he masked his truth for the reality he wanted us to see.

I cried. It stung, bad. *What the fuck?* He was my age. Most producers would be like, "Wow, that's really sad," but I was crippled with real emotions, because I genuinely fucking cared about people. I truly did not understand. I was staring at his face, but now I was supposed to comprehend this reality that he was actually dead. I was supposed to do my job, wipe away the tears, and think of how I move forward telling a different story and removing his existence from all of it. Because he was here and a part of the story, but then, he was gone.

It made no sense. It didn't feel real.

But, it was real life—and my job was to tell *reality*.

It's what I was expected to do.

So that's what I had to do.

Not just in the world of TV, but in my real life too.

"Darling"

One of the hardest moments in my life came shortly after Crosby was born. I knew I was supposed to go back to work eventually. Work was all I had ever known. I busted my ass to be at the point in my career I was at, making more money than anyone at my position in the company I was doing freelance producing work for. I never in my life, ever, imagined myself as a stay-at-home-mom. Being a mom had always been a dream of mine, but staying home full-time was something I never planned to do.

When Crosby was on the brink of three months old, I was rocking him to sleep. As he was snuggled in my arms, I looked in his sleepy eyes and just broke down crying. Something bigger than me or my career whispered, "He needs you here." It was not an easy decision, but I decided to put a pin in my career and didn't go back to producing TV.

In making this decision, I was giving up my job, my career, my title, my paycheck, my identity, everything I worked for, everything that supposedly defined me as a person to be there for him every minute of every day. I gave up the *biggest* part of myself for the *best* part of myself.

And, as time would eventually come to tell, he really did need me home.

My husband was my biggest fan. He believed in me when I didn't even believe in myself. Don't get me wrong—our relationship was far from perfect. We challenged each other on the daily, but also loved each other with everything we had. We might've fought, a lot, about really stupid shit, but we always had each other's backs when it came to what was most important in life. There was no pressure either way on this decision to be home with Crosby. We both knew the kind of life we lived before when we were both working on shows together, and knew we couldn't keep up at that level now with a baby. It wasn't that we *couldn't*, but for us to be able to make that happen would require a lot of assistance and creative scheduling—and not only would we be paying for that help, but we would also never be around for our boy. Financially, living the life we did in L.A., my paycheck would primarily be going toward someone else taking care of my baby, and both of his parents being away from him easily twelve hours a day. Why would we bring a child into this world just to pay someone else to raise him, and with our work load, miss out on most of his life? It was an absolute no-brainer to make the decision we made.

Until one night, when my husband really pissed me off.

"Have You Ever Seen the Rain?"

It was getting toward the end of the workday for Adam, but in our industry, you never knew what would come up last minute. The commute from our home to the office was about forty-five minutes—and that's with zero L.A. traffic. Realistically, it would take up to one and a half hours, sometimes each way. That day, I was beyond tired, but I tried to channel an inner calm while secretly panicking in excitement—could the Chicago Cubs actually do this and win the World Series?! Crosby was dressed in his little "Waited my whole life for a Championship" onesie. Rough life, kid—you waited a couple months; try over three decades here for Momma!

This was 2016, and—for those of you who know absolutely nothing about baseball—the Cubs did win the World Series, for the first time after a 108-year drought, in Game 7, in the tenth inning. That was even better than when the Bulls got their second three-peat (which was epic in itself). I told Crosby he was the Cubs' good luck charm! *He turned three months old the day after they won.*

Anyway, we hadn't won the World Series yet the night Adam really pissed me off, and aside from the intense stress of being a Cubs fan, the stresses of being a new mom just waiting for my husband to come home and snuggle his son up for a few so I could maybe go take a shower for the first time in days was wearing my patience thin. A little before the workday was going to end, Adam texted me, "I think I'm going to go for a drink after work at a place down the street." What really bugged me was what he said next, so quickly that he didn't allow me the opportunity to respond: "I deserve it."

Oh, oh, *oooohhhhh, no!*

As Crosby and I sat watching the Cubs in the World Series, seeing Adam's "I deserve it" text to why he was thinking of going to get a drink after work just unleashed a full-on bat-out-of-hell, pissed-off new momma.

I lashed out on him via text: "You deserve it? YOU deserve it?" That night, I had breastmilk stained on my tank top from pumping, I hadn't eaten all day, and Crosby was so needy that I didn't even have time to go swap the laundry or do the dishes, including endless bottles and pump parts that had taken over in the sink. I had barely slept because there was no such thing as napping for me. I was beyond tired, but he deserved it?! His texts unleashed a beast:

> "I'm sorry your commute sucks, but every day you're stuck
> in that truck, YOU get to have catch-up adult conversations

on the phone—all I get is coos. YOU get to go out to lunch or sit in silence in your office and eat—I can barely get to the grocery store without a Crosby having a massive blowout. YOU get to shower every single morning because you claim you can't function if you don't—I have to shower with the curtain open and put Croz in his damn puppy thing cuz I'm psycho and won't just leave our new baby in the other room. YOU get to go down to the second floor of your office building, which was my old office building too, because it's less crowded and YOU get the privilege of shitting in peace—I have to bring our son in the bathroom with me when I need to poop. Oh wait, YOU, while you're annoyed with most human beings and don't like them, YOU get to actually have human interactions with people at the job you got because of me with the people I worked with before you ever came along and now I put my career on hold and there is not an ounce of that for me because I am taking care of everything and my body is still dealing with postpartum stuff and a new little baby who just looks at me and needs all of me and haven't gotten to do one single thing for myself in months…but YOU deserve to go out after work for a drink?!"

His text response to me was just: "Fine."

Fine. I fucking hate that word.

I wasn't trying to be a bitch, but he just wasn't stepping back and *seeing* the reality of what life had become for me.

That was when the postpartum started to get really bad—because I finally admitted it out loud. I had the most precious thing in my arms, the baby I wanted more than anything in the world, and yet I never felt so lost, so alone. I couldn't recognize who was staring back at me in the mirror. I couldn't talk about it to anyone, because we, as women, aren't supposed to feel these things, right?! It's not how I was *supposed* to feel; it wasn't what was *expected*.

"Human"

When a baby comes into this world, it's all about the baby. Everyone wants to know the baby's name, wants to hold the baby, wants to buy gifts for the baby. Rarely does anyone look at Mom. Did anyone stop to acknowledge what I just had to go through or what I go through every single moment of every day? No one asked me if I was *okay*—people just wanted to know how Crosby was doing or would text me just wanting me to send pictures of him. Never, ever stopping to consider my personal struggles—physically, mentally, and emotionally. And there was certainly no one sending food to my house to help my already hard new *mom life* a little easier on me. Adam would come home from work, and the shift happened—he would go to see the baby first and ask how Crosby did today. If I got a kiss hello, it was a good day. I was never asked, "Are you feeling okay today? Is there anything I can do to help make life easier and give you a break?"

But the honest truth is, I never asked anyone either. I never wanted to be a burden to someone else's life, so I just suffered quietly in my own struggles. Yet, I secretly wished for someone to just *see* without me having to ask.

We mothers slowly get to a place of just *existing*. We, who are needed for so much, but never thought to be enough to be noticed. And if we dare admit just how hard this *hard* is, we've failed, right!? Because we're just expected to handle it all, to do it all and with grace and a smile on our face—that's the fucked-up idea society has burned into our brains, because it's what our *role* is.

I had my little family. I had my husband. I had my beautiful baby boy who I wanted more than anything in the world. I was surrounded by so much love in my life and joy in my heart, yet often I just felt so alone. I was slowly suffocating—and no one was knocking on our door trying to give me the release I needed just to breathe.

People who say, "It takes a village to raise a child," make me want to scream my face off. *Where's my village?* My husband was there, but he was off at work most of the time, so it was really all me. I didn't have daily help. I didn't get the luxury of people—a mother, a grandmother, a mother-in-law, a cousin, friends—popping by. My sister was there, but she was also working full-time, and I couldn't expect my twenty-something-year-old sister to be the kind of recurring support I needed to define my "village" because I was there to help raise her, and I knew she also needed to live her own life. So without paying for hired help, there was no one to do things during the day to help make life easier, make us a meal, or just play with him for twenty minutes so I could shower in peace, fold the laundry that'd been sitting there in a basket for days, or rock Crosby so I could nap. A nap? *What the fuck is that?* I hear of these moms who get relief because they have a *village,* and all I can think of is what a glorified privilege that they get to nap. Ya know, maybe if I got to nap I wouldn't have been so bitchy with my husband or cared that he went for a drink one random time after work. But I got bitchy because I was beyond tired and handling it all on my own—and no one ever cared to notice, because all eyes were on the baby.

So no, it doesn't take a "village" to raise a child. Because even if I was bitchy and tired, I did it without one.

Just as my assistant camera operator did, just as all the moms who had a village to give them the ability to go off and take a nap in peace—what they did was take the time for themselves to reset and recharge so they could emerge a more restored human being. I never got that, and no one ever told me it was okay to take that time for me. No one ever gave me permission to take care of myself; not even my own self.

After I flipped out on Adam for his "I deserve it" message, it all made sense. In finally just snapping, I was putting the reality of this hard thing out there. Marriage is hard. Having a child is hard. And what that moment was for me really, was me begging for something for myself, beyond just being a newly stay-at-home mom, a role I never planned for in my life. For some people, that's all they ever wanted—that's their dream, and they're crushing it in that life. For me, I needed an ounce of something for myself to make me feel like a human being again, beyond just being Crosby's mom and Adam's wife. I needed a reminder that I was still in there somewhere, in that reflection of this unknown person I saw in the mirror.

But, aside from a quick stint with dancing with the devil, my "own business" venture with a cult-like clothing company that will surely be talked about in part two of this book series, I wasn't really able to give anything to myself because as time would come to show, I was right—my baby boy needed me home more than I knew at the time.

"Fireflies"

Adam always said he felt Crosby was dealing with more than we knew when he was younger. I wasn't really looking for any signs when he was a baby because a child with autism wasn't something I really knew about or was familiar with. In my eyes, we had this beautiful, absolutely loving, hilarious, sassy boy who had a lot of traits that were made up from both his parents—like my stubbornness, which I will fully credit to both of us being Leos.

Crosby was right on the target with a lot of things, as far as developmental milestones go. In the areas he was behind, there wasn't much concern. He crawled at nine months, though it took him until fourteen and a half months to walk. Crosby was babbling a lot by his first birthday. I have videos of him trying nonstop to talk to me in his high chair, having conversations in his own way with me. Shortly after his first birthday, his vocal communication started to regress. Around the same time, I began noticing some different behaviors—like how he began throwing toys kind of hard, which was uncharacteristic of his usually calm temperament.

I felt pretty defeated. I'm Crosby's momma, and I could see something was going on, but I had no clue how to navigate what this was. So, I started asking questions and tried to gather more info, and one of the common things I read was if a child was having issues with hearing, behaviors such as speech regressing and throwing objects hard often occurred out of the child's attempt to cause some sort of reaction. We went to his pediatrician so I could have her check him out and raise my concerns about what might be going on with him. My worries and suggested scenarios for him were met with her comment, "Don't be one of those moms who just look things up on Google. His ears are perfect. Don't be *that* mom."

Okay. I won't be *that mom,* and I'll trust the doctor.

By eighteen months old, things had gotten worse. All his babbling had completely disappeared. I tried not to be *that mom,* but I knew something was up. And yes, while Adam had been bringing up some signs of autism for quite a while now, my intuition was telling me there was more going on.

We finally said, "Screw it," and took him to an ear, nose, and throat doctor to get his hearing thoroughly checked out. Lo and behold, my concerns over the past six months were spot on, and his hearing test results showed that, in both ears, he had been hearing at extremely negative levels—as though he was swimming underwater for probably the past six months. So if everything he was hearing was muffled—no wonder when I would say to him, "I love you," he responded only with *tones* that mimicked my words. He couldn't tell us because he couldn't hear properly, and his trying to communicate any way he could was met with our confused reactions and him having no clue why we couldn't understand. For at least six months he was going through that, six months of a crucial developmental stage in his young life.

Fuck, fuck, *fuck*! I knew it! I fucking *knew* it. I cannot even express the rage that came over me inside at that point. I was so angry and so upset and felt like I failed him as his mom. I hated myself—I didn't follow my instincts as I should have. I was his mom—these *knowings* inside of me came with that. And I didn't listen to what I knew to be true about my baby boy. Instead, I listened to some doctor we were supposed to trust, who took my concerns and met them with a warning to not be *that mom. Fuck!*

Well, let me tell you—do be one of those moms or dads or caregivers and listen to what your inner voice is telling you! I did what was expected of me, and his doctor discredited my intuition and made me feel bad about myself for worrying about my son. I listened to the person we were supposed to trust, the one who supposedly knew it all—and my son suffered because of it. Because of someone else's ignorance—and my voice not being strong enough to fight back.

Over five years later, I still carry the weight of that guilt with me every single day.

Over five years later, I still feel like I failed him.

I will never fail him again.

It should be pretty obvious to say we were done with that pediatrician at this point. I should have sued for malpractice, but I just couldn't fight that fight. I knew I needed my energy for what was to come next.

"You Are the Reason"

We found a new doctor who *listened*. He listened to Crosby's story, he made notes, and he offered proactive suggestions. This was around the time Crosby turned two and had already started early intervention services with our regional center, receiving infant stimulation therapy, speech therapy, occupational therapy, and was put in an early education program where he received physical therapy as well. While so many other kiddos his age were starting their first dance classes or soccer practices and having play dates with their friends, Crosby's schedule filled up with endless appointments to help him try and catch up in life.

His new pediatrician wanted us to get another hearing test done from a hearing center, a different test than the pressure test the ENT did. This test could help determine if sound was being blocked and not able to enter his ears or if sounds were entering his ears and his mind just wasn't processing it. He also referred us to a neurologist and wanted us to go meet with this well-known doctor who did a lot of work with Children's Hospital L.A.

Crosby got the hearing test done first. They put him in some enclosed room, and he needed to respond appropriately to objects and sounds and indicate what directions they were coming from. After having tubes put in both ears a few months prior to help alleviate the pressure, the results showed, "He's now hearing well enough that it shouldn't affect his speech." That's the only takeaway we got from there.

When we first met with the neurologist, it was a bit of a different experience. Instead of asking all the typical questions I'd been asked over and over again, he just observed Crosby's natural behaviors. The neurologist scheduled us to have an electroencephalogram (EEG), which gives a recording of the brain's electrical activity. The test actually looked scarier than it was—especially to a two-year-old who struggled with anything new, having suction cups placed all over his head with wires sticking out of each and then his entire head being gauzed so that the sensors didn't move was a bit terrifying for him (and me). Holding him in my arms while the technician performed the test, I was uneasy. I didn't like not knowing what the wavelengths meant in regard to our son's brain activity.

When we were done, we had to just wait for our follow-up meeting with the neurologist.

We'd become good at waiting by this point.

The following week, I took Crosby back to the neurologist to talk about the results from the EEG exam. He confirmed that everything looked pretty normal, and there wasn't anything to make him think that Crosby was dealing with bigger issues we didn't know about. He looked at me and probably recognized the "worn thin" expression I was carrying around, an expression he probably saw often on mothers' faces. In a very calm, reassuring, grandpa-like tone, our wonderful neurologist said that he truly believed Crosby was just delayed and that he would be *okay*. And to just, as parents, keep doing what we'd been doing. The very nice gentleman got up to walk us out, but before leaving, he turned around to tell us a story:

> *When I was four years old, my mother brought my baby sister home for the first time from the hospital. And when I looked at my sister, I asked my mom, "Why is she not speaking?" And those were the first words I ever spoke in my life. At four years old.*

Someone who understood. Who had been there. Finally, it felt like we had someone on our side. And some hope.

Crosby was two years old when the doctor told us this story. He was two years, eight months old when he was diagnosed with autism. He's now seven.

I'll never give up hope.

"Something Beautiful"

May 20th, 2019, was the day Crosby was given the official autism spectrum disorder diagnosis. I had just waddled out of Quest Diagnostics where I had gotten my blood drawn because I was six months pregnant with his baby brother and it was a high-risk pregnancy. As I got to my car, my phone rang with an unknown number calling. I usually never answer an unknown number, but something told me to pick it up this time—it was the doctor who evaluated Crosby calling me. I answered the phone, and she said, "I just wanted to call and let you know so you didn't have to wait around until the paperwork arrived in the mail, but I want to tell you that my report will reflect an official ASD diagnosis."

Twelve hours prior, we had been sitting in Honolulu International Airport after the best little getaway in Hawaii. Twelve hours after our vacation, I could already feel my stress slowly creeping back into my body. I couldn't really say much to the doctor. I sort of just listened. I thanked her. I hung up. Then I broke down crying, right there in my car.

I never planned for that call. I don't think a parent with a child with special needs, in many cases, ever prepares for the possibility of it. I couldn't *produce* that. It was just life, happening.

It could have been so easy to find myself in the spiral. But I couldn't do that. As I felt overwhelmed and panic started to creep through my entire body, all I could do was close my eyes and take some deep breaths.

I pulled out my phone to send Adam a quick text:

Done with my bloodwork. Got a call from the doctor at regional center... she gave Croz an official autism diagnosis. I'll
be home soon.

I didn't race home. I sat there in my car, crying after hearing of
Crosby's official ASD diagnosis. It wasn't because of her officially *la-
beling* him as having "autism." It wasn't something that by any means
changed who this incredible little boy of ours was in our minds or
how we saw, accepted, and loved him just for who he was. It was just
that everything came crashing down on me as I was reflecting back
on all of these other pieces of this giant enigma. I was, all at once,
trying to make sense of what all of this was and what it all meant, and
realizing how it felt like a lot of the "work" we did didn't really help.
But now we have this official "answer," and it was overwhelming—
mostly because I didn't know what steps to take from there.

The official ASD diagnosis was given like, "Here it finally is, and
off you go," without anyone steering us on this new path. There was
no manual telling us where to go from there, and suddenly, we were
thrust into figuring out this unknown territory that we were now
officially a part of. It was emotional and unsettling—here I was, his
mom, limited in what I could do to help him. We would always advocate for him and fight for what he needed and be his biggest fans,
and I knew somehow it would be okay—but in that moment, I just
wished we were back at our little cabana in Hawaii, hidden away
from our real life. Our little place where he just looked out to the
ocean hoping to finally find Moana—where we could just be, away
from it all, and just exist, as us.

After Croz was given his ASD diagnosis, suddenly everywhere I
looked, I saw puzzle piece images, attached to the saying, "Until all
the pieces fit." A puzzle piece logo is the symbol that was chosen to
represent Autism. At first we bought into it all. We went with the
majority. We were completely lost in navigating this new world, so

we followed in the direction our Google searches seemed to be going. We definitely drank the Kool-Aid, we raised the money for the walk, we plastered puzzle pieces everywhere and then—I just got angry. A puzzle piece?! "Until all the pieces fit," as if implying that someone who is on the spectrum, my child who is on the spectrum, isn't whole. Why? Because he has autism?

My child has autism and his brain doesn't make sense to some people, so his "puzzle," his whole self, isn't complete?—yet I'm over here, not on the spectrum, just trying to shove my own puzzle pieces into places they don't belong.

Crosby is a living, breathing, walking representation of much more of a whole person than most humans I know. Why is his puzzle not complete, simply because his brain works differently? Most geniuses and forward-thinking individuals have brains who "think differently," who see beauty in a way that others cannot and live with more goodness, authenticity, clarity, and enlightenment than most of us will ever do in a lifetime. Different shouldn't mean "incomplete."

And who decided being *incomplete* was a bad thing, anyway? A complete puzzle does not mean whole—it just means done, finished, over. What's left then? The world might try and tell you you're broken when, in reality, you're just freaking beautiful.

Crosby doesn't need a missing piece to be found. He's the purest soul I've ever seen. If anyone needed fixing, it was me. I was more broken than he would ever be. Because I let the world break me. *I will never let the world break him.*

Thankfully, things have evolved and the world is expanding beyond the image of a puzzle piece—transitioning to the "infinity" symbol to represent neurodiversity and inclusivity, with gold being the main color to symbolize autism awareness. On the periodic table of the elements, *gold* is represented by the symbol "Au," which is also the first two letters in the word autism.

I'm grateful for minds who think beyond the limits others want them to believe.

"True Colors"

When I pulled up to our home, after getting the news of Crosby's diagnosis, I sat in my car, crying. I couldn't bring myself to go inside because going inside meant acknowledging life was now expected to change. Getting out of the car meant opening the door and stepping out into this new reality that would be our life moving forward, a new reality that our two-and-a-half-year-old son would now always be known as having autism. Like an asterisk next to his name, a label that cannot easily be defined. I tried my hardest to channel the calm, but I'm human—so I cried and I rubbed my pregnant belly as now new fears really came to surface. Six months pregnant, I felt like I was drowning. You see, having one child with autism greatly raises the odds of having another child with autism. And if the sibling was a boy, the chances were even higher now.

So I sat, tears streaming down my face, overwhelmed but needing to remember I had his little brother and a true miracle growing inside of me. Given my history of pregnancies and being high risk, I needed to not overwhelm myself too much. I didn't know what to do, I didn't know how to feel, and I surely didn't know what to think—all I knew was what was expected of me to do as a mom, to make everything okay. Knowing that, I wiped my tears away and quickly brushed a little blush on my cheeks so it didn't look so obvious there had been so many tears. Then I got out of the car, and upon reaching the front door, I took another deep breath.

I went inside and smiled as I saw Crosby standing in the room. I grabbed him and just hugged him. I didn't want to let go. Crosby was still in the phase when he didn't really notice when you came home from being gone and really didn't acknowledge it either—until you went up to him and hugged him. When I hugged him, he smiled, and the room lit up—it was the absolute best feeling in the world. As I hugged him, I held on a little tighter and a little longer, and tears welled up in my eyes again. I told him I loved him, I reminded him that he was my best friend in the whole world, and then I looked at Adam, the question in my eyes. He gave a look back that said, "We'll figure this out. It's okay."

We'll figure this out. It's okay.

Our concern came not just from the official ASD diagnosis we just got for Croz, or me being over six months pregnant with his brother, but also knowing the timeline in front of us, the life changes that were about to happen, and the instant stress of the heavy weight of the question, *What are we going to do?*

You see, at least in the state of California, when a child turns three years old, that child has to transition out of early intervention therapies and becomes the responsibility of the school district. Your kid has to go through more testing and assessments in order to get an IEP, which is an individualized education plan for any child in the United States who is enrolled in the public school system and has special needs. We went through the process with Crosby because that's what we were told we had to do. We were never given a choice of an alternative option for him. And when the school district met with us for his IEP meeting to go over the results of the assessment, we were told they were giving him a primary diagnosis of autism and a secondary diagnosis of "intellectual disability (ID)." Not only were his therapy hours slashed, he was going to be put in an all-autism classroom. I was super pregnant with Wylder at the time, and we had no one at the IEP meeting there to advocate for us, so we signed the damn thing just to keep Crosby moving forward. *And because we didn't know any better.*

There was so much that didn't sit right with me about the IEP, and it wasn't until later that day when I consulted one of Crosby's therapists, who spent a lot of time with him, that I learned an "intellectual disability" in our modern society is what used to be known as "mental retardation."

A wave of emotions ran through me as I looked at him sitting next to me. I started to cry to her. "I know my son, and that is not my son. He doesn't have an ID; that's not what is going on with him. Yes, I can accept he has autism. Yes, I will say he has a neurological disorder. Yes, at this time, he cannot verbally communicate his words, but he's also extremely intelligent—it's just others keep limiting his abilities and not giving him the chance to show what he's capable of because small minds don't know how to think outside a damn box."

She agreed with me. She believed it was ridiculous of them to put that ID label on him. But what was I supposed to do? At this point, I was eight months pregnant with his brother, and I didn't have the energy to fight that fight. We had already signed the IEP, and now were at the mercy of other people—people who barely spent any quality time with my son, telling us once again what was best for him and what the plan was going to be moving forward.

I knew we were failing him by signing that IEP. And the weight of it was heavy. Because I had made a promise to never fail him again.

"I Hope You Dance"

On the cusp of Crosby turning three years old and me being over eight months pregnant with his brother, we were doubting the IEP and whether to actually put him in the program or retract our decision and not put him in school at all. Adam was familiar with the world of ABA therapy; I was not. He brought it up to me as a possible different route Crosby could go down should we decide to not put him in the school district and have him instead do forty hours a week of applied behavior analysis therapy, which is the only evidence-based therapy that exists based on the science of learning and human behavior.

When he brought the idea up to me, I was against it even though I actually didn't know much about it except the things I heard about it during the past year and a half of early intervention, when I would be surrounded by other moms that would unwelcomingly thrust their opinions of "how bad" it was onto us new, vulnerable moms who were just beginning to navigate the world of *special needs*. But the terrible, awful, horrific things they said, comparing it to "child abuse," was enough to make me believe something like ABA therapy would be worse for our son than the "ID" label the school district slapped on him.

Knowing Adam's stance on ABA but thinking about what this new journey with the IEP we signed would mean for him—at this point, I had to take a step back and really look at the past year and a half of our lives since Crosby entered early intervention therapies from a logistical standpoint and what kind of support he was given—two times a week of speech therapy, two times a week of occupational therapy, one time a week of physical therapy, and an early childhood education program of just a couple hours a few days a week. When you do the math, it's not that much support, and his one-on-one time totaled only about five hours a week. For a child who was now severely delayed, how much impact and progress was that really making on his life? Not much at all. And now, due to his age, and the state of California wanting him to transition into the school district—his one-on-one therapy time was going to be cut down even more or, in some circumstances, become a "small group" therapy during his already short class time. I knew he needed more than the situation the school district was offering him, but I was about to give birth to his brother. So, we were in a stressful situation and had to make the easiest decision in that moment to keep Crosby moving forward with some sort of support while focusing on bringing his baby brother safely into this world.

Crosby did go into the school district program, following what was reflected in his IEP, just two weeks before his baby brother was born. Navigating this new journey for Crosby while having a newborn at home was a lot of *new* at once, and all I could do was hope we made the right decision for him. I would drop Crosby off and pick him up with his baby brother along for the ride, and the feedback I would get from school was, "He did good today." But then I started to pay more attention to what wasn't so obvious—every time I would look at the pictures they would share with the parents, all I could see was how *lost* my boy looked in his eyes. It's like his body was there, but his spirit was elsewhere; I couldn't see the light in his bright eyes. There he was in an all-autism classroom, surrounded by only other kids who also struggled with their own things or unable to communicate with words as well and no real one-on-one attention. I knew something had to change. I couldn't leave him in that situation any longer. And while I knew I had my own feelings about ABA therapy after hearing that "It's hard on the kids because it's so intense and kids need to be kids so play-based is the only way, and ABA is just child abuse."—all I could do was hear the *I know everything* mom voices that were stuck in my head, but I needed to trust one voice more, the one who was in it with me and who fought every day alongside me—Adam, who said, "I know it's going to be a lot for him, and it's going to be hard, but he won't remember this *hard* time. We will."

I could handle all the hard things for my son if it finally set him on the right path. So, after a short stint, we pulled Crosby out of school, got him into full-time ABA therapy, and he was finally on his way moving forward, in the right direction for him.

"Don't Give Up On Me"

The most important thing we instantly discovered after the first few ABA sessions—the biggest issue Crosby was really dealing with was needing to learn the skill of "learning." All he needed was someone to give him the attention and have the patience to show him *how to learn* and he was able to show just what he was capable of, what he had locked inside of him but no one gave him that chance until now. Once his ABA therapists started pulling it out of him and he started being able to show what he was truly capable of and what he knew, it was like his entire world lit up. He was full of life. He was so proud every time he got something right, and he had this newfound excitement to want to learn more. For the kid who at three years old couldn't do a simple two-piece, interlocking jigsaw puzzle, well, he proved everyone wrong when a year later he could do 100-piece ones. And once this kid showed just how easily he could *learn* new things, he took off and started mastering programs and new skills within a day!

As parents, making the decision to pull him out of school at that young of an age and go the route of ABA therapy was not an easy one. There's a huge stigma that surrounds ABA therapy and a deeply drawn line in the sand between parents who are in favor of it or against it. I would never, ever push something onto someone else because that's not who I am. What I can do is talk openly about our life, our decisions, and explain why something works for us, providing a different perspective. But our family is not anyone else's family, so I would never try to force our decisions in life onto anyone

I think there's a huge misconception about ABA therapy, and I think it's the "behavior" aspect that bumps people the wrong way. What a lot of people don't understand is the "behavior" aspect of it is focused on the skills needed in order to live and survive in this world, and on altering the ones that can be causing harm. For example, Crosby never would wear sunglasses, ever. But Crosby also has extremely sensitive eyes, and when he's in the sun, it really bothers him. So, I asked his supervisor if she could create a "program" for him to learn the skill of wearing sunglasses. He was so against it the first time they tried. He flipped out and wouldn't let them near his face. But everything is a step—and it starts with just a few seconds. A few seconds—that's it. They told him to count along with them with just the sunglasses near his face: "One, two, three, four, five." And when he was able to do that, the time increased more and more until finally he was able to put them on his face, and then it became counting how many seconds he would allow the sunglasses to be on his face for. They worked on this a lot that first day, slowly increasing the time and having the patience to find his comfort in it, while also making sure to track data every step of the way.

The very next day, I was in the kitchen making lunch, and his therapist yelled to me, "Hey, Mom, Crosby wants to show you something." And in the kitchen he walks, with a little saunter in his step, wearing his sunglasses in the house like he was a legendary rockstar. They created a program, they tracked the data, he did the work, and in one day, he changed a *behavior*, and in doing so, learned a new skill that was able to help him in life, instead of continuing to struggle because doing the work was just "too hard on him."

But it's not just sunglasses—riding a scooter, trying new foods, wearing a Band-Aid, wearing a hat, putting on sunscreen, recognizing the faces of people in his family, playing with a simple toy, opening up a wrapped present, giving a high five, having a friend, brushing his teeth, getting his hair trimmed, taking a bath, taking his temperature, and oh hell, giving medicine could result in a full-blown panic attack for everyone involved—every single thing Crosby has learned to do in our home, at school, and in life was a program that had to be developed for him. He has to learn a "skill" that so easily comes to the majority of the world. It can be exhausting, and a lot of people are too consumed with their own selves to ever understand, but that's ok—we went the "hard" route because he is our son and we will always do all the hard things we need to do in order for him to have a fighting chance in this world. He breathes life into us and gives us purpose, but no, it is not easy. And that's okay—I've never been one to choose the easy route.

Forty hours a week that child started doing ABA therapy, working harder than most adults I know just to be able to have a fighting chance in this life. Yes, it's hard. But the people who said, "It's too hard on him," were projecting their own ideas onto our situation. And here's the reality—it's *our* situation, no one else's. Crosby doesn't look at it as "hard"—he loves it and is learning, growing, and communicating in ways he never could communicate before. It's frustrating that sometimes other people's *know it all* opinions are just thrust onto the emotional insecurities of vulnerable parents. There's a difference in speaking openly about your journey vs just projecting your opinions onto others as if that's the only truth.

I'm so thankful I became strong enough to turn down the damn noise and listen to the only voice whose opinion really mattered, my husband's. We made the absolute next best decision for our son, and it scares me to think where he would have been today if we didn't.

It's funny because there's many versions of a saying out there about "love" being a skill that needs to be learned. Yet, for Crosby, *love* is perhaps one of the only—and most important—skills he never had to learn. He just knows love. That kid loves without limits, and it is contagious. He is the most loving, the happiest, the most inspiring soul I have ever met—and I'm the luckiest because he is my son. His energy is contagious. We all need a dose of his beautiful spirit—everyone who meets him, whose lives are made a little better simply by knowing him, adores him. And I'm not just saying this because

I'm his mom. As his parents, we may be his biggest fans, but that kid has a stadium full of people cheering his name.

"Blessings"

There's a reason the divorce rate is high for parents of children with autism. When we made the decision to go the ABA route for Crosby and pull him out of the school district at three years old, we knew it was going to be the hard route, and we knew it would be even harder on us. What I didn't plan for was the math of forty hours a week, eight hours every single week day. I couldn't leave the house, as the therapy had to be supervised—I was essentially quarantined, well before the COVID-19 pandemic. And let me tell you, it is *hard*. When your child has autism, some days can challenge every ounce of you and your partner's being. Adam and I have most certainly been tested time and time again, always trying to not let the spiral consume us.

No one knows what my life feels like on a daily basis. The truth is, I cry every single day, because I can't make Crosby's journey any easier and I can't *fix* even the smallest things that a mom should be able to. There is not an ounce of me that would ever want to change my beautiful boy—I just know how cruel the world can be, and I just wish life didn't have to be so hard for him.

Navigating Crosby's journey is an everyday constant, and as his momma, all I can ever do is hope I'm doing everything I can to make sure he has the best fighting chance. Even though there are hard days, even though there are super emotional days, and even though I can't do a single thing to make his hard things not so *hard*, I know we are blessed. He was my first miracle.

When you can step back even for a moment and look around, you see that, yeah, we've all had some hard shit thrown our way, but there are so many other people dealing with much harder battles. That puts a lot in perspective. I have seen kids with tubes in their necks, I have seen kids confined to wheelchairs and needing help one hundred percent of the time, I have seen kids rolling an oxygen tank through the grocery store, and kids with body parts missing, I have seen kids with holes in their hearts who shouldn't have probably made it to this earth, but who did because kids are incredible. I have seen people struggle for a long time trying to carry a baby of their own and not be able to. I know being able to bring healthy and happy babies into this world, regardless of what label others want to put on them, means I am lucky. I am grateful that I get to hold my babies every night—because not everyone can. There isn't a single day that goes by, even in the hardest moments we face, that I do not have gratitude for my life, for my kids, and for the good and the hard because there's something to be grateful for in all of it.

Crosby may have to fight the rest of his life to prove he can do anything; he just does it in his own way. He will do it, though. I know he will, because he's a fighter, and he's a fighter because he's my son, and I'm a fighter. I don't know if he will always be "nonverbal," but I tell you, this kid is fighting every day. We can accept life's challenges with grace or we can fall apart. And yeah, there are a lot of times I have fallen apart, but *grace* is how I am able to be strong enough to share this piece of my story.

Oh, and by the way, three years after Crosby's initial assessment, leading up to his sixth birthday, the school district actually removed the "intellectual disability" label that was slapped on him when he was nearly three years old and said that definitely didn't reflect who he is—proving what I have known about my son all along, that he cannot be defined by someone else's idea of who he is, for he is so much more than the limitations others want to put on him. I truly believe Crosby exists to change the world and shine his radiant light on the blindfolds over some people's eyes.

Being a parent in today's world is hard, but being the parent of a child with special needs—until you actually live this scary, intriguing, complex, awakening, misunderstood, absolutely beautiful world that is being a part of the autism spectrum in some way, you can't begin to understand just how hard the *hard* is. The list of names in which I can trust another human with my child, especially him being nonverbal, is not even an inch long. It is not easy talking about our journey, but as the mom of an incredible soul who is on the spectrum, I do talk in hopes that if speaking openly about our journey helps someone in some way, then the vulnerability is worth it.

Although I know what this beautifully complex world is like, I still don't know even a fraction of it. And I can't assume to ever fully know because everyone's life is different. That's why it's a spectrum. I try to live with my eyes open and see what other children go through and I try to have compassion for other families because, as much as I feel like I know what living in the world of "special needs" means, I'm still learning new things every single day. I try hard not to have assumptions or show ignorance or be judgmental toward others because I have never navigated anyone else's life. And because, I don't want people to have assumptions or be ignorant or judgmental toward our life either. It goes both ways.

It's easy to beat myself up for choices we made, but the reality is, I can't change the past. I didn't listen to my gut, my intuition, when I knew something was going on with Crosby. I can't go back in time and make different choices to have spoken louder and fought harder for my boy when I knew something was wrong. From his doctor telling me not to be *that mom* or the school professionals trying to tell me my son was something he wasn't—I can't fix any of what happened, but I can learn from it and choose to find some sort of beauty within it. And the beauty is remembering that I do have a voice. The lesson is to fucking use it—no matter who tries to silence me, because my kid deserves to be heard, even if I have to be the one to *speak* for him.

While I want to be pissed off most days, I have to be thankful for the lessons I've learned.

It's the only way to try and move forward.

More than anything, what Crosby's journey thus far has taught me is the importance of just being a kind person. When we say things like, "kindness matters"—it really, truly does.

MAYBE, TUESDAY?

"Unfold"

Way back in 2008, Madison and I were living in a tiny two-bedroom apartment in North Hollywood when I got bit by a creative bug so hard I ended up locking myself in my bedroom, and within three days, I wrote the entire first draft for my screenplay called *Perfectly Imperfect.*

> Synopsis: A romantic comedy set in Chicago, Perfectly Imperfect tells the story of two lovers who have suffered a failed relationship and how to deal with one another within their close circle of friends as their two best friends are headed to the altar. Based on the idea that you can spend your entire life searching for this ideal "perfect person"... what you come to find is, in time, it's a person's "imperfections" that make them *perfect* for you after all.

> Tagline: Aren't we all, simply, *Perfectly Imperfect?*

My plan was solid—write the script, cast my talented group of friends, and make one freaking awesome movie. I became obsessed with it. I could see the entire thing playing out frame by frame in my mind. I had my dream cast in mind, a budget planned, and a soundtrack laid out, including an original song (appropriately titled

"Perfectly Imperfect") written by Madison and her ex-boyfriend. With an epic karaoke collab to "I'd Do Anything for Love (But I Won't Do That)," a drunken poker night showdown to "Chicken Fried," and wishlist cameos by Vince Vaughn and Jon Favreau playing rival hot dog vendors at a Cubs game, this was destined to be what the fading rom-com genre needed to keep it alive.

So what happened?

Fear got in the way. Imposter syndrome once again took over. I hid that script in my "Dream Box" and just gave up, thinking I wasn't enough to make it happen. The climb was too steep, the stars too far out of reach. Who out there would believe in little me and my little dream? I let my own doubts get in my way, and I didn't believe in my own voice enough to think it was something others wanted to hear. I convinced myself that I couldn't do that today, but someday I will. Maybe someday—just not today. That was fear talking, but I listened—and I shoved it away. And now, fifteen years of "maybe somedays" later, *Perfectly Imperfect* has become such an overused phrase that it haunts me daily for letting fear consume me, when I had something so original in my hands.

Why do we let fear stop us from going for it?

I've been putting off my "maybe someday" dreams for so many years now. Not just with *Perfectly Imperfect* but with almost every aspect of my life, every dream I've had, every creation I've created. I get so far, and then I allow fear to get the best of me. I have so many great ideas, I go all-in, and then I just stop. I let *the noise* remind me I'm not *enough* or convince me that I can't do it, or I'm not the one who that can happen to. *Am I deserving?* No. *Can I be the one to inspire change?* Fuck no. *Who am I?* I'm just me.

We've all been there before. Maybe someday I will get off my ass and get to the gym. Maybe someday I'll have the courage to talk to my crush. Maybe someday I'll actually get that raise I've been too scared to ask for. Maybe one day. Maybe today. Maybe, Tuesday?

"The Middle"

I said, "Maybe, Tuesday?" because if I was ever given a tiny sliver of help during the week, before the pandemic hit, it was on Tuesday, when my mother-in-law could come up from Long Beach and oversee Crosby's therapies going on in our home. During that time, while Adam was at work, I could sneak away to do all the Target, grocery store, gift buying, and laundry things—not to escape and get a massage or have a wine and cheese date with girlfriends. And never did I just get to go get my nails done. She was able to provide me a few hours of relief so I could get the obligatory life happenings done without outsourcing them. It might not seem like a big deal to go do things like that by myself, but it was a huge deal.

What most people don't realize is being the parent of a child with special needs, in almost all scenarios, I instantly default to *survival mode*. I do what I have to do to just do it. When I did have to take Croz with me to run errands, he would always be in a stroller with his iPad, and I would push the stroller with one hand while pulling an overflowing cart behind me with another. I've gotten many comments from people applauding me for being the mom who could do this and what a genius idea that was—yet, no one understood I wasn't a hero. I had no choice. When you have a child who isn't able to verbally communicate with words, my constant, daily, every-waking-moment living fear is if he wandered off and couldn't tell a single person who he was or who his family is, I might never see him again. So, my superhero power of pushing a stroller while pulling a cart had nothing to do with trying to be cute or clever—it was always me, in full-blown survival mode. Knowing my stroller-loving kid was perfectly chill, strapped in, safe in one place preoccupied with his iPad equaled me not having to deal with the stress of my fears.

Yet, I can't tell you how many nasty looks I got from other parents because my child was consumed with watching his iPad instead of running through the aisles pulling toys off the shelves. The amount of judgmental nastiness I got shot at me for years would sometimes make me beeline to the very corner of the store and just cry in peace for a moment—where no one could see me break down, as if I was a failure of a mom, in the "As Seen on TV" section of Target. All I was doing was just trying to survive—yet I couldn't even do that without the judgments of others.

So, on the Tuesdays my mother-in-law was able to come up to Burbank and I could escape to be just another typical mom in Target blending in with all the others, the weightless feeling of being able to do that without the shrewdness from others was more relaxing than any massage could have ever been.

"Born To Be Wild"

Since I've met my husband, every Christmas, he has gifted me a necklace. One year, it was a Chicago Bears helmet necklace. Other years, it was a cheese grater necklace for my intense hatred for the Packers (thanks to Aaron Rodgers), a Swiss army knife necklace, a harmonica necklace, and even a single match necklace, each with their own special meaning. On Christmas of 2018, Adam gave me one of the most profound necklaces yet—a compass necklace, with a note attached. He never gave a note, so this was something different. Before I even read it, I knew it meant something more than any other necklace he had given me before. You see, just a year prior, I suffered my second miscarriage.

I carried that loss differently.

It was October 2017 when a positive pregnancy test confirmed Crosby was going to be a big brother. Just after Thanksgiving, our doctor "called it," and with no growth and no heartbeat, we said goodbye to Baby Number 3. While we once again had to trust that *life* had another plan, this was the most traumatic loss yet. Even though my body knew what to expect, it felt like hope was lost, a dream was gone—but I tried to listen to what the universe was telling me. Maybe Crosby's *stuff* was just too much, and he needed all of our attention at that point in time.

I had to deal with the physical and emotional pain every day, yet I was coaxed back into the routine because I had my boy and, while it felt my life was stuck in the heartache of going through that again, other people's lives around us were forcing me to just keep moving forward with a fake smile on my face.

Sometimes, when people would see Crosby, they would say, "You should have another baby. You two made a cute kid." All I could do was smile through the tears. Every time there was another pregnant woman belly rub happening in front of my face or a "show me your bump" trend happening on Instagram, I wanted to throw up.

Baby Number 3 really showed me just how much I let fear consume me. Fear of the depth of Crosby's situation, which we were slowly starting to become aware of, fear of what my body would be capable of after suffering another loss, fear of the unknown, fear everywhere. And it consumed Adam with fear too because he couldn't lose me. While I knew how blessed I was to be able to bring Crosby into this world, and I know that kind of fortune is never worth taking for granted—the dark truth was fear consumed us. We just did a really good job of hiding it from others.

A year later, as we were deep in navigating Crosby's early intervention therapies and trying our best to heal from the pain of losing Baby Number 3, I found myself pregnant once again, and suddenly there was newfound *hope*. With that hope, all the fear came rushing back in.

That's why Adam gave me a compass necklace on December 25, 2018, and with his Christmas gift, the note which said:

My Love,

This year's necklace may be the most significant yet. It really made me think about where we have been, as well as where we are going.

We've been through some of the most amazing times together but also some of our most challenging. However, we've always stayed the course. We've always had each other's backs.

Our journey has brought us the most amazing gift either of us have ever had in life, and life just may double down on us because it knows how much love we have to give.

I love our journey. I love where we've been. I love where we are going. Most of all, I love you. Forever and always, let's stay the course.

Love, Adam

That's what we did. We stayed the course. Despite my fear of going through it again, we held on to hope one more time. And life double downed on us.

My "Maybe, Tuesday?" did come true. Wylder McCoy was born on August 13, 2019.

Which just so happened to be a Tuesday.

And because none of us are perfect, and I hope by now we're friends, I will let you in on a truth that not many people know about yet, unless you actually know us. Wylder is also on the autism spectrum and was given an official diagnosis at an early age, just like Crosby. Our boys are the example that just because someone may think they know or have met someone with autism, doesn't mean they know "autism." I said earlier when it was just about Crosby, it's a spectrum. And I'm learning new things every single day because I have been gifted this beautiful life of being their momma.

We never needed a manual. We just needed our boys—their laughter and love are the light guiding us as we navigate this life.

And what a fucking magical one it is.

FIVE.

The Darkness

THE HARDEST HIT

"Secrets"

Early on a January morning in 2018, which was about a year and a half after cutting my mother out of my life, I woke up to a text message from my uncle that just said, "Are you ready for life to never be the same again?"

I started panicking, thinking someone had died.

We were living at our pool house above Glenoaks at the time. Crosby's seventeen-month-old self was nestled into my back and sound asleep in between Adam and me, so I had to ninja-like maneuver my way out of the bed to a more private space to process the next complicated text my uncle had sent me.

As I started to read the image in the text that followed, a screenshot of a Facebook post, I almost threw up all over myself.

My mother did it—she dropped the biggest bomb on our family via a social media post.

I really despise social media.

At fifty-six years old, she revealed to the world that after never feeling like she "belonged" and digging into her ancestry, she discovered my papa was not her biological father. Instead, another man was—a man that my grandmother had been with and who she got pregnant by just before meeting my papa. But my papa and my grandma agreed to take the secret to their graves and that he would raise my mother as his own daughter, forever.

All the times she was a bitch to him, all the times she wreaked havoc on his world, all the times she only wanted money from him—he put up with her shit for fifty-six years, loving her first and foremost as "his daughter" and keeping the promise he made to my grandmother to protect my mother, love her, take care of her as his own. And how does my mother repay him? By blowing up our entire family with a fucking Facebook post—because, to her, the world of social media had always been more important than actual human relationships.

I don't care that I had cut her off from my life; she knew how to use a damn phone and reach me if she had to via my husband. I don't care that her siblings lashed out at her in pain, my uncle calling her *selfish* and texting her, "Who do you think you are, Mother fucking Teresa?" I don't care that people lied to cover truths for their own reasons. I wanted to feel sorry for her at that moment, having empathy for my own mother not knowing the truth of her life, and therefore of her kids' lives, our entire lives. I truly wanted to show compassion and give grace for what she must have gone through in that moment. But I couldn't— because of how she went about revealing that information. Because she took to social media, bashed my papa (altering the post after the fact), posting photos of her, my grandmother, her biological father, and at fifty-six years old, instantly calling him "my daddy." That's how my family found out—because one person saw her post and it spread like pink eye through our phones one early January morning in 2018.

Because the people who didn't really matter in life, people she didn't know of beyond the name of on a screen, mattered more to her than anyone else. Because the likes and the comments she needed from others to fill some void in her mattered more than just doing one thing right for once. She revealed this truth to a cold screen instead of to the people who she had hurt, but who would have still been there for her regardless of the pain.

As her daughter, I have the right to say that's fucking gross.

Ugh, it's hard to sit here and breathe normally just writing this. The heaviness is unbearable at times.

The funny thing about technology is even with the ability to "block" someone, you sometimes can't actually *block* them. Even when you make the hard decisions to delete their info or try some *Eternal Sunshine of the Spotless Mind* method, you don't *block* everyone. So, there's always a way for someone to still be able to creep back in and hurt you no matter how hard you try to not allow them to do so, even if it's from the thoughts in your own head.

And my mother constantly found a way to do so.

My mother's Facebook profile is public, and yes, I'm fucking human, so maybe I went onto her account a few times after her bomb-drop on our family to see the follow-up for myself. And I saw the photos of her making amends with my grandmother. And I saw the photos of her meeting her biological father for the first time. And I saw the photos of the reunion she got with her *daddy* before he passed away. I saw it all—the trips she took around the world, the selfies she posted endlessly, the persona she wanted the world to believe—a person starved for *likes*.

Yet she had her first grandchild breathing in this world—and everything else was more important than to try and make things right or try to be a better human for that innocent child. And yeah, I have moments when maybe I'm a little bit bitter about that. But I'm honest enough to admit it. And then, I just get sad—for her—because she's the one who missed out on a child's beautiful life.

The one thing I don't think my mother will ever be selfless enough to realize is that she ultimately got her one day to say goodbye, her last word, one last hug from her "Daddy." She got her *one day*—because she didn't care who she hurt in her pursuit of what she wanted in life.

I never will.

And I don't know if I can ever forgive her for that.

Yeah, my "one day" really mattered. But now it's too late.

You can't bring someone back from the dead.

"Ghosts That We Knew"

In January of 2020, about exactly two years after my mother's lovely "secrets exposed" bomb drop, I kept having a recurring dream that was so vivid I would wake up in sweats questioning if it was reality or just a dream.

I remember myself clearly. We were living in our little transitional apartment in Burbank. The dream itself always started off on the weekend, and I know that because Adam wasn't in the office but rather working from our family room couch because there are no boundaries for work when it comes to the entertainment business. And as he watched Croz playing on his swing in the open space next to him, I was watching both of them from our recliner while I rocked a sleeping baby Wylder in my arms. There was a quiet calm in the air, unusually quiet for a small apartment usually filled with therapists and chaos during the weekdays. As I was slowly dozing off soaking in Wylder's snuggles, my phone was vibrating on the table next to me. With Wylder snuggled in my arms, I couldn't just reach over and grab it, but I could see who it was calling me.

My brother.

His timing was never good, but I'll always answer. *Guilt has a way of doing that to you.*

I hadn't heard from him in years. In fact, I hadn't heard from him since he told me he wouldn't be coming to my wedding because he was still hell bent on some bitch that he was no longer even with. But that's what my family does—prioritizes relationships that will never last over the ones that are supposed to. But now, nearly five years later, out of the blue—here he was calling me.

I couldn't pick up right away because if I moved too quickly, Wylder would wake up. So, I had to wave to get Adam's attention.

I mouthed to him, "My brother is calling me. Can you come get Wylder?"

Adam gave me a "that's weird" reaction but then came over, cuddled Wylder up in his arms, and traded places with me as I headed to our bedroom to call him back.

I sat on our bed, and with an uneasiness ripping through my body, called my brother back. The phone rang once before he picked it up and, in his over-dominant Italian way, just said, "Dad is sick."

Mind you, I hadn't heard from our "dad," my biological father, in ohhhh, about twenty-seven years at this point. He did not raise me, like he did my brother.

"Okay," I said, then paused for a long time. "Okay, what is going on, and where is he?"

My brother told me our father's liver was failing him, apparently the bottle was doing him in, and he was too stubborn to make better changes for his life. Apparently our father had skipped out on paying child support to some younger half-sibling of ours that may or may not actually be the "junior" of him, so our father had to flee Illinois and was never allowed back because of bullshit with one of his exes— so he had been hiding away in Georgia, living out of his RV, in some motorhome park.

As I listened to my brother on the other end of the phone, his words started to become scrambled because all I could do was now relive the past decades of my father not being in my life. Part of me has always, always believed that no matter how *bad* of a man people told me he was, at the core of him, he is my father. He's 50 percent of why I exist, and I know I'm a good person, so there has to be good in him somewhere.

There has to be. Right?

Holding on to that ounce of possible goodness that existed in this man I barely knew yet whose eyes I carry with me every single day, I knew, in this possible final act of his life, I needed one final moment with him.

I had never been away from either of my babies for more than one night, but I knew this was important. I had to be brave enough and trust enough in my husband to take care of things at home, because I needed this time with my father before it was too late. As I was preparing to make the journey to Georgia by myself, I was met with my husband standing by our car with his own duffle bag packed. "We're all in this together," he said. "I'm here with you and for you, and we got you." A part of me just wanted to go and not deal with any responsibilities other than having to deal with my past, but a part of me knew I needed my boys with me more.

Road trips have always been a special thing for Adam and me— to drive and listen to music and be free from the constraints of the world. Just as we did on our road trip to Napa—even in this most heart-wrenching of circumstances, we drove and listened to the *soundtrack of my life*. We drove and drove, the boys cried and cried, it took way longer with pit stops, hotel sleepovers, diaper changes, and all that, but we were headed to Georgia. I was on my way to hopefully heal the past decades of wounds. And if this was really his end, at least I could say *goodbye*.

It was a long journey from California, but I knew it was all going to be worth it for just one single day with him, if that's all we got. If he was really sick and he was headed toward the end of his story in this life, I knew I was willing to risk it all for just one moment. Maybe just one conversation. Maybe just one hug from his grandkids. Maybe Wylder could make him "ha ha" laugh one last time. Maybe Crosby could forehead kiss him to let him know he was loved. Maybe Adam could have a single moment to tell him how loved his baby girl is. Maybe I could get no answers if it came to it, but just a look from his eyes so like my own—his eyes both myself and my boys have—to let me know he's always been with me even when he hasn't been. Just one day, that's all. Whatever life was going to bring in that day, that's what we were taking this chance for.

Just one day.

"All That Really Matters"

We pulled up to the trailer park in Georgia that his RV was camped out in. I had waited so long for this moment to see *my father*. I had no idea what I was going to say to him, what I truly needed from him, but here I was, finally, steps away from my father who was sick and too stubborn to get help because life hadn't always been on his side. But, here we were.

This was happening.

For the past twenty-seven years of my life, I thought about what I would say to my father at this moment. I wondered for so long how he would react to seeing his firstborn daughter after nearly three decades of never so much as hugging her. What would he think of the woman I'd become? Would he actually see any part of me in him? I wanted to know if all the unkind stories of him were true. Was he really such a bad man? Did he do all those awful things like push my mother down the stairs when she was pregnant with me, and that's why I was born six weeks early? Did he really burn down their own video store just to collect the insurance money? Did he really not want me and only wanted my brother? Was I really never enough for him?

But more than that, I just wanted to know if he loved me. I wanted to know if he was proud of me. I wanted to know what that moment would be like when he saw his grandsons for the first time. I thought about what it would be like for Adam to shake the hand of the man who helped create me. I envisioned maybe a moment with my boys on their mother's father's lap and maybe something within him helped break through to Crosby in a way no one had ever been able to do before. I imagined this moment, and in it, Crosby spoke a real sentence for the first time in his life, to his grandfather he had never met and would never get to spend time with beyond perhaps this one day. And that would be a moment to change our entire world—to heal a part of the past and to give us a beautiful step forward toward a new tomorrow.

Even though I spent most of my life hating my father because of what my mother wanted me to believe, I never stopped loving him. And I just really needed one day, one moment, to let him know that even when he felt so alone, and even with all the pain, that he was loved.

But the reality was that day never came.

And it would never come.

Ever.

Because it was all just a dream.

Just a recurring dream I had for weeks. A dream so vivid, I questioned the possibility of its reality every single time I opened my eyes. A dream I told Adam about and went to him one day and said, "I really have this overwhelming something inside of me that's pulling at me, wanting to reach out and find my father and make peace. I think I need that." And Adam said to me, "I think you should. And I think you do too."

Two months later, the world got shut down due to the coronavirus pandemic.

Two months after that, my father was found dead.

"Day Is Gone"

After the coronavirus pandemic hit, a good chunk of time went by before we physically saw any of our immediate family in the flesh. We followed a pretty tight "safer at home" policy, because we couldn't afford to jeopardize losing any of Crosby's therapies since they were done in our home. So whether or not people thought it was an easy choice for us to keep such a strict distance, by no means was saying "no" an easy thing—but we had to do right by our family so we wouldn't chance getting sick and so Crosby wouldn't regress. The four of us were our own little "inner circle," and we had to do what was best for us.

When we finally saw my in-laws for the first time during the pandemic, we drove from our apartment in Burbank down to Long Beach early in the day to surprise my brother-in-law—socially distant, of course—for his birthday. It was Saturday, May 23, 2020, when we showed up in Long Beach for his Hawaiian-themed birthday gathering—making sure to safely deliver gifts across the lawn, which involved a thoughtfully planned DIY Hawaiian Mai Tai basket so he could enjoy some tasty treats from our favorite place in Hawaii.

At 2:41 p.m., I received a missed call from my own brother.

I saw the call come through, but I did not answer because, frankly, I hadn't heard from my own brother since 2015, when I did have to force out of him that he wasn't coming to my wedding. So, when I saw his name appear as an incoming call on my phone four and a half years after I last heard from him, I knew, based on our family history, something was up. In my dream I swore I would always pick up whenever I saw his name—but in real life, I just couldn't at that moment. Crosby had my phone when the call came in, and I quickly grabbed it from him and sent it to voicemail to avoid awkwardness.

But then the text came in: "Call me back when you're free."

That only could mean one of two things: either he was drunk and wanting to be dramatic about something in his life—or something bad really did happen.

After an hour of telling my kids, "No, you can't go over there," and holding them back from their grandparents, our boys were both starting to just lose it. Honestly, I was internally losing it just listening to them losing it. I couldn't think straight. Trying to calm them while wondering *why* my brother called after nearly five years of no words, I just needed to get out of there, so my husband, our boys, and I air-hugged my in-laws *goodbye*.

We got in the car.

We got on the freeway.

I called my brother back.

He picked up, before the first ring finished. "Just had to call and let you know... Dad died."

I didn't know how to process this. *Our father is fifty-nine years old. Was.*

How do I process this?

I don't know how to handle this. I don't know a thing in this moment.

My father? MY father. DEAD?! No. No. NO.

This one hurts. It really...fucking...hurts.

Just stop. Like, can life please just fucking STOP, everything in this moment just freeze, please just freeze so I can just attempt to wrap my head around this blow?!

Whatever a text version of the game "telephone" is, that's what happened next. My mother texted my grandmother telling her to text my aunt Julie to text me and let me know that my father died. But I already knew—because even though I hadn't talked to my brother in four and a half years, he knew what the adult thing to do was. Pick up the phone and fucking call. While my mother still couldn't physically call me because she was blocked, she had every ability to pick up the phone and call my husband. My own grandmother didn't call me. It was just her text to her text to her text. My father died. That was a shitty way for a "long line of strong, independent women" to pass that memo along.

That day my brother called me, that day I will never forget, May 23, 2020, what surprised me the most about his phone call was not the news of our father dying; it was how hard it hit me. This isn't at all how I thought I would feel when this day was to come at some point in life.

A man I was raised to hate. A man so many people, including his own family, "hated."

I shouldn't be crying.

But...

I can't stop.

After all, he is—correction, *was* my father. No matter how hurt I'd been all these years or the pain, anger, hatred, uncertainty, or unknown resentment—all the emotions wrapped up into a ball of major fucking grief, and it still didn't make sense and didn't seem real.

He was fifty-nine.

And died alone.

In a motorhome.

In Georgia.

Found in his RV, after being dead for days inside of there, in the heat.

And no matter what he had done or others said he had done, I couldn't be okay with that.

I was so mad and so upset, and I didn't know how to process this all—like, how?!

I didn't care what people said about him my entire life—that's not how a story is supposed to end.

"Piece by Piece"

The day after I found out my biological father died, I woke up feeling like a ton of bricks fell on me. I couldn't text anyone back, I didn't want to talk to anyone, I could hardly get out of bed. I was struggling, bad. My husband, our boys, and I went for a walk and ended up walking for six miles. Along the way, we found this cute little shop in our town, a little boutique named Tansy, that I had never noticed before but I was instantly drawn to. Adam said, "Let's go in." So, we went in, and I ended up finding a beautiful, cascading houseplant with heart-shaped leaves that I was drawn to and wanted to purchase, as a physical reminder to honor my father, which they planted for us in a macramé hanging planter that we loved. We then walked it back to our home.

After we got my father's plant home, I learned that it was a golden pothos, which also goes by the nickname the "devil's ivy" since it's so hard to kill and can grow in the dark. *That's a little ironic to me.*

I had never before owned a plant. Crazy, I know, but I wanted something to honor him in our home, memorabilia of sorts, and this seemed perfect. I don't know what it was about this plant embracing the spirit of my father, but since his death, I have talked to the plant, fallen to my knees asking it for answers, cried, screamed, laughed, prayed to that plant—to my father. Because of this plant, I have had a better relationship with my father, with his soul in his next lifetime, than I ever did with him in this one.

I don't know how to word this properly because I don't want it to be about religious or spiritual beliefs, but I have to believe there's more beyond here, call it what you shall. The moment I locked eyes with my husband, it was so strong it was as though I knew him in lifetimes before. When I look into my children's eyes and hold them into me, my heart knows we've chosen each other once again but in this lifetime. I have to believe because when we sit with our emotions without the noise around us, *life* tells us so.

My father helped bring me into this world, and for that I'm eternally thankful. Because of him, my children are here. I married a blue-eyed boy with dreams of having blue-eyed babies because I always hated just how deep and dark my own eyes are. And funny enough, I didn't end up with blue-eyed babies—they ended up with deep, dark, Italian brown eyes because of my father. Every time I look in their eyes or at my own reflection in the mirror, I see him there in our eyes—I see him staring back at me. That plant has brought me up from some dark places since his death, and I know he has been on the other side, finally being the "dad" he should have been here on earth but life didn't allow him to be—but beyond this earth, he could be. *I know he's finally watching out for me.*

The pandemic had tried my marriage and had challenged us at times, but since I got the news that completely, unexpectedly made my world crash down, my husband was the epitome of a rock, of support, of a best friend and my love. He hadn't asked questions. When we got home from buying the plant, so sweaty after walking six miles in ninety-degree weather with two cranky kids—I went to the bathroom and I broke down, crying my eyes out. Then, I came back out to the family room to find Adam screwing in the hook and hanging our first ever plant, the one in memory of my father, in the corner above our couch.

It reminded me why I love him so much.

The days following the news of my father's death, Adam naturally handled the boys and allowed me to slip away just to cry in my own space. He didn't force me to talk about my feelings but rather sat patiently waiting till I broke, and was there to catch my tears. Adam barely knows the complexity of my family history but had been a part of enough to feel quite a few slivers of it. He let me cry, he let me be angry, and he gave me the directive space to just breathe.

He's the reason I've chosen to rewrite my story, our story—so that our boys have a future full of pure love and not the heartache of the past I've had to endure. While I can't physically change my past, I can rewrite the narrative so they are told a different story, one with a little more light, not the depths of the ugliness I was made to believe my entire life.

And I'm certainly doing my best to write a more beautiful tomorrow for my children.

The mold had to be broken.

"Demons"

May 23, 2020, will now always be a day I can never forget. It was not the day my father's soul left this earth, nor was it the date the funeral home marked to the right side of the *dash* of his life—but it sure was the day that altered mine.

I held on to hope that maybe one day, maybe someday, I would be enough for my biological father to risk it all to reach out and make things right. At thirty-eight years old, that hope was gone. *How can I let go of the weight of an outcome I can never change?*

I couldn't forgive. I couldn't forget. All I could do was continually grieve for multiple decades of wrong doings. I didn't choose this. My brother didn't choose this. We were too young. Our lives were chosen for us, and we were ripped apart.

I couldn't help but struggle with the quite possible reality that I wasn't enough. Why wasn't I *enough*? I was a child. I had no choice, and even now, decades later, I'd discovered the things I was told were lies. My entire life growing up was a lie, in a sense, because it was driven by the intents of what was best for others, not myself. My life was based upon what benefited everyone but me and the control they needed in their own lives.

After my father's passing, I started finding out some truths from his side of the family; people who have been torn up for years that they didn't get to grow up knowing me. I found out my paternal grandparents actually won that court battle—which was just for the right to take me on vacation with them to Florida. But I was always told my parents won against their fight for "grandparents' rights." I learned that even after I was no longer coming around Melrose Park, my paternal grandmother, aka "the witch" as my mother called her, did something special for me every year on my birthday—just in case I happened to show up. And when it comes to my father, although it's not his words, I got a message that said "regardless of the shit show our family has been, I know he loved and thought of you often, so please take comfort in knowing that."

It had been twenty-seven years since I last saw my father—because I chose to always do right by my mother, never wanting to be the one to cause her the kind of pain I felt for decades. I couldn't hurt her by being the one to reach out to him, no matter how much I wanted to—I just couldn't do that to her. Even though I had written her off, I still respect the choices my mother made—and that's my damn fault. So, I never reached out to him—always holding on to hope that maybe one day he could, and that he would wake up, defy the demons of the past, and say, "Hey, my girl is worth it."

But I never was, and now it was too late.

The guilt I carry every day for never picking up the phone and making one single call is crushing most days. The weight of that on my heart is unbearable.

The guilt is heavy, as I sit here wondering if my loyalty to my mother and the pain I could have caused her outweighs this pain I now have to carry through the rest of my days.

And let me tell you, this pain fucking hurts. But that's why, as a mom, I will always do everything in my power to make the world a little less painful for my kids. Yes, they will feel pain, but I will carry as much of it as I have to so they don't ever know just how bad it can all hurt.

That is why this is by far the hardest hit of my life—I just needed one damn day. One day to just be with him. To just exist. To not have to say a thing, if he didn't want to, but just be in his presence as his grown-up baby girl who was now a wife, a mother, a TV/film producer, his daughter who grew up and who, I think, he would be really fucking proud of.

I'll never get one day.

If a relationship holds a weight on your heart, make it right—in the definition of what "right" means for you. Even if it terrifies you, I promise you what you will feel when that "one day" is no longer possible isn't worth the hurt that could come if you just took the chance—even if the outcome hurts more. You don't need to go to the extreme of face to face or disrupt your home life for the uncomfortableness of it all—just be sure you are the one who is writing your story.

In order to move on, I have to let go and forgive this part of the journey—and forgive myself for never trying to forgive until now.

Only problem is, I don't know how to begin to forgive.

And, I don't know how to let go.

But what really scares me—even though he didn't raise me—I'm terrified I'm more like my father than I know. Because I have his DNA—and his demons run through my soul.

"Head Above Water"

Four months after I got the call that my biological father was found dead, I found myself hunched over in pain. I was light-headed, and my body was overheating like a California wildfire. I could hear my baby boy screaming from his pack-n-play, while at the other end of the house, my four-year-old was sitting across from his ABA therapist just trying to push the "I" sound out of his mouth. I could also hear my best friend, Madison, talking to me through the faint sound of my iPhone, all while swiftly falling to the ground. I crashed down on my knees, and it felt as though daggers were stabbing me from the back of my right shoulder blade through my breast bone to the front of my chest. *I could hardly breathe.*

In this crippling moment, tears streaming down my face, I couldn't catch my breath. Somehow, Madison knew to stop her story to listen to my breathing, and said, "Nic, you're having a panic attack."

Through the pain, I tried to laugh it off because versions of this feeling (albeit, much milder ones) had become a recurring, daily pain over the last six months, and no one around me, not even my husband, said a thing toward acknowledging any of it. Yet there Madison was, 3,000 miles away, seeing what was really going on in my life—no one else had noticed, but she could *feel* it.

In an absolute fog, those words echoed through my mind, *Nic, you're having a panic attack…a panic attack…a panic attack,* as if I were Alice falling down the rabbit hole.

But then she followed up with, "I know because I've been there. You need to breathe."

Even with my baby crying, even with my toddler now having a meltdown with his therapist, I found myself in a physical position to mentally tell myself to just listen to Madison. *Shit, I need to breathe.*

But I couldn't.

The tightness on the right side of my chest got worse, the stabbing feeling intensified, and at that point, I didn't care about the therapist's protocol or what the CDC would say—I ripped that mask off my face and curled myself into our old wooden floors, finding myself in child's pose, sitting on my knees with my arms out in front of me, my back pushing into my stomach, toward the ground. I closed my eyes. Trying to drown out the noise, I took a quick but deep breath in.

As I breathed in, everything that had happened lately whizzed through my mind—the coronavirus pandemic, the protests over social injustice, the upcoming presidential election, having to probably disappoint my in-laws with canceling plans because of social distancing but seeing via social media other people doing whatever the fuck they wanted regardless of concerns for others, which certainly didn't align with my own little family's values, stressing about if my husband would send the email to quit the new gig he just got that was slowly killing him from stress, and he only took it because the pandemic hadn't been financially kind—wanting nothing more than to just give my sister, Demi, a hug, but I couldn't because of social distancing while being so annoyed from reading remarks from people on Facebook about how easy it was to get pregnant and now thinking of my babies I lost, and now I was forced to think about that time my mother blew up our entire family's history when she took to Facebook to expose hidden secrets, me no longer having my professional identity I worked so hard for, continually just feeling *lost*, why had men always made me feel like I was never enough? Am I never enough? Oh and, yeah, my biological father unexpectedly dying, and not hearing from my mother who I hadn't talked to in over four years now. Maybe Vick was right, maybe life couldn't be a fairy-tale. I couldn't fix the past, I couldn't fix anything. Wylder wouldn't talk because his older brother was "nonverbal," because Crosby has autism and there was not a damn thing in the world I could do to make things easier for him—and not just him, but also my husband who I was not able to give what he needed in life because I was just exhausted at this point and trying to hold on to not only my marriage but also my sanity, yet how could I give him what he needed when no one on this earth, including myself, was giving me a simple something for *me*?! Who was I even at this point?! *Fuck!* FUCK!

All of that ran through my mind in one simple moment between inhaling a breath and exhaling. And when I exhaled, I didn't feel any better.

"Just quiet your mind," Madison said, trying to help.

But I could not quiet my mind.

"I don't know how," I whispered. "It never stops."

"Nic, stay with me. Keep breathing. You can do it," she said.

I didn't believe her, but I tried—and I breathed. And then I breathed again.

It was at that moment I realized that I was not Alice falling down the rabbit hole toward Wonderland. I was Nicole, climbing out of the rabbit hole and waking up to the reality of my life.

"Out of My Head"

We get to a point sometimes when we can no longer just handle it all, no matter how strong we are. That day was not my darkest point; but it was my breaking point, and it became a day I will never forget. I thought it would be another typical, *nontypical* afternoon—yet I found myself face down in child's pose, surrendering to life and what the universe had been trying to tell me.

For years and years and years, I had been carrying the weight of the world on my back. I couldn't easily just let things go and, instead, was carrying everything—the good and the bad—with me. And worse, I had been living by what others had wanted and expected of me for nearly my entire life. *Life* had made me anxious. It was at that moment I knew...

Something had to change.

I had to change.

Life had to change.

This was the universe saying to me, *Wake up, Nicole!* The spot on my back where I felt those stabbing feelings over and over had now become an invisible tattoo. I carried the pain with me every day, and when the anxiety creeped in, I knew exactly the spot it was going to trigger. That spot right there on the lower left side of my right shoulder blade, a translucent scar I wore that no one but me could see.

I don't mean to speak in terms of everyone in the world but I also, personally, don't know a single person who hasn't, at some point in their life, had a moment where they knew their life needed to change. The more we experience, the more we worry, the more we question. We begin to think at even deeper levels than the deep levels we previously claimed to be thinking at. As we grow older, we grow to be a constant juxtaposition of our own selves. We think we're "okay" just coasting as we've been doing, yet a louder voice in our mind is screaming at us that it's time to change. And when these two personalities, these two sides, these two parts of us clash—well, I guess that is when we get our wake-up call. For me, that was in the form of a massive panic attack.

As I came back to myself and found my breath, as I realized things needed to change, something clicked. That moment made me reflect on all of my past, it made the present clearer, and it made me rethink my tomorrow. Let me correct myself there—it made me rethink *our* tomorrow.

During that panic attack when I took that short breath in, all those worries I described just rushed in. I didn't even give you all of them, but just enough to feel the heaviness of it all. Holding onto all that pain all those years of my life up until that point, got me to a crippling moment where I could hardly breathe. Admitting all of that was just the beginning. But that's just it, only the beginning. *Just the admitting.*

There was no fixing anything at that moment. I was carrying nearly forty years worth of life experiences on me, never having let any of it go. In a perfect world it would be nice to say I had one specific moment where I had a major awakening and knew life needed to change and it did. Or I convinced myself I wasn't enough then changed that narrative. Or I decided to live for myself for once instead of the expectations of others. But a lot of the emotional experiences we go through in life are not one-time things. As we continually grow into the person we are becoming in different seasons of life, sure the hope is we take the lessons of the past and do the work to become a truer version of ourselves—but life isn't this linear course where something happens once and you're like "check that emotional box off." As we evolve and grow, we're going to cycle back to some of these emotions again. And where I was wrong most of my life, was thinking I made the changes but I actually never did. Because in order to truly change, you have to do the work to heal the past. I've never healed my past. So how could I change?

On the floor, surrendering to life—that was the moment I finally saw from an eagle-eye perspective the things that were leading me deeper into the shadows of my life.

It was during this panic attack that I realized I had been held down by an unbearable weight, the weight of my entire life I was choosing to carry. A weight that made it hard to breathe at times, especially in this moment. I would think a breaking point would be my awakening moment to force me to grab hold of the light and finally make the choice to change my life.

But my light had already dimmed so much by this point that the only thing this moment did for me was send me straight into the darkness.

The depths to which I began to feel I was drowning weren't the lowest point of all—I could still get bursts of air. What this was, was the beginning of the storm. And I was already deep in the spiral.

GARY

"No Hard Feelings"

I think the hardest things we have to go through in this life are those moments we never see coming, those moments we could have never planned for. I credit my husband to being the one who always miraculously seems to hold it all together even when the world starts falling apart. Until the day his did.

On Sunday, April 11, 2021, nearly a year after my father died, I woke up exhausted. Adam had been up late watching TV in the family room, and I was in our bed with Wylder, but I was having crazy, disruptive dreams. I found myself awake around 2:00 a.m. just sitting up in bed, disturbed and confused. Wylder was also having a restless night and kept waking himself up and crying out of the blue. So, I was up like every thirty minutes that night, continually in and out of sleep, which is not normal for me, nor a toddler who typically slept soundly for eleven hours at night.

After finally falling asleep for a stint longer than thirty minutes and looking at the clock, hoping that Wylder would maybe sleep in after a restless night, I kept hearing Adam's phone go off. Just before 7:00 a.m. our time, his phone finally startled him in such a way he got up and checked it, but then he did something he'd never done— answered it while still in bed and, without hesitation, jumped up.

At this point, we had been together for over seven and a half years, and I had never, ever once seen him frantically get out of bed like this, unless there was an earthquake. In a single flash, he disappeared from the bedroom. I sat there wide-eyed, unsure if I should get up, confused about what was happening, delirious from no sleep. After about ten minutes, I walked out of the room, through the hallway, across our dining room, into the kitchen, and opened up the back door, where I saw Adam abruptly turn toward me, mouthing something. I couldn't hear his voice—and all I could see was the river of tears streaming down his face.

My husband is not a crier. I can count on two hands the number of times in our relationship that I've seen him break down and cry. Even with all the scares and losses we'd experienced in life, I had never once seen him cry like this.

He looked me in the eyes and said, "*Gary...*"

I was so confused. Why was he jumping out of bed, acting like this, crying nonstop, and mentioning *Gary*?

His response to my puzzled face as his eyes swelled with more tears was, "...is dead."

And he choked up and broke down, turning away from me.

It was as if a tidal wave was coming at me from every direction. I had no clue which way to turn or whether to jump up or dip below and hold my breath or just let it wash me away. My father dying might have been my hardest hit thus far, but this, this was bad—like really, really, *really* bad.

My husband just found out his best friend was dead.

Do I go outside and hug him? Do I go inside and go lay back in bed and just wait? What was I supposed to do, knowing I couldn't fix this? How do I navigate this? Fuck, what is happening?

I just froze. All I could think about was our restless night—while it was still very early that Sunday morning in Indy when *Gary* died, Adam was still awake the night before here in L.A. *Gary's* soul was passing from this earth and here we were, awake, but unable to do a damn thing to help him.

That night, I was so worried about Adam. A state of worry so deep, I was terrified to leave him alone. I knew what he needed more than anything was to escape this new reality, so instead of going to sleep after an emotional day, I stayed up with him. His surviving the darkness pretty much depended on me doing so. That night, we didn't talk much—we drank and listened to music, which consisted mostly of Staind and Fleetwood Mac. At one point, Adam said to me, "This is what *Gary* would have wanted. This is exactly what *Gary* would have fucking wanted."

Gary's death was a big blow. It was one of those hits that shatter you, one of the real "you don't come back from this" moments in life—*Gary* wasn't just Adam's best friend; he was the *brother* life chose for him. He was to Adam what Madison is to me. Adam didn't just lose his best friend that day; he lost a piece of his heart.

I knew I couldn't fix this one for him, but I could do everything possible to help his heart hopefully hurt a little less.

Up to this point, we hadn't traveled during the pandemic—but there was no way we weren't getting on a plane to be there in person and celebrate *Gary's* life.

"Forever Young"

My husband is an introvert who doesn't ever want to command the attention of the room; he's the guy who holds his cards close to his chest. But the day of *Gary's* "Celebration of Life" back in Indy, Adam was the first one to grab the microphone and speak of his best friend.

Wearing a black Incubus T-shirt from their high school days and black hat that simply said "GARY," I stood in the back, holding our boys and started crying at the sight of him so bravely standing before this massive crowd. And when he spoke—there wasn't a dry eye under that tent.

"*Gary* wasn't a friend to me. He was, literally, a brother. I've known him my entire life. This was a hard, hard hit. And ugh, he never met my son before. In fact, at Justin's wedding, he runs up to my wife and grabs my child out of her arms and holds him all night—like he was his own. Just those little moments. I think it was the trust with *Gary*. I trusted him with my life. Everything you experience growing up together—we did it every fucking step of the way.

There's not going to be a day that goes by that I don't think of him. I'm not a religious guy by any means, but I feel *Gary* all the time now. And, I love that. I wish he could have met my other little boy—so he could have been in his presence. Cuz he was a special guy. A very, very special guy."

For a guy who usually keeps his feelings locked up—those words hit deep.

After Wylder threw up warm milk all over one of my husband's childhood friends, everyone under that tent went outside in the open air, grabbed a hold of a white balloon with the words, "You are loved. You are missed. You are remembered," written on each one, and together, we released them into the air in honor of *Gary*.

We all just stood there, watching the balloons float away, slowly becoming tiny specs against the clouds.

As I could see others heading back inside to grab another drink, I stayed in this moment for a bit longer than everyone else. I stared at the clouds and the balloons flying toward them—and I thought about my father for a moment. And as I stood there watching the balloons float towards the clouds, I felt the sun shining down and couldn't help but feel a small sense of peace; perhaps my father was actually, finally, truly watching over me and if he was, may he take care of *Gary* for us all. And if they were together, may they pour one out for all of us down here just trying to do our best at living this thing called life.

Every single piece of what *Gary's* closest friends and family did that day was to honor a tremendous heart gone too soon. He was a good man who loved others with everything he had. It's a damn shame the darkness took his light.

Gary, may we continue to find ways to keep your spirit alive, and wherever you are, may you watch over all of us. Because we sure as hell need you to. And, we love you.

The death of Adam's best friend hit us hard. What I didn't prepare for was how losing *Gary* would change our marriage. In some ways, it made us stronger, but in other ways, it pushed us further apart.

As tragedy often brings our own demons to the surface, the days and months following were not easy for our marriage. Adam started taking his heartbreak, guilt and grief out on me, and I started to see him pulling away from the kids and me. While I couldn't possibly understand the pain my husband was personally feeling, I understood that in the hardest of times, you lash out at the ones closest to you. And while it wasn't okay how he had started treating me, I had to be okay with carrying his pain—because if I wasn't the one to do so, I didn't know if he would rise up from this life-altering blow.

The sobering reality is—it's in the most devastating losses that we must be reminded that life is just too short to continue going down the same path.

If there was any hope for us to make it out of these dark times, we needed to listen to the wake-up calls the universe had been giving us.

But we didn't, and I found myself spiraling toward the darkest part of the darkness.

"Trying My Best"

The night after *Gary's* celebration of life in Indy, it was after 10 p.m. and we had to be up at three o'clock in the morning to make our flight back to California.

We were at Adam's grandma's house. I had all the suitcases laid out in her family room, clothes spread out everywhere, I was trying to figure out which snacks to bring with us, which snacks to leave for the cousins, making sure two iPads, two tablets, two computers, four portable chargers and Crosby's "Chat," which is the device he communicates through, all of that was plugged in and trying to wrangle two overly tired kids who were still awake, crying for snacks, demanding their devices, emotionally spinning around and around—while everyone else was sitting around watching *American Idol*, and I was getting no help. Don't get me wrong, I was rooting for Chayce to win the whole season, but it felt like I was on the fucking Tilt-A-Whirl all by myself and no one could see the vomiting-inducing situation I was in.

This reality caused more tension and bickering between my husband and me. He thought I should just flat out tell him what to do, but I also wanted him to be the father and husband I knew he was and just *see* the entirety of the situation we were under after a super emotional week without having to slap him upside the head because he was just sitting among the chaos cracking jokes via text with friends, who he had just left a couple hours ago, signing off into *Adam's World*. It was the "I want you to want to do the dishes" moment—but no one ever wants to fucking do the dishes, nor does anyone ever want to willingly jump into the storm if they can stay dry inside and watch from the window.

Everyone in that room was dry—except for me.

Look, I know how emotional Adam was after coming face to face with his best friend's death and the rush of emotions from the past few days in Indy. I was the one person living it with him every single day since we got that call over a month prior. If he had come to me and asked me to just handle it all because he was struggling, that would have been one thing. But he didn't, and he was lying on his stomach cracking jokes with his childhood friends, completely losing sight of his responsibilities in life. I had given him the benefit of the doubt over and over again in his time of grief. But this was ridiculous—so, yeah, I was a little pissed.

In moments like this, I can see how women claim they have to "train" their men to be the way they want them to be. But my husband is not a dog, and if I had that kind of energy, we'd get a real one.

I needed off this damn emotional roller coaster, and the only way to do so was to flat out tell Adam to look around. I could have been a bitch and barked at him, demanding what I wanted him to do, but I didn't. I chose a gentler approach, which still caused a scene when I said, "Get off your phone. Do you not see what's going on in front of you? Do you not see the massive amount of shit that still needs to be done to get us ready to be at the airport in five hours from now? Your children are still up and losing their damn minds—and you're sitting there on your phone cracking jokes with *The Dipshits*. Fucking help me. *Please.*"

Adam walked out of the room. *He can be really fucking moody when he wants to be.* So, I was left with the tension in the room and the burning question if Chayce was going to win *American Idol.*

I stayed unreactive for a moment. I just closed my eyes and took a deep breath as my attempt to try and hold back the tears from the overwhelming amount of emotions inside of me. Because while we were all dealing with the pain of losing *Gary* in real-time, I was also battling the internal pain of my father's death—which I got the call about exactly one year ago to that day. No one in that room remembered to think about that, especially not my husband.

I wiped the few tears that managed to escape and went up to Adam's mom and grandma. I apologized for getting upset and frustrated. It was an emotional week, I was sleep deprived, I thought I was going to have more help those past few days, but I was once again doing most of it on my own—including being my husband's emotional support. And I was exhausted. With time running out before our flight, suitcases not packed, kids still awake, and no one looking at me thinking to help me—I believe many women in my situation would have felt my emotions were justified. Really, the apology was me begging for a way for someone just to *see* me at that moment. But, the response I got was:

> Mother-in-law: "I always pack for (her husband). Always. On every trip."

> Grandmother-in-law: "I always packed for (her husband)."

I shook my head in more frustration, trying not to once again have the urge to just scream it all out and, instead, walked out of the room. This wasn't about packing for my husband. He's a grown-ass man and can pack his own suitcase. This was about my husband, the father of my young children who have a lot of extra needs, preferring to lie on his ass, texting his friends and editing photos from the weekend and just bullshitting around instead of saying, "Hey, I should *help* my wife because this family is my responsibility too," when we had a countdown of hours until we had to be up, and I was over here freaking drowning, and there were other adults in the room and not one of them saw the reality happening in front of them to offer to help me.

I'm the mom. I'm the wife. It's on me to do it all—always.

That was what was *expected* of me.

But don't worry—as always, I got it all taken care of.

And yes, Chayce won *American Idol.*

"That's The Kind Of Woman"

It can be an overwhelming burden to feel compelled to meet the societal ideals and standards assigned to women.

I'm married, yes—therefore, I am a wife.

I have children, yes—therefore, I am a mother.

My husband chose to marry me for who I am, not for conforming to someone else's beliefs of how our life should be.

He put a ring on my finger. A *Mrs.* was put in front of my name. And I became *his wife.* But what people forget is there's *my* life too beyond all of that. I don't exist simply because I married a man and I'm *his wife.* I have a life too—and it matters. I'm a person too—and I matter. I love with every ounce of my being—just not in the way societal pressure expects me to do so.

A good friend of ours once said to me, "If you let Adam come get drinks with us for my birthday (this night), then he will *babysit* so you can come to the gathering (the next night) for my other birthday thing." Let me say this—my husband will never babysit our children. Ever. Because he is not a babysitter. He is their father, and it is his responsibility to organically help take care of and *parent* his own kids. It is not solely my responsibility, simply because I am Mom. He doesn't provide some *babysitting* relief, as if he's getting paid to do so and is not equally responsible for them in this partnership. I know our friend did not mean for her choice of word to come across that way, but it did and it really triggered me because it was yet another example of how society tries to define what a woman's "role" is in the world or, rather, what is expected of *her*—the mom, the wife, the daughter. And sometimes it's exhausting trying to keep up with the expectations that come along with being a woman.

So, no, I will never, ever let my husband babysit our children. Rather, I will co-parent our children *with* my husband and live our life the way we promised one another, as partners in it together—*us against the world*.

And sometimes it makes me sad for my husband, that he didn't marry the kind of woman who is okay just being defined by the *Mrs.* version of him. Someone who goes to the extreme to present a "perfect" image to the world of a life that isn't real. Someone who is okay just slaving her life away on her hands and knees but feels some kind of ounce of worth when her arm is wrapped in his. Someone who takes care of it all behind the scenes, while he basks in the light. But that's not who I am. He married someone extremely independent, who has a voice of her own, who has dreams and goals bigger than he even knows of, who never had to rely on another person for anything, who may not present this idea of a "picture-perfect wife" to the world—but who doesn't have to hide behind a false reality, who isn't afraid to just look like a hot mess, because at least I'm being real. And yeah, a lot of times our toilets aren't sparkling and our clean laundry baskets sit there for a few extra days, but I'm in it with him, equally as me. That's who I am.

And he knows who he married—even though sometimes I wonder if he prefers his life to be a little easier having married someone willing to just be okay playing the part. I know he wouldn't, but the expectations of others surely put doubt in my mind. A lot of times the noise makes me feel like I'm failing him as a wife, like I'm failing my kids as a mom—regardless if the person I'm actually failing is myself, in the moments I try to convince myself maybe I should be someone other than me just to play the part—to be who others want me to be.

At times I wish I could, but I just can't be that woman. Actually, it's not that I can't be. I just don't want to be. I spent most of my life being an actor. I'm done playing some role in life that isn't true to who I am.

The problem is—I don't always know how to live that authentic life without disappointing everybody else. So, a lot of times I just end up disappointing myself at least trying to play the role others wanted to see, even though inside it was killing me.

The weight of the expectations others had been putting on me my entire life—since that crown was first placed on my head and being told I had to be a good girl and a good wife and a good mother and to always please others and do what others wanted me to do because I was told my voice didn't matter and I would never be enough nor anything more than the limits others put on me and I was far from this external image of *perfection*—I was carrying well over thirty years of emotional baggage on me and the weight of it all became an unbearable heaviness to live with. So heavy that it finally pushed me straight into the absolute darkest time in my life.

"We Belong"

A week after we got back from *Gary*'s Celebration of Life, I had an unexpected health scare that really shook me up. My husband had just lost his best friend, and as I laid on the cold operating table, the thought that came to my mind was, *He can't lose me too.* As I closed my eyes and whispered, "Please get me through this. My boys need me," a single tear streamed down my left cheek. The nurse grabbed hold of my hand and started rubbing it to comfort me, while an oxygen mask was placed over my face. As she kept holding my hand, she said, "You're gonna be okay, Momma. You're gonna be okay."

I have to be okay.

When I opened my eyes, I was in a hospital room, and Adam was by my side. I hadn't seen him this worried about me in a long time. He grabbed my hand and said, "You scared me." With tears welling up in his eyes, he whispered, "I can't do this life without you."

I promised him, "I'm not going anywhere."

Later that night, I was doing my fart laps after having emergency appendicitis surgery. Yes, "fart laps" are a thing, and since I was on the gastro floor, it was just our mutual awareness that every person in their hospital gown, pulling their IV cart with one hand while holding their gown closed with the other, was doing circles because we had one mission—to fart, because farts meant things were beginning to properly work in there again after your insides got shifted around during surgery.

I thought about how I should have been taking advantage of this glorified "quiet time," even with the pain I was in, but the reality was I couldn't sleep. I was struggling with missing my boys. It was Memorial Day weekend, so I understood things could take longer, but my boys needed me, and I needed to be home, even in the chaos I knew home was. Life was writing me a permission slip to take the few days I needed for me, to heal my body and recharge—and I couldn't take it. I couldn't exist in that kind of calm. I had become a master of living a life that was *calm in the chaos*. I didn't know how to exist without it.

Before getting discharged, my surgeon called, and she gave me a pretty serious warning. She said, "I want to let you know that on your MRI results, I also noticed a few decent-sized kidney stones on each one of them. They're small enough to probably pass on their own, but I want you to take extra care of yourself; especially after the surgery you just had. I know you have young children at home, but for at least three days, you need to not pick your kids up or strain your abdominal muscles. You really need to rely on other people to help you so that you can heal properly."

I got home from the hospital, and when I looked around, I was right back in it—no time to heal, as my doctor told me I needed to do. Mom was home, so everything would be *okay*.

My stepdad texted me, asking if I was home safe. I said, "Yep. Back home, back in full swing with everyone needing everything from me, even though my doctor told me to be sure to rest for a few days."

His text back was "That's what mothers do."

That's what mothers do.

"*Live Forever*"

A few months after I had my emergency appendicitis surgery, Adam was out of town and I was alone to handle the house, the kids and my new TV show I thankfully was able to be working on remotely. The day was an emotional one—Crosby was learning a brand new program so his frustrations were high, Wylder was in the early stages of potty training and was throwing tantrums with his bare butt in the air because he refused to put his underwear on by himself, I was scrambling to rework an entire storyline and get my editor what he needed but with all the chaos of the kids' stuff happening around me, and my office in the tiny corner of our dining room, there was no separating any one person's emotions from the other.

It was getting toward the end of the boys' sessions for the night when all hell just broke loose in my house. I was trying to get dinner cooked so they could start eating before their therapists left, Crosby was trying to be vocal but often times the sounds he pushed out would be triggering for Wylder, so Wylder started losing his damn mind, screaming and crying in absolute hysterics because of his brother; to then which Crosby started losing his damn mind, screaming and crying in absolute hysterics because Wylder was doing so in response to him—all the while I was running in and out of the kitchen taking care of their foods while dodging the phone calls that kept coming in from my boss and my editor. I waved off their two therapists and told them to have a good night and for about the next five minutes I kept running around in circles; my body completely out of sorts with my mind, listening to both of my kids still having full blown tantrum meltdowns. Wylder grabbed his plate and chucked it across the table towards Crosby because he was upsetting him so bad, which only upset Crosby even more. That's when I stopped and finally noticed I wasn't alone in the house with the kids. Their supervisor was still standing there.

Holding back the tears I knew I had to control, I said to her, "Wait. You're in overtime. It's after six o'clock, you have to go." And she looked me dead in the eyes and said, "Nicole. There is absolutely no way I am leaving you alone in this situation." She used her hand to gesture around the room, wanting me to acknowledge the reality of my life. Then she said, "This... this is a lot. Like, a lot. And I know you can handle a lot but I'm not just going to walk out of here and leave you like this. There's no way."

And I broke down crying.

She told me to go take some deep breaths, while she sat with the boys and tried to calm them.

I walked to my bedroom and emotionally collapsed. She was the only person to ever see that much of our real life, and the only person to ever acknowledge any part of it enough to tell me to go breathe. She handled my hard for me that day because she knew I was going to break if she didn't.

Their supervisor loved my kids and our family so much that she would go out of her way to do small things to make sure we were always just a little more than *okay*. I know I claim I never had "a village," in terms of this massive support system I could rely on to help and be there all the time and in any way possible, but if there was anything close to a tiny existence of one—it was her. I couldn't have navigated those years of therapies, a pandemic and the boys' lives if it weren't for her, being there for our family in ways she wasn't obligated to do. She was like a living angel that gave me a flicker of hope in what started to become the absolute darkest of times.

While the boys' supervisor helped diffuse what could have been emotional destruction in our home that day—I went to bed that night anything but okay. And as I laid in my bed with my two boys finally, peacefully sleeping next to me, I drank a glass of wine and the deep thoughts that came to my mind proved I was anything but all right.

"Lonely"

These were the thoughts I wrote that night:

People are always telling me I'm Superwoman. They can't understand how I do it all!

While I light-heartedly say I had become the superhero of my story and had to become indestructible for my little family—the truth is, I sacrifice everything. Not one thing gets even 50 percent of my energy and attention. I'm told what an amazing mom I am, yet I feel like I'm failing them. I'm praised on my TV show for being damn good at what I do, yet I feel like I'm doing far from my best. I try to do all the things a wife is supposed to do, yet every day I fall short of those expectations. I tell myself, "Nicole, tomorrow you will do better"—yet every single day, I fail myself. I'm spread so thin. And as many people by now have told me, "Nicole, this is a lot—like, *a lot* for anyone to handle," what am I supposed to do? It's my life—and I need it all. Yet, I don't know if there's a way to balance it all without making sacrifices. *Usually at the expense of my mental and physical health.*

This is my one wild and precious, *amazing crazy* life, and I'm the one chosen to hold it all together. No one else could hold this together. No one else can do what I do. No one else can fool the world into thinking it's all under control—that I can be a wife and a momma to two young kids with special needs and a sister and a daughter and a friend all while being a damn good producer, with no village and no hired help, and in this carousel of life, I try to be myself yet default to doing what is often times just expected of me by others because, literally, the thought of disappointing someone else is more exhausting than just meeting their expectations. The worst part is, even if people get an inside look into this reality, they only see a glimpse. A glimmer. A tiny ray of the sunlight peeking in through an overcast sky. They only see what I allow them to see: "a lot" or "too much" or "more than one person can handle." Yet, that glimpse is nothing compared to our full reality. "It's a lot," I'm told by many people. Yes, it's a lot, but it's my life.

Please, nothing can happen to me.

"Good Job"

I looked over to my sleeping boys, ran my hand over Crosby's head, kissed Wylder on his cheek, took a few sips of my wine, and then continued writing my thoughts:

> The only thing I have control over anymore that I feel I can hold on to is choosing whether or not to pour that glass of wine. *That's all I can control.* That choice, regardless of the consequences.

> I can't quiet my mind enough to meditate at night—there's no hope in that. Some people smoke a bowl. Others shop online. Many brew a cup of tea. Others watch too much TV, or porn. You may sit there and do a puzzle, or spend hours gaming away or trading cards online. Everyone needs something. Some form of escape. I can't just go for a run and get fresh air at ten o'clock at night when I've got two small kids and some crazy coyotes and homeless people lurking in my "beautiful" Burbank streets. I can't just pick up the phone and call someone because when my brain just needs a moment to itself, a phone call usually becomes about someone else. Some people scroll social media as their escape, but that only adds to the negativity in my life at this point in time.

> So yeah, I have my nightcap, which leads to another, and sometimes another—because that's my moment for me; that's my escape. Even though I know every ounce of me is probably suffering for it. *I know.*

The excuse has become to numb the pain, to mask the *hard parts* of life as though I'm just putting another fucking Band-Aid over yet another fucking wound—to see this night through hoping to see the sunrise, hoping that tomorrow will give us a fresh start. The sun always rises, but the nights always turn dark. There's no village. I'm Super Mom. I can—I must—handle it all. Others placed the "I come from a long line of strong, independent women" label on my back, so even if I break— the world knows I can get back up. Because it's what I have to do. Even if everything is crumbling around me—*Nicole, get back up.*

Sometimes I don't want to get back up. I just want to lie here and cry. I just want someone to notice. I just want someone to reach their hand out and pull me up out of this *hard part*—without for once having to be the hand to do it myself. But there is no one doing that. It's like a pier full of people watching me struggle to catch my breath in the middle of the ocean, but no one is throwing me a life raft. So I take a drink. I numb the pain just enough to grab hold of my own hand and pull myself back up—just like I did that day in the Grand Canyon.

I'm pretty sure Superwoman had a hidden flask or some microdosing pills hidden in that gold belt of hers because there's absolutely no way anyone, superhero or not, could handle it all without some form of escape. And sadly, junk food and trashy television isn't my thing.

Yet, even in the lowest of lows, the hardest of hards, the darkest of dark nights when I don't know how I can possibly keep going, I look over at my beautiful boys sleeping peacefully.

Wylder will suddenly stir and just wrap his arms around me while off in dreamland, or Crosby will pull me into him, holding on to me as though life depended on it. And I want nothing more than those baby cuddles because no matter how hard life is on the daily basis, no matter the extent to which my life is *a lot*, no matter how much I have to grieve the idea of a "typical" life for the beauty of a non-typical one, no matter that no one will ever truly understand any of it, even though they expect me to think of their situations first—that pull, that hug, that snuggle and cuddle is the best thing in the world. Somehow, even without a drink, even without an escape—my boys make all the hard all right.

I've just finally realized… I don't need to be Super Mom.

I just need to be all right.

"Shallow"

About a month after that night, Adam and I hit our lowest point in the eight years we had been together thus far.

My husband has stopped seeing me, I said to myself.

As I stared at the chipped painted ceiling with my body halfway between the old wooden floors in our hallway and the cold tile in the boys' bathroom, I thought to myself, *Is this what it feels like to die alone?*

At that moment, I couldn't help but think of my father. And of *Gary*. All I could feel around me was death. And while I knew I would get through this moment, it was inside of me that felt I was dying.

It wasn't COVID-19; it was a flu worse than any flu I'd ever experienced, and it was ripping through our home. Crosby and I spent ten minutes throwing up in the same bucket, Wylder throwing up all over his sheets, and me. My body was so weak, but my only priority was to take care of them—to get them content enough to just sleep. *Because that is what Mom is supposed to do.* Adam was pissed at me for wrapping the puke-soaked bedsheets up and throwing them in the wash, but I was so sick myself, if I didn't just do what my fainting body was capable of doing, I didn't know how we would get through this. Yet, even in my own sickness, I had to find grace because I knew how bad my husband was still grieving the loss of his best friend.

I finally got the kids to sleep for enough moments that I was able to escape their room. That's when I find myself lying on the floor, halfway between their bathroom and the hallway. The floor was cold; it felt good there. My throat was so dry I needed water, but I knew if I took a single sip of water, I was going to throw up. Yet, if I got up off the floor and laid back in bed with Wylder, I knew it would all come rushing out the other end. I was that sick. So, on the coldness I laid—half on wood, half on tile.

That's when it happened.

My husband came walking into the hallway to go into our room and pee—and just stepped over me. My body, lying on the ground so sick, and he just stepped over me.

He's stopped seeing me.

By the time he finished his business, he walked past me on the way back to the family room, and I laid there, still staring at the ceiling. Not sure which way to move, so I just laid there. Alone.

Moments passed, and I could hear the audio resume on the Netflix comedy special he had been watching. I heard his laughter echoing through our tiny home from the other room. He was laughing, and I was just trying to make it through this horrific night—wondering at what point one of the kids would awaken and start throwing up again, panicked because I was down to one clean towel left in the house that I could swap out a soiled one with. Because that's what my job was, right? That's what everyone always says—even when you're sick, even when you're in pain, even when your husband is physically fine in the other room yet you are just praying the last vomiting-while-shitting incident for you and both your babies was the last time it would happen—it's Mom's job to just "handle it all." *And I'm Mom.*

It was taking every ounce of me not to get sick again, so I just laid still on that cold floor, staring at that old sunken ceiling, hearing the laughter of my husband coming from the other room at one o'clock in the morning. A sad thought came to my mind, and I couldn't help but wonder, *Is this what it felt like for Gary, before his life was taken too soon? Is this what it felt like for my father to die alone?*

As I laid on that floor, so sick, and my husband just walked over me, I knew that he had started not seeing me. He had become consumed with his phone, his texts and Instagram chain with his other best friends, Justin and Matt. Instead of giving his attention to his family, his attention was going toward everyone else. Our marriage got to a bad place, not because of them or their love of *Gary*, but because of what Adam couldn't see—my pain.

This was the moment in my life I could feel the closest I had ever felt to death and as I closed my eyes and took a deep breath, hoping to once again not get sick, I could hear a whisper in my ear that was so profound it really shook me up. It was my inner-knowing— just wanting to speak and be heard. And *she* said:

Most people are just living to die. Here I am, just dying to live.

I think that whisper was the true *me* that was in there, still alive and begging to be set free.

Obviously, I didn't die that night—but I felt so fucking invisible.

"Rise Up"

A few days after the kids and I were finally healthy again, I spoke the truth Adam didn't want to hear. With tears pouring down from my eyes, I told him I was sorry.

> "I'm sorry. I'm sorry that I can't bring *Gary* back. He's gone, and I can't do anything to fix that for you. I can't even begin to understand that pain for you because when I think of the alternative, had I lost Madison—I can't even think of that. So I am so sorry. But what you're not seeing is that in losing *Gary*, in not being able to save him, you've ever since so tightly held on to Justin and Matt because you're so damn afraid of losing another best friend. All you've been doing is giving them all your attention, completely ignoring your family. And if you don't wake up and realize how you've been living, especially not giving these kids what they need from their dad—or just stepping over my body as I lie so sick on the floor by myself scared how I'm going to make it through the night—if you don't wake up and realize how you've been living, one day you're going to look up and we will be gone. Because we deserve so much more than what you've been giving us—which is nothing."

It wasn't an ultimatum; it was just me telling him the truth—he was holding on so tightly to what he couldn't change, while letting the family we created slip away before his unawakened eyes.

The easier thing would be to not share any part of this, but this is one of those pieces that is too important not to share. Grief affects us all, and we all experience it in different ways. We can let guilt and sadness consume us, which we have certainly done with losing *Gary*. However, there's also a turning point when you will be able to smile for the first time, seeing the beauty in life again. One day, you will feel gratitude for the blessing of having someone in your life for the time that you did. One day, you will decide to move past overwhelming grief and come back to your life—and, if needed, take care of your sick wife and children.

While I wish I could say that is the truth of our story through this great loss, we're not there yet. At this point of our story, there was no resolving anything. Life just revolved over the course of a grieving husband's wife writing some of the stories of her life, during the height of a pandemic—and I can't write about healing that hasn't happened yet. The pain is still very deep, very real, and I see it affect my husband every day.

In a perfect editorial world of life, I'd have a great solution for you on how we got through this and life just somehow got better or moved on to greener pastures. But that's not how life works, and that's not how I've chosen to write this book series. It's a journey. As I stared into my husband's eyes and told him, "If you don't wake up and realize how you've been living, one day you're going to look up and we will be gone," that was when I started to see the truth of our reality, if we didn't change *our* lives, our life as a family—we weren't going to make it through the darkness.

There was no way it could change overnight. I knew that. Grief this deep doesn't just get better. I knew I could continue to take on the emotional burden, knowing that this wasn't going to heal right away, but believing at some point in time it would. Because I love him that much, and I know how important this family is to him. While it may work for some people, for us, there was no magical pill to pop to numb this one, and a Band-Aid certainly wasn't going to do that job. We were so inside of our own minds and pain that the only thing we could think to do was wrap a few layers of a thick, elastic bandage over the emotional wound, giving us just enough support to not hurt so bad but keep pushing forward, *for now*, trying to do better and be more present with each other, even with the pain there every single day.

I know the day will come when we need to take that bandage wrap off and really clean out the wounds, and it's going to hurt like hell. But that day just isn't today.

Grief doesn't just go away because the world expects you to no longer feel it. Grief is a journey every individual experiences differently. While the grief, anxiety, expectations, fears, stress and absolute overwhelm of life is still on my back and in my heart daily, I have to find an ounce of gratitude in this dark time.

Because, well, at least I woke up today—not everyone did.

And because of that, I have no choice but to hold onto hope and believe that even in the darkest times when it's hard to see the light, I have to believe and hold onto that hope. Because I also know—there are diamonds beneath the darkness.

SIX.

The Storm

STAY THE COURSE

"Imagine"

When I was ten years old, competing for that crown, a small piece that was required of us was coming up with a motto, an idea that we wanted to stand for and that would represent who we each were to the world. It wasn't fully original because every aspiring queen had to finish the sentence, "Believe in yourself...," as that was the pageant's theme. Mine came pretty easy to me, and my motto became:

"Believe in yourself... and your dreams will come true!"

Look at you, ten-year-old me—something so simple, and yet so powerful! Yet this is definitely something we forget along our journeys in life. The harder things get, the more that's drained out of us, the more we stop dreaming, and we stop believing. However, I was right—the only way to make our dreams come true is by believing they will. And that starts with believing in ourselves.

Richard Linklater's *Waking Life* was one of my favorite movies in college. I was fascinated with it. The movie poses the question: "Dreams. What are they? An escape from reality or reality itself?" What I appreciate with this film is it doesn't give us an answer; it is up to us to determine and seek out those answers for who we are as individuals. Our dreams are personal to our own beings. And so, how can anyone expect our dreams to take on the shape of theirs?

But sadly, people *do* expect you to want what they want you to want, and if you dare share your own dreams, they are not always supported. People can't always separate their projected wants for your life from your own desires.

One of my absolute favorite quotes from *Waking Life* is, "Things have been tough lately for dreamers. They say dreaming is dead; no one does it anymore. It's not dead; it's just that it's been forgotten, removed from our language. Nobody teaches it, so nobody knows it exists. The dreamer is banished to obscurity. Well, I'm trying to change all that—and I hope you are too. By dreaming, every day. Dreaming with our hands and dreaming with our minds."

I have a tattoo on the back of my neck, in my handwriting, that says, "Dare to Dream." Yet, all these years later, I had forgotten how to do that—dream.

It was one night shortly after I had that massive panic attack during the pandemic that my husband and I were making small talk as the kids were settling down, and really out of nowhere, I said, "What are our future goals? What are *our* future dreams?"

He sat quiet for a moment, and then said, "I'm good. I'm good, just (hand gesture in a kinda straight line) coasting."

Well, that was not true. I know my husband better than anyone. *Don't tell my mother-in-law I said that.* If I had never seen the *dreamer* in him, I may never have married him because since day one, we have talked of dreams, many, many of them. But the reality of life as-is had kicked in. We have the responsibility of a huge overhead every month that needs to be paid for. We have two young boys with special needs and that gets a lot of our focus, energy, and resources. We have a production company with a slate of original projects that are all in different stages of development, yet we constantly push them to the side because our "work" time needs to go to the freelance jobs we get, which keeps us afloat in this ridiculously expensive place. We are fascinated with the idea of just escaping and moving away from it all, but life is "comfortable" in California because it's what we've known for nearly two decades. And we were existing so deep in the darkness, we no longer had the ability to *imagine* a life beyond the one we were just "coasting" in.

The depths of our desires are often overshadowed because the fear of the unknown is greater. We've had so many desires, so many big dreams—from living by way of a fill-it-yourself egg rolls food truck on the North Shore of Oahu to opening up *His & Hers*, a split-identity restaurant, to pouring everything we have into our biggest passion project of all, *Songs of Hope*. He is a dreamer, so hearing him say, "I'm good, just coasting," broke my heart. Yet, the sad reality is hearing that made me have to admit to myself, *I had stopped dreaming too.*

Then it made me ask the hardest question of all: *When did my dreams become about someone else?*

"Peace"

The thing about life is we only allow others to see what we choose to show them. People may think they know what someone else's life is like, but they have no clue, no matter who the person is. I'm a big believer in the truth that assumptions are a very dangerous thing. And, they are. Assumptions go hand in hand with expectations—because you assume something, you expect a certain outcome.

No one truly knows another person's life, and people certainly didn't know ours. They know what we shared in conversations, what we posted about on social media, some of what I've written on all these pages—but we never showed our true cards.

The awakening moment for me came during that crippling panic attack, when I realized I was just surviving in the eye of the tornado. The chaos was never ending, and I was the center of it all. Though, in reality, it was more like I became the tornado, and the eye was the hope of a better life I knew existed somewhere out there but couldn't find the answer to what that quite meant—because I became consumed with only existing in the darkness of it all. And every day, every year that went by—the tornado grew stronger, and the eye started to shrink. I felt so alone in all of this. No one could see my pain. No one heard my cries. I was self-medicating just to escape it all, missing out on truly living the precious moments of my life, and I couldn't find a way out. Until one day…

It was early in June 2022, when Adam went golfing with one of our dearest friends for his birthday. I couldn't get a hold of him for hours, and I had an uneasy feeling about that because, especially having young kids, if you have a partner to rely on you need to be able to rely on them and know everything is okay.

Six hours later, he finally called and said he was on his way home, but I could hear in his voice a tone unfamiliar to me. I told him to just be careful and get home safe. When he got home, he wasn't quite himself. Actually, he wanted to just go unwind by himself and fell asleep on the couch for an afternoon nap.

Days later, he opened up to me about what happened that day. It was the most vulnerable I had seen him in a long time and, perhaps, one of the most honest conversations we'd ever had. *Finally* all our fears had come to surface and met each other on the same level. That day he was golfing, he said he felt off, and after golf, they went to grab lunch. Something came over him, and he couldn't control that feeling; it was that bad. He just got up and left. He couldn't be there. He didn't even leave money to pay for the birthday lunch. He just needed out. *Sometimes we just need out.* When he called me on his way back, he wasn't in a good place. His body and mind weren't aligned. He was overwhelmed with an unexplainable sensation—he was having a panic attack.

This was a difficult moment for me—because I could have taken the easy, selfish route so many take and make it about myself like people often do. I had been having panic attacks for nearly two years now, internally begging for my husband to say he saw me and would help me through it. Not tell me to just take a tiny pill because that was the easy thing to do, when I'd known all along the root of what was causing them. But he never quieted the noise in his own head to stop and hear the pain in mine. And here I was, face to face with my husband, the father of my children, my partner in this lifetime, and he was saying to me what I had been begging for him to notice all this time. Whether or not he acknowledged or understood what I had been going through, I couldn't let him get to where I had been. Something had to be done.

With tears about to fall down my face, I held his hands, looked him in the eyes, and said, "You haven't been the same since *Gary* died. Losing him has hit you hard, and it's affected our entire family. But in losing him the way we did, you haven't changed a thing about your life. Our life is stressful. Our life is overwhelming, and we both self-medicate to get through it, missing out on just how beautiful it fucking is. We are *go, go, go* nonstop every single day, draining ourselves of just living our life because it's constantly so much. And everyone just constantly needs things from us, expecting us to live our own life by their wants. And you have this grief you're carrying with you every day, and maybe these feelings and this anxiety and panic is happening because you know life is trying to give you a wake-up call that you just aren't wanting to wake up to. What you've described to me is what I've been feeling nonstop for almost two years, begging for you to see me and help me, but you've been consumed in your own darkness. This whole time I thought it was just me in an endless downward spiral whipping around like the tornado of my life—but it's actually both of us in an endless chaotic state of stress and anxiety. If we don't grab hold of the hope and calm I know there is in the eye of our own storms, we're going to collide. And I fear if we collide, it will be permanent destruction—and I don't know if there will be any saving us."

He stared at me, unable to say a thing except just pull me into him and say, "Can I have a hug? Please."

"Breathe"

When one of us comes up to the other and asks for a hug like this, it isn't your usual hug. This is a look deep in each other's eyes, completely present face to face, "Can I have a hug? *Please*," kind of hug. It's a raw moment in which everything the other person is feeling and cannot express in words is laid out. It's a I'm *holding on to you as tightly and deeply as I can, telling you all these things I cannot say, but I have to believe it's going to be okay, and I'm not letting go* kind of hug. It's a hug that lasts until we have felt and said with unspoken words everything we needed the other person to feel. It's our reminder that no matter how hard things may get and no matter the challenges thrown our way, we're in it together.

Crosby is the one who taught us how to *hug* like this.

Without verbal words—*We're in it together, no matter how hard it may get. Always.*

But, it's hard, his hug told me.

I know, my hug said back. *But we'll figure it out. Together.*

A few days later, Adam had a one-day work trip he needed to take. He woke up early around four o'clock in the morning to give me a kiss goodbye before he headed off on the short ten-minute Uber ride from our house to Burbank Airport.

About an hour later, my phone kept buzzing. I had a bunch of texts from Adam saying he made it to the airport. He was having a Bloody Mary cocktail at the airport bar at 5:00 a.m. while having something to eat. He said that he was rapidly having anxiety because he couldn't have too much to drink since he had a full day of filming ahead of him. He was struggling, unable to self-medicate enough to get on that plane without his family.

I sent him a text, "Be smart, be careful, and I love you." Then I laid back down, knowing I needed a little more sleep to be able to, once again, handle the day's workload for my show and two kids, with all of their stuff, by myself.

Maybe twenty minutes later, my phone was ringing—Adam. I answered and heard a deepness in his breath I had never heard before. "I'm coming home. I can't get on the plane."

"Just get home," I told him.

Just get home.

That was the day we had an honest conversation about our lives, agreeing we probably needed out of whatever this life had become, as far and fast as we could. That was the day we both knew our life had to finally, for real, change.

See, before it was me who had that awakening. But now, it was both of us. To get out and survive as a family, we had to do it together; by our own choosing.

A few days later, during my morning meditations, I could see so clearly that there was somewhere else we were supposed to be. I saw myself in an open-concept kitchen looking to my left with open windows, the snow softly falling outside as I smiled and cooked a meal in a house full of warmth and love—looking over and seeing Adam on the couch, in front of a fireplace with our boys snuggled in his arms watching football. This wasn't a dream. This was my glimpse into the life that was waiting for us. This was our real life—if only we could find a way to let go of what we couldn't control. And break free from the storm, break free from our own selves.

"Anywhere Away from Here"

A few nights after the day we talked when Adam didn't get on that plane, for really no reason at all—oh, except the massive amounts of pressure coming down on me, my recurring anxiety, and Adam's panic attacks—as I was rocking Wylder to sleep, I turned toward Adam and said, "But for real, like serious talk here, if we were to leave L.A., like really move our family away from here—to just break free from all of it and just go—where would you, for real, consider actually moving to? We've light-heartedly talked about it now and then since we've met—but for real talk here."

I did this to him a lot—dropped these *for real* talks on him when he wasn't expecting it. Sometimes he would be in the mood to play along, sometimes he clearly let me know he was not. That night, he was more than serious and actually wanted to engage in the conversation about our possible future.

"I don't know. It's a lot to think about. Where would you want to go?" he asked.

Without a single ounce of hesitation, I said, "Hawaii. Hands down. I don't even care which island. Like, let's sell everything we own, take the kids, and go live a life of *aloha* in our favorite place, riding our bikes to go buy fresh fruit every day, and just exist on island time."

"No," he said in a kind of somber and shocking way. I was so surprised at how quickly he nixed my dreamy idea of moving to Hawaii, considering Adam, myself, and my sister, Demi, had this plan to move there a year after we got married, but once we realized I was pregnant with Crosby, all those fun "let's move to Hawaii" dreams just went away.

"I don't wanna move to Hawaii," he then continued with the conversation. "Because that's our special place. And I don't want to ruin what that means to us, if we lived there full-time. Maybe one day, but it's not the right time now. Plus, they don't have the level of support the boys need with their therapies at this time in life."

"You're right. That makes sense. Okay, well... What about South Carolina? Madison loves it there, I miss my best friend, she has such a special bond with the boys."

"No." Again, matter-of-factly. "I do not want to live in the south. I hate the weather there in summer."

"But what about Nashville then? We love Nashville, and Matt's there. You'd be close to one of your best friends, and how fun would it be if our kids could grow up together and you and Matt can go dick off doing whatever fishing things people do in Tennessee."

"I said I don't want to live in the south," he quickly reminded me.

"Ooooookkkkkkaaayyy... No to the south. Okay, what about Chicago then? You love Chicago, I love Chicago, my family is there, it would be a great blend of all the things we love around us, and have the support the boys need if we raised them there."

"No. I don't want to raise them in Chicago, and I also have no interest in moving back to Indy. So don't mention that option because we're not doing that."

"Well, if we were to stay in Southern California and chose to get out of Burbank, the only two places I have any interest in ever moving to, the only places at this point in time I would consider staying in SoCal for, are Malibu or Manhattan Beach."

"I agree," he quickly chimed in. "But, those two places are even more expensive than where we are now."

"Right." I sat in deep thought for a moment, really thinking about all our options and the research I had been doing for years now. "Okay, then what about Colorado? Fresh air, open space, we could give our boys the kind of life they deserve—without the fear of drug busts happening next door and drag racing accidents just up the street. This place isn't what it used to be—and neither are we."

"Growing up, I always loved going to Colorado. It really is an awesome place," he said.

"And as we know, the state is very supportive and inclusive when it comes to autism. Which is incredible."

And then Adam continued to go deeper with the conversation, "I guess one of the good things that has come out of this pandemic is we both can work remotely now. I would probably have to come back and show my face at the office now and then, but—We could definitely afford to buy a house there and stop pissing away thousands and thousands of dollars on rent. We'd have seasons again…"

To which I cut him off in excitement, "Oh my gosh, and we can have a fireplace in a home of our very own and be able to put the Christmas tree right next to it and just snuggle up while the snow is falling outside. And we could have open space and breathe fresh air."

"It would be the slow down we need."

"The *slow down*," I repeated.

"I obviously know Fort Collins really well because that's where we used to spend our time when we went to visit my grandparents," he mentioned as I could see the wheels now really turning in his mind.

"Wilderness"

The next morning, I woke up, and while everyone was still asleep, I did an early morning meditation, as part of my "The Miracle Morning" routine. As I was listening to that day's *Daily Trip With Jeff Warren* via the Calm app, my eyes were closed, only the glow of the candlelight seeping in through my eyelids, and as I focused on my breath, he said:

"If you trust you are the ocean, you won't be afraid of the waves."

My eyes popped open. I stared at the candle illuminating in front of me; it reminded me of the candlelight from my early childhood—when we had no power, when my mother and I didn't know how we were sometimes going to get through the night. In the darkest of nights, the flicker of the candle was what gave me hope that no matter whether you can see it or not, there is always a way out of the darkness.

With an unfamiliar sense of tranquility throughout the house, I repeated that piece of the meditation multiple times, yet it evolved into words of my own: "If you trust you are the ocean, you won't be afraid of the waves. If *I* believe *I am* the ocean, *I* will not fear the waves." *Holy fuck!* If I trust myself and act with the truth of who I am, all this *stuff,* all these *things* that turned me into a freaking storm—if I am the ocean, this is all a part of me. The ocean is in charge of itself and deals with the other elements thrust into its existence. The ocean doesn't fear anything, because the ocean controls everything. The storm can get bad; it can be ugly, and you better get out of the damn way because it's not stopping for anyone. But when the storm passes, the ocean is still there, and once again calm, beautiful, full of depth and life. Humans everywhere look out at the vast ocean and need a piece of it to help heal their own souls. All of this chaos, all of these *things* are just a part of life, a part of me.

I am the ocean. And I do not fear the waves.

After everyone was finally awake and in the groove of the day, I ventured into our bedroom closet, and pulled out a hidden storage bin beneath my hanging dresses. I wiped the dust bunnies off the top of it and uncovered some of my cherished items: Madison's maroon "red carpet" she gave me for my first movie premier, a glitzy mask I wore in Las Vegas on my 25th birthday, my childhood tap shoes, and a signed Christina Aguilera CD. Underneath all of that, I found what I was looking for—my Dream Box. Yep, that same Dream Box I made in college and filled with all my hopes, dreams, poems, quotes, letters and bits of inspiration. Among those things, I found it—the reminder I was searching for, the reminder I needed after I allowed myself to get to such a dark place because I let the world break me and take my light. *It was the one reminder I needed.* As I held in my hand the senior-year photo of my high school sweetheart, when I flipped the photo over, I rubbed my thumb over his handwriting and it was almost as if he was right there whispering in my ear, "Don't stop short on any of your goals. You can do whatever you want to."

I took a deep breath and closed my eyes.

This is my life. I can do whatever I want to.

These are our lives. We can do whatever we want to.

It was at that moment I realized—I no longer knew what it meant to have a dream. I was a dreamer who got lost in life's reality—and I didn't want to exist in *reality.* I wanted the freedom to know what it meant to once again have a dream of my own, after my life became so much of what others wanted it to be.

I just wanted to dream again.

And so, I decided to dust off my spontaneity hat and planned a surprise trip.

Later that day, I handed Adam an envelope and told him, "Here. I know the timing isn't ideal with work trips and life happenings right now, so don't be mad. But, here—it's a surprise."

When he opened the envelope, inside was a note that said, "Let's take a chance and see...," along with the printouts of four airplane tickets to fly to Denver that weekend. He looked at me like I was batshit crazy, and I said, "Let's go and see what we think. I haven't been to Colorado since we were first dating, and the boys have never been. If we're having this serious *is there something more out there that's better for our family* talk—then let's just go. So we know if it's worth talking about more or if we should just stay put. But we're not going to know the answer unless we try—we always said we wanted to be where we wanted to be by the time Crosby was in real big boy school. He just turned six, and our backs are against the wall. Our window of time is closing for us to make that decision because the school district wants answers from us. If it's here, then it's here, and we make it work, and we start the war for the life our son deserves. And if it's not, then we need to go. But we won't know if we don't go, the four of us together."

He thought about what I said. He looked at the tickets. And the next thing out of his mouth was, "Okay. Let's do it."

And for a moment, I saw that spark in him that I hadn't seen in a long time. I saw *life* coming back into his eyes. I saw the man I married.

"Colorado"

On August 7, 2022, we landed in Denver and after we got the kids and our luggage into the rental car, I was headed to get in the passenger seat when Adam said to me, "Wait. I need you to drive."

"What? Why? I don't know how to navigate getting out of Denver. The plan was you were going to drive," I said to him.

"I just… I can't do this. I'm having those feelings right now. I just physically and mentally am not in the right headspace, and this feeling inside of my body. I need you to get behind the wheel," he said to me with an anxious, trembling sound in his voice.

I didn't fight him. I just grabbed the keys out of his hand and got myself settled in the driver's seat. When I looked up, Adam was still standing in the parking lot. As I sat behind the wheel watching him outside the car needing to take a moment and some deep breaths, I could see that something was triggering him. He was overwhelmed. He was having a panic attack, which was why he needed me to drive, and I was watching it happen right in front of me.

But I couldn't intervene.

Something inside of me just said, *You need to let him figure this one out on his own.*

We didn't say much on the hour drive. I just focused on the road and on getting my family safely to our destination. I looked out the window and saw the sun shining down on the gorgeous mountains and felt a sense of calm in the air.

As we got closer to Fort Collins, I could begin to see a shift in Adam happen. This was a familiar place. A safe place. He knew this place. While it would be a new beginning, it had a feeling of *home* since he had some family who lived here. That gave him an emotional crutch, in a sense, and I think that's why the shift was happening in him.

We drove past CSU, and for a moment I thought, *Wow, is that where Crosby could go to college one day? The place where Temple Grandin is doing amazing work with horses and for individuals with autism. Wow, look at that football stadium! Wylder would love to run all over that.* We were quite hungry so the first thing we decided to do was go to Old Town, which is the charming downtown area that Main Street USA at Disneyland is actually modeled after. We walked around with the boys, stopping at little shops I hadn't seen in the eight years it had been since my first visit to Fort Collins with him, and it was just as I remembered it—so much character, art, fresh air, views of the mountains, and a sense of community surrounded us.

But then, when we went to lunch, suddenly his anxiety creeped back in.

When I asked him what was going on with him, he said, "I'm just processing all of it," as he then excused himself to go to the bathroom

The boys were distracted with their iPads and, as I waited for Adam to come back from the bathroom, I sat alone with my own thoughts processing my own fears in real time:

We've both lived in California for over seventeen years. That is what we know. California is where our careers are. *Though now we could work remotely.*

Adam's parents moved all the way across the country to be there a year after Crosby was born. *Though they actually live by his brother, and we don't see them that much.*

Some of our closest friends are in California. *Though everyone is spread out all over the place, and we really haven't seen people much because of the pandemic.*

The boys have an incredible team of therapists, and we would have been lost these past years without their supervisor, who we owe a lifetime of gratitude for. *Though people on his team came and went over the years for their own reasons, so there's no guarantee in that—but maybe I could convince their supervisor to come with us!*

But we know Los Angeles; and it's the devil we know how to navigate as we are in the process of transitioning Crosby back into the school district. *Though I promised I would never fail him again—and we've got lawyers on hold to fight the war if*

*we choose to, to give our boy the life we know he deserves, a life
beyond just the fucking ASD box he checks.*

Adam made it back to the table and I could see his emotional sickness now physically affecting him. I asked the waiter for our
check and after I paid, we left—Adam never once touching his lunch.

"This Life"

After we left lunch, we drove over to a park Adam knew well,
as it was the park just down the street from where his uncle lived.
Growing up, he used to walk to this park all the time when his family
would come and visit from Indiana. When we got out of the car and
started walking the boys to the playground area, it was almost as if
I started having an out-of-body experience. I could feel the fresh air
hitting my face. I noticed people smiling, just enjoying their lives.
A couple our age were on a walk with their young kids and waved
hello to us. An old man tipped his hat, smiled, and said, "I hope
you have a lovely day." Wait, someone actually was hoping we had
a lovely day, and there was no ulterior motive attached to his kind
comment? Adam was smiling, running with Wylder toward the slide.
Crosby was skipping toward the swings and then wanting to actually
explore and try out the balance beams with me. When I looked over
at Adam, the sun was beaming and it was like light was radiating
from him; seeing him so free, seeing the weight of what he had been
carrying lifted off of him for a moment.

This was our family just living our life, as us—without any expectations and external pressure weighing us down—the feeling closest
to what we feel when we escape to Hawaii. This was a glimpse of the
slow down we were needing in life. What was it about this place,

in this moment, that I was able to finally notice the life happening around me?

The next day, we met up with our real estate agent we had just started working with. We weren't sure what we were doing, but we knew if we were serious about making a huge life change that we needed to get ahead of ourselves and really see what kind of options we had. We had been looking on Zillow, comparing all different areas and price points and with every one we virtually looked at, there was one house that we just kept circling back to. And while other houses were getting swept up in days, somehow this specific house that we were drawn to just sat there untouched. I took this as a sign from the universe and so, we met up with our real estate agent to do a walk-through of the house in person.

The house was beautiful, in a community with open space and fresh air, with a bike path just beyond the backyard—it felt safe to me.

This house would have easily priced for nearly $2 million in L.A. And here we were standing in a house that felt like we belonged in it, a house with stairs that Wylder was freaking out over exploring because we didn't have stairs in our tiny pool house rental, a house Crosby was running around the backyard in because there was grass and a real yard, a house Adam wouldn't stop messing with all the small things first time home buyers need to pay attention to, a house with a small room that had French doors and could finally be my own private office space. I could see us in that house, together. But it was just a house. A very nice house full of very nice things, but that's not what was important to us. If we were going to make the decision to completely uproot our family and the life we built in California, we needed to make sure it felt like *home*, not just a house.

When we went out back to check out the walking path, Wylder took off running. Adam chased ahead to grab him and, instead of bringing him back, he grabbed hold of Wylder's hand and they just kept walking. Without a care in the world, they were just enjoying the moment as it was happening. And I just stood there watching them walk towards the sunlight.

While there was no way to make the decision about our lives at that moment, it was the moment I knew if we were going to get out of the storm, the only place we would be going was Fort Collins, Colorado.

"Landslide"

My journal entry from August 9, 2022:

> As I write this, I'm on a plane with my family. We're flying back from Denver, Colorado, to Burbank, California, for what could possibly be our last time making this trip. In one of the hardest decisions of our life thus far, we're having the real conversations that, just shy of eighteen years living in L.A., it might be time for a fresh start, a new beginning. We want to give our kids a better life—and that starts with both of us being better. And at this point in time, I don't see how that can happen while still living in Burbank, Los Angeles or California. But as I sit here writing this, I can't help but be overcome with emotions. Doubt. Fear of the unknown. As I look out the window and see blue skies and clouds of fluff, I can't help but once again feel lost.
>
> Burbank is what we know. What's so terrible about continuing to rent? Even though it's at a $4,000 a month price tag just for the rental alone—at least we'd still have the pool to escape into for our "grill and chill and too many White

Claw" weekends that seem to do an okay job masking the pain. Even though we'd have to fight with the school district, we'd have our therapy team supporting us every step of the way. My sister no longer lives there but Adam's family is there. Our friends are there. Even with remote work, it's easier to network being there. Yet even in the comfort of those things, I still can't help but feel like life is squeezing us to the point it feels like we're being stuffed inside the termite-infested pool shack.

And yet—We just viewed in person the house we fell in love with. A house surrounded by community, with a charming artisan village just up the road and a school district focused on inclusiveness. A house with windows opening out to the backyard with an open kitchen looking into a family room with a fireplace, and a perfect little corner for our Christmas tree. A house that could become our chosen *home*. The house I saw in my waking dream. Adam couldn't believe this house was still on the market, and all I could keep telling him was, "If this is what we're supposed to do and if it's meant to be our house, it will be our *home*." I was trying to channel Little Miss Sunshine even though I was terrified inside. We joyfully imagined what a life elsewhere could be, but now the fear is really setting in. With how complex our life is, there's so many layers to think about.

Could we really do this?

But as I sit on this plane heading back to the place that's been our "home" for nearly two decades, the feeling of being lost sneaks back in because doubt and fear have creeped to the surface. Could we really do this? Are we being selfish in wanting this, or is this really what's best for our kids? What if the remote opportunities stop, and we leave California and are an hour from the opportunities in Denver? What if the school situation for Crosby isn't what we think and it's more of the situation he would have been in if we stay—is that really any better? We will have no friends around us and limited family support, so it's really, once again, the four of us—can we get through this hard time and be strong enough for each other? *Us against the world*—can we make it through the tough times to come? Can we finally heal from all the grief and the pain and work toward being better versions of ourselves?

Can life actually change for the better?

Are we willing to trust that life has something more beautiful waiting for us when we make it through to the other side of the storm?

I don't even know if we will like Colorado. If we move, I don't know if it will be forever. But I feel like—I believe we need to try.

I don't know. *I just don't know.*

"Once Upon a Poolside"

We got home from Colorado and the reality of our life just came rushing back. That night, after we put the boys to bed, we went outside and looked each other in the eyes. With tears welling up in my eyes,

I said to Adam, "What are we doing? We can't continue on like this, with one foot in two different directions—with one foot rooted and the other just wanting to fly. What are we doing? We have to choose."

He didn't respond.

So I said, "I don't know if Colorado is the answer. I don't know if we will like it there. I guess our safety net is, we can always come back if we end up realizing it's not where we're meant to be. What's worse—trying and it not working out? Or living with the regret we never did?"

Adam just stood staring at me.

Suddenly, my entire body became overwhelmed with emotions. Tears now pouring out of my eyes, I looked at Adam and said, "The school district won't even entertain talking with us and our lawyers, they just wanna shove him in a multi-grade autism program just because there's dollar signs over his head because he checks the ASD box—and he is so much more than a fucking checked box. They want him to stay behind in kindergarten because they think he can only count to four, when this kid can count into the hundreds and in increments of 10. Oh, and them thinking he only showed what he was capable of was because 'Mom was around,' well good fucking thing I was around to show people who should know better how to see things from a different perspective. And that fucking speech therapist—I'm supposed to trust that woman with my son? When her reaction to him in the IEP meeting was laughing and saying 'well, he's really cute.' A fucking speech therapist said that about our *nonverbal* son. I can't... I just... I will never again let the world limit him, and I will do whatever it takes to fight for him. I will always fight for him, as hard as we have to—but I have to question, is this the fight we want to fight?"

Adam didn't say a thing. And I couldn't stop talking.

"I can't do this anymore. We're not in control of our lives anymore. You're having anxiety. I'm having anxiety. You're having panic attacks. I'm having panic attacks. What kind of life are we giving our kids if we're not even giving ourselves a good life? The deep end of our pool is nowhere near comparable to the depths it feels like we're drowning. I married you, you married me, and it's the pressure of the world crashing down on us expecting all these things from us, and it feels like our hands are up on every wall and our feet are out holding down with all our might the foundation of this house we built for ourselves, and I see the faces of everybody and everything screaming at us, clawing at us, and we're not in control of anything—and if we don't grab our kids and jump the fuck out of the storm and run as fast as we can towards the glimmer of light in the distance I can still see, it's all gonna come crashing down on us. And we won't rise up from that disaster. I feel like I can't breathe anymore, and if we don't get out, we're not going to survive this together. Our backs are up against a wall. Time is running out, so I'm asking you, what are we going to do?"

The truth I was saying internally was that I just wanted peace. I didn't want to live any longer in this version of what our lives had become. I felt like a prisoner in my own life. And I wanted to be set free.

Adam got frustrated and went off into the garage, which often became his man cave late at night when he just couldn't deal with the hard things of life. And I did something I hadn't done in the two years we had now lived in our pool house.

I stood there, staring at the pool lit in the darkness of the night, and I once again heard *his* words, "You can do whatever you want to."

And, I did.

I pulled down my sweatpants, I took off my tank top, and by the moonlit sky above me, I went into our pool in my bralette and underwear. And there was, for once, a calmness in the air. A calm I hadn't felt for years. Stripped down, without the fire from the pressures of our lives burning through me—my body was content, and it felt good in there.

Then I wondered, *What would it feel like to just dip below the surface?*

Adam and I both went to bed that evening without ever saying *good night.*

"Our Love"

The next morning, I woke up to a text from Adam that he had sent me after I went to sleep. In the text was the link to a song. He knew this band wasn't one of my faves because while we both love music, we don't always have the same go-to musical taste. My husband often listens to what I like to jokingly call "scream-o" music. I literally walked into our garage once in the middle of the night to find him and our buddy standing on the furniture with music blasting, and they were head-banging alone to their air guitars like they were in a garage band in high school with a cloud of pot smoke lingering around them. But, given the conversations we'd been having and knowing the mental state we had both been in, I decided to listen to this song because music is our family's way of expressing what our souls are saying when we can't always, or aren't able to, find the verbal words to explain.

Plus, along with the link, his text message said, "This is the song I've been listening to a lot lately, and it's important to me at this point in time."

So, I clicked the link and listened to "Our Love"—and that song said everything I needed to hear that my husband couldn't find the words to say.

That was it. All I needed to hear were the lyrics in that song. They weren't words he wrote, but they were the most perfect words he could have ever told me in his own way in the moment I needed to hear them the most.

It was a no-brainer, the easiest decision we could make, one we should have made years ago, and one we didn't want to wake up years from now and regret we never did.

And by the end of listening to that song once through, the decision was made that we were leaving California and moving to Colorado.

"Defying Gravity"

At this point in my life, Los Angeles was one of the longest relationships I'd ever had of my own choosing. The twenty-year-old version of myself fell in love with this city. The forty-year-old version of myself was suffocating because of it.

I'm not placing blame on L.A.—Los Angeles was just the vessel, holding onto everything I had been through until this point in time of being face to face with that choice to stay the same or pivot in the direction of a new beginning. "The world," "life"— it's not just a person or a place or an energy or emotions or circumstances I had no control over; it was all of it, combined. It was everything I could no longer control and I felt out of control because of it.

I wish I could agree with the people who believe if you follow these very specific steps and do what you're told to do, it will get better. But I don't believe that. I believe we all have to figure out this thing called *life* our own way because we're all on our own journey. And no one's path looks the same. Even in the darkest of the darkness, I still had a very strong inner-knowing. And I knew what I needed to do in order to take back control of my life. And in doing so, reclaim my voice. And nothing would have changed for me, if life didn't change. There was no way to change when we were just stuck in the life we were living. In order to change, I needed to once again be free to just roam.

It's not to say we weren't happy or we weren't blessed with having a fortunate life full of careers we loved and good relationships around us, but years and years and years of the hits and the stress that we could never let go of and the emotional weight we carried with us every day, made us feel as though we were drowning. We could see the light coming through the crack, but no one was ever holding out a hand to help pull us out of the downward spiral. The spiral was never going to end on its own—we had to jump out of the storm if we were going to survive.

I just need life to slow the fuck down.

In thinking about our L.A. journey of nearly the past two decades, perhaps one of the biggest discoveries of all was that we have stayed there so long based on the dreams of the twenty-year-old versions of ourselves. The reality was we were no longer those people. We stayed for who we were, not who we had become. And who we had become had outgrown Los Angeles, just as often we outgrow clothes, toys, and even relationships. People hold on to things for so long because there's a sentimental attachment to them, not thinking that perhaps our letting go of what no longer contributes positively to our lives is what ultimately will save us. And I had to learn to let go of perhaps the biggest expectations of all, the ones I put on myself. I had to stop expecting my forty-year-old self to live by the dreams I had when I was a twenty-year-old starlet-wannabe. My own expectations were bigger than anything others could have ever put on me. And it was time I got out of my own way.

The thing that made the most sense for our lives, from an outside perspective, would have been to stay in California. But I knew that if we didn't leave at that moment in time, the stress, the anxiety, the grief, the panic attacks, the darkness—would have killed us. That's how bad it was. I could have chosen to stay as life was, we had a good life—but I didn't want to die. I was begging to live.

So, it was time to finally say goodbye to one of the longest relationships in my life, and with that, let go of who I had been to make space for *who I am becoming.*

We made the one decision no one expected us to ever make—and a month shy of eighteen years in Los Angeles, we left it all behind, never looking back.

"All I Know So Far"

We knew that leaving California was the only way we had a fighting chance and the only way we'd make it out of the storm alive.

Because while we were in L.A., I had been living a lie.

My own lie.

This entire time I had been walking through life, I was writing all these words in this book, thinking and believing I was living my best, truest, most authentic life. But the joke was on me. I wasn't. It wasn't until the day we pulled away from our pool house in Burbank and, with Adam and his dad in the moving truck in front of us, and me in my car with my boys strapped in the back seat—somewhere within the sun setting in the mountains of Arizona, the moment happened for me...when I realized we had finally left a deceiving life behind and were stepping into our real one. It was a surreal moment during a terrifying drive, so I pulled out the compass necklace Adam gave me that Christmas I was pregnant with Wylder. I hung it on my rearview mirror, looking to my right at my father's plant sitting shotgun with me, to give me the strength I needed to get through this hard part, and that's when I heard his whisper:

"... stay the course."

We just left our life behind. All I could do was keep going forward. It was up to me to push through. So I put on my "soundtrack of my life" playlist and blasted P!nk's "All I Know So Far." And when the first chorus kicked in, I grabbed a hold of that compass necklace with one hand while holding with all my might to my steering wheel with the other. As we started to descend through the most picturesque mountains I'd ever seen in my life, the sun continued to set—and I just let it all out. No L.A. in my rearview mirror. Just fucking freedom. While belting at the top of my lungs the chorus of that song, it happened.

I found me. I did it. I finally found *me*.

Every plan, every path, every idea, every expectation, every everything in my life up until that moment—I decided to be done with it all. I was free of it all, and in that moment, I was finally found. Me, who I am—here and now. And I finally started to *live*.

Leaving L.A.—I was leaving behind the person I once was, the person others told me to be, the person I never really chose because even in all the times I thought I was choosing for myself, it was still with the consideration of others behind those choices. All this time, I was living for the expectations of everyone else, never realizing the biggest expectation I was living by of all was that of a twenty-year-old version of myself. And the ten-year-old version of myself I was so jealous of. And the thirty-year-old version of myself who thought she was finally getting it right but still was never living for herself. I take with me the scars of all these versions of myself because I wouldn't be who I am becoming without them. But I also release their expectations of who they thought I was supposed to be because the only person I'm supposed to be is who I, here and now, choose to be. I'm tired of the masks, the lies, the expectations, the assumptions, the past—I woke up today. I'm breathing. I'm here. And *here* is what I have.

This is my life. And finally, in that car, holding on to that compass necklace my husband gave me when he needed me to just hold on through the hard and *stay the course*, for the first time in my life, I finally knew what it felt like to just be living my life as *me*.

I had no clue where we were going beyond the address I had input in my phone. But that was okay. For once, I wasn't lost. Here, in the middle of nowhere, I was found. I was on *Somewhere Road*—and it was guiding me *home*. Home to myself. Who I was, without who the world expected me to be.

My scars—all of them physically, emotionally, every piece of me that had led me to this moment; the world we knew had been blown up finally by our own doing, and I rose up from it.

We think all these things life throws at us can destroy us, but we are so much stronger than we know.

You see, there were always diamonds beneath the darkness—because there was always me. A diamond, the toughest natural substance, is virtually unbreakable; not even lava can melt one. Though a diamond doesn't shatter if it's dropped, it can break if there's too much built up pressure. And just like a diamond, I am fucking strong. Yea, I may have allowed the world to mold a version of me that wasn't always authentic at times or allowed others to dim my light because they were too insecure to shine on their own—but the one thing no one else could do was break me; only I could have done that to myself.

But I know the value of my soul—and it's way too rare to exist hidden underneath a mountain.

So World, I'm giving you back your darkness—and I'm taking back my light.

This is my life. I can do whatever I want to.
I am the ocean. And I do not fear the waves.
I am a diamond.
And it's time to fucking sparkle.

SEVEN.

The Wrap Up

AFTER THE STORM

"Better Days"

For nearly two years during the COVID-19 pandemic, I wore a red The Giving Keys necklace around my neck every single day. I had the word *breathe* custom inscribed on it as my reminder that when life gets overwhelming, to just stop and breathe, because *everything will be okay.* I wore my red key necklace every single day, I grabbed hold of it in the moments I needed it most, and it pushed me through that final stretch of leaving Los Angeles and journeying toward an unknown future ahead of us.

The day we made it to Colorado, closed on our house, and moved into our new *home*, among boxes and the chaos of moving, navigating life as first-time homeowners in a whole new place—it was the first time in forever that I could feel the overwhelm of stuff going on, but I wasn't overwhelmed. It was the first time a stressful situation was happening around me, but I wasn't stressed. It was the first time fear of the unknown was staring us right in the face, but I didn't let the fear get to me; instead, I controlled the fear. For once, I didn't know what tomorrow was going to bring, but I was perfectly okay with that. I was finally living in the moment, and even though all the things we were still struggling with weren't going to change overnight, the days suddenly became longer, the quality of time together got wider, and the storm disappeared, revealing a double rainbow.

Crosby and Wylder slept in our bed that first night. I stood there staring at them sleeping peacefully in our new home. I ran my hand over Wylder's head and kissed him on the forehead. "I love you, my sweet boy," is what I whispered to him. Then I went over to Crosby. After snuggling his blankie into him, I kissed him on the forehead and whispered, "I love you, my sweet boy. You're my best friend. I promised… I would never fail you again."

I stood in our new bathroom staring at myself, processing what I just accomplished on my own on that drive with my boys in the back seat, soaking in the reality that we just left our life behind. I took my red *breathe* key necklace off and never put it on again.

I could finally breathe. All on my own.

As I stood there breathing on my own, I realized what it was I needed all this time…

I needed a clean slate. I needed a blank canvas. I needed the chance to begin again, to flip the script and in the freeing of the past, breathe fresh air, feel the sun shine down on my face, realize time is just energy and I needed to soak up all the positive energy I could. I needed to be able to just be me. Even in the darkness, I knew others could still see my light. But I need others to not just see my light, I needed to feel my light. I needed to guide myself back home to me and do the work to change the narrative I have been telling myself all this time, the narratives I allowed others to convince me to believe were my truths.

I don't have all the answers. I'm a work in progress toward *becoming* and that's okay. I don't need all the answers. What I needed was the chance to *live*. I needed to be able to run free in the wilderness of my own life. I needed the freedom to dream again, dream bigger dreams than I've ever had for myself, and I couldn't do that trapped inside the storm—trapped inside my own mind. People often think of a storm as a bad thing. I actually find beauty in it; there's a calm—if you're willing to just sit in it for a while. Lightning strikes and it can shake you up, but it can also light the way if you trust in *the knowing* that there's beauty waiting on the other side.

I cannot, I will not, look back on my life and say I didn't fucking take the chance, I didn't live for me, I didn't try—even if I faceplant on this next road I travel down, at least I can say I tried. Isn't that what life should be about?

I can't quite say the exact moment when the switch happened. It just did. One day, in one moment it just hit me and I realized, "Damn, this is life. This is *my* life. My *one* life. And I'm going to fucking live it."

This time, I finally drew a line in the sand and promised myself I wouldn't cross back over to life as it was before—because my kids are depending on me to keep pushing forward, going all-in on myself.

So I chose today, not someday.

And I rolled the dice on me for a change.

I like my odds.

Ya know, here's the thing about everything I've shared—I realized that I'm actually okay with those words my mother said to me when I was twenty years old. I'm okay with being "a dime a dozen." Because a *dime* was classically referred to as a woman who had a special kind of light about her that could capture a room. So, as my mother told me I was back then, if I am, indeed, "a dime a dozen"—it means I'm a bright spot within a small group. And if there's one little bright spot per every dozen of everyone in the world, then that's a lot of little bright spots shining their positive light onto a very darkened world. And we all need more of that; for in the darkness, all these little bright spots will guide us *home.*

"Message to the World"

My friends, you have made it to the end of the first book in my **Life thru Lyrics** series… the journey to become.

Diamonds Beneath the Darkness has been about laying it all out there, everything since the beginning of my life that got me to that severe panic attack I had, just some of the heavy things I carry on my back and in my heart every day, and what, ultimately, contributed to us choosing to leave Los Angeles. But just because we left L.A., I finally could breathe, and felt an ounce of freedom as I drove my kids through those mountains to an unknown future—just because I let go of that heavy thing doesn't mean life just instantly changed. Life is complex, with many layers to work through. All it was, was letting go of that one heavy thing, letting go of Los Angeles. That was just step one. The real work begins now.

I set myself free—and now, I'm finally ready to heal.

Life thru Lyrics, part two will embrace the next season of life—showing what it means to forgive, to release, to heal, to finally not just learn to let go but actually *let go.*

I hope you continue to join me on this journey—because healing is a process just as becoming a truer version of ourselves is a process. It won't happen overnight. I know it's time to rip off those Band-Aids and do the hard work to clean out the wounds and push through the pain so I can continue to evolve into who I am *becoming.*

In this moment, you're here—remember that. Look around you. Notice life and breathe it in. No matter what you may have discovered about yourself, and your own life, along this first part of the journey and no matter the work you know is waiting to be done in the future—you're here right now. Hold on to this moment—this is the moment you're tuning out the noise and turning up the music inside of you.

Growing up, we're often asked, "What's your plan?" Then your answer is followed with, "Okay, but what if Plan A doesn't happen? What's your Plan B?"

In college, we're encouraged to not just have a major but also a minor, so you have something to "fall back on," something you have just enough knowledge in but isn't your primary focus.

There is always supposed to be a backup plan, yet we're told there's only one life. And, when life doesn't go as planned, some give the excuse that life got in the way. So again, let's all stop saying "life got in the way." Truth is, life doesn't get in the way—life is the way. Every moment is life happening. You can't plan for life; life *is* the plan! This is me reminding you that, as far as we know, we only have this one wild, *amazing crazy* and beautiful life to live. So just fucking live it! And live it for you, without the pressures and expectations of the outside world telling you that you should be anything other than who you're meant to be. Let's stop shoving people into black-and-white boxes they don't belong in and, instead, start awakening to the truth that every single one of us is an individual with a story that matters.

As someone who has spent her career with a burning passion to tell stories I believe others need to hear, I finally woke up and realized that maybe those stories have always been my own. Isn't that the most beautiful gift of all? To use our experiences to help inspire others to just go out there and live their own lives.

We're all storytellers. We all have something to say, but we all say it in different ways—some of us choose to tell our stories through movies, some through music, art, life experience, teaching, inventing, or love. Our purpose as humans is to be compassionate, and connect with others, making one another laugh and cry, but most importantly, making others feel something *real* and reminding anyone out there willing to listen that it's okay to have a dream, it's okay to switch paths in life, and damn it, please do get a little lost along the way. And stop waiting for *someday*—because one day, your somedays will run out. Whatever scares you right now, let it scare you, and then go after it. Take the chance; let the fear fuel you. Because worse than letting fear stop you is looking back at the end of your life, regretting you never took that leap of faith! Take the path less traveled—there's too much noise where everyone else is going.

I was terrified to put these stories out there, to be so honest, and be real, raw, and imperfect with all of you. I had "Imposter Syndrome" come close to stopping me so many times, delaying me for years before publishing some of these stories I had written—putting my life and my truths out there, being so completely vulnerable in doing so, knowing that the world could stomp on me and attack me in return. But my *Why* was greater than any of my fears—I wanted all of you to know that you have never been alone in life. Someone has always been there. My voice just wasn't strong enough to tell you that until now.

What kept me writing was so that you know—I get you, I see you, I'm here for you and with you. And for that, finally speaking my truths was worth it all.

If you don't have someone in your life who can encourage you to share your stories, I will be that person for you. These pages you're holding are your reminder. If I could do this my own way, so can you! Sometimes we just need to get out of our own heads and stop worrying about how others might respond because the truth is that those negative people are the same people who are too damn scared to just go for it and live their own lives. They are the people who hide behind masks, who truly don't know who they are, so it's easier to talk about others instead of taking a chance on life and putting their true self out there into the world. Once you break free from that kind of life and start running toward who you're becoming, there's no going back.

Come run with me.

ACKNOWLEDGEMENTS

"Fight Song"

T hank you to everyone out there who helped make this possible, and who believed in me when I was losing hope and didn't think I would ever make this dream a reality; when I didn't know I had the strength to use my voice, reclaim my life and share my stories.

Thank you to everyone who loves me and supports me, unconditionally—to those of you who accept me, just as I am—*Perfectly Imperfect* and all.

And thank you to everyone out there who ever told me, "No," who told me I wasn't enough, who made me believe not only did I not have a voice but that it wasn't important enough to be heard. Thank you to everyone who made me feel so small, who pushed me further down instead of helping pull me up, who never quieted their own mouths to listen to my cries, who expected me to just do things the way they wanted them done, or who thought they knew it all, and I knew nothing. Thank you for your negativity—because from that, I got my fire. You gave me the courage to rise up, light that match, and blow it all up. Without you, I truly would not be becoming the *me* I know I'm meant to be. I am fucking proud of myself for no longer choosing to allow any of you to get in my way again. This strength I have today is because of you. Out of all that dirt and darkness and ugliness has emerged a woman hellbent on making sure others don't ever feel the same way.

This book has first and foremost been for Crosby—and for all my people out there who I love so much and who love me for speaking my truth. And it's for everyone who needs to be reminded that every voice, no matter how big or small, matters. Just as I promised my children to always fight for their voices, and for my own, I promise to keep doing everything I can to make sure you know that all of you have such strength within you and deserve to be heard as well.

So, thank you to Crosby for helping me find my voice.

And thank you to all of you for giving me the strength I needed to finally speak.

Remember, you're a diamond—now go fucking sparkle!

I love you.

CONNECT WITH NICOLE

Hi Friends!

Of all the things I've produced, this book series has been the hardest thing I've ever created and equally the most beautifully rewarding. I have put my heart and soul onto these pages for all of you and truly hope you enjoyed part one: ***Diamonds Beneath the Darkness***. It would mean the world to me if you'd take a few moments to write a review and share your thoughts with myself and others. Your feedback is greatly appreciated and will help me make what's to come on this next part of the journey even more impactful.

Please take a few moments to leave a review
www.lifethrulyrics.com/review

And since we're on this journey together, don't be a stranger! Let's stay in touch—I'd love to directly hear from you! You can connect with me in various ways:

Email: hello@lifethrulyrics.com
Instagram: @its_nicoledanielle
TikTok: @its_nicoledanielle
Book Bub: @its_nicoledanielle
Good Reads: Nicole Danielle
Patreon: Life thru Lyrics: the untold stories

See you again soon in book form! *Life thru Lyrics, part two* is coming your way in 2024!

With endless love & gratitude...

XO,

Nicole

WHAT READERS ARE SAYING...

"Where do I start? This book had it all! Nicole Danielle shows up authentically from the start. She is the best friend or sister every woman needs as she navigates through the twists and turns of life."

"I just cried. This book is so beautiful and amazing. I was having so much anxiety about feeling lost and putting all this pressure on myself. I don't even have words. The author has a pure talent for writing and making people feel things."

"I'm reminded to think that this life will be good and beautiful, but not without heartbreak. Pain is the cost of living, it reminds us that we're alive."

"As you watch this beautiful human on her self-discovery journey to *become*, you'll find a wealth of inspiring and relatable moments where, if you look closely, you may just discover something about yourself. The author had me in all my feels from page one!"

"The hurt, the sadness, the hope - I feel it ALL. The best part is... it's REAL! And you can't help BUT feel it. You feel what she's describing. And when she talks about wanting to 'break the mold,' you feel the hope and love for the life the author is going to create and you can't help but cheer and root for her, because the way I see it,... NICOLE DANIELLE is the hope. SHE is the love."

"While reading I had moments of needing to just breathe. Many different emotions came upon me while reading and breathing in each sentence. (The author) sharing intimate details of her life and being vulnerable is her showing her authentic self."

"**Diamonds Beneath the Darkness** is so soul quenching. It's not just a 'look, here's my story' book – it's "this WAS my story—and I'm better and stronger for it. I'm grateful for all the lessons, good and bad." **Diamonds Beneath the Darkness** is a journey of self-worth, discovery, loss, hurt, pain – pain so deep that as you're reading it, you can physically feel the left side of your chest ache as you're crying—and finally, forgiveness and redemption, all the while learning, growing and evolving in the process."

For a little taste of what's coming next in the **Life thru Lyrics** series, just scan the code to get your sneak peek from **Life thru Lyrics, part two**.

Or sign up here
www.lifethrulyrics.com

www.ingramcontent.com/pod-product-compliance
Lightning Source LLC
Chambersburg PA
CBHW030400130626
46549CB00004B/1572